05

STUDY GUIDE

to accompany

Edwards & Wattenberg & Lineberry

GOVERNMENT IN AMERICA

People, Politics, and Policy

Thirteenth Edition

to accompany Comprehensive and Texas editions

Charles S. Matzke
Michigan State University

Heidi Lange
Tom Haymes
Houston Community College

New York Boston San Francisco
London Toronto Sydney Tokyo Singapore Madrid
Mexico City Munich Paris Cape Town Hong Kong Montreal

Study Guide to accompany Edwards/Wattenberg/Lineberry, *Government in America: People, Politics, and Policy, Thirteenth Comprehensive and Texas Editions*

Copyright ©2008 Pearson Education, Inc.

ISBN: 0-321-48299-9

3 4 5 6 7 8 9 10–OPM–10 09 08 07

Foreword

This Study Guide is designed to assist the student in understanding and learning the material presented in the text, *Government in America, People, Politics and Policy,* Thirteenth Edition by George C. Edwards III, Martin P. Wattenberg, and Robert L. Lineberry. Each chapter in the Study Guide is divided into six sections: Chapter Outline, Learning Objectives, Key Terms, Using Your Understanding, Review Questions, and Essay Questions.

The Chapter Outline section presents a brief summary of the chapter in outline form. Key terms in the chapter are presented in bold type. This section serves as a quick review of the major topics of the chapter. The outline is not meant to substitute for a thorough reading of the chapter.

Learning objectives are listed in the second section. After studying the chapter the student should be able to understand and discuss these objectives. Several exercises are presented to help the student better understand and meet these objectives.

The section on key terms provides a space to identify and describe each key term from the chapter and compare and contrast related terms. "Name that term" reverses "identify and describe" by presenting a definition or example of a term for the student to name.

The Using Your Understanding section is designed to give the student the opportunity to delve deeper into a subject presented in the text. Most of these exercises require some outside research beyond the information found in the text. These exercises may be used as the basis for a term paper.

The Review Questions section consists of various numbers of multiple choice and true/false questions. These questions will help the student test their knowledge of the information presented in the text and prepare for exams. Two multiple choice questions in each chapter are labeled "bonus." These questions cover obscure or fun facts found in the text. The answers to the review questions as well as the page in the text where the answer can be found are listed in the back of the Study Guide.

The final section of the Study Guide presents a number of essay questions. These questions are designed to take a closer look at particular topics covered in the chapter. The questions test the students' understanding of the subject matters presented in the chapter and may help the student prepare for essay exams.

Table of Contents

TEXAS EDITION CHAPTERS

CHAPTER 1

INTRODUCING GOVERNMENT IN AMERICA

CHAPTER OUTLINE

I.   Introduction (pp. 2-8)

II.   Government (pp. 8-10)
    A. The institutions that make authoritative decisions for any given society are collectively known as **government.**
    B. Two fundamental questions about governing serve as themes of this book.
        1. How should we govern?
        2. What should government do?
    C. All national governments have certain functions in common:
        1. Governments maintain national defense.
        2. Governments provide public services called **public goods.**
        3. Governments preserve order.
        4. Governments socialize the young.
        5. Governments collect taxes.

III.   Politics (p. 10)
    A   **Politics** determines whom we select as our governmental leaders and what policies they pursue.
    B. The ways in which people get involved in politics make up their **political participation**.
    C. **Single-issue groups** are so concerned with one issue that their members will cast their votes on the basis of that issue only.

IV.   The Policymaking System (pp. 11-13)
    A. People Shape Policy
        1. The **policymaking system** is the process by which policy comes into being and evolves over time. (See Figure 1.4)
        2. Political parties, elections, interest groups, and the media are key **linkage institutions** that transmit the preferences of Americans to the policymakers in government.
        3. The **policy agenda** consists of the issues that attract the serious attention of public officials and other people actively involved in politics at a given time.
        4. A **political issue** arises when people disagree about a problem or about a public policy choice made to fix a problem.
        5. Policymakers work within the three **policymaking institutions** (the

6. Congress, the presidency, and the courts as established by the U.S. Constitution).
B. Policies Impact People
    1. Every decision that government makes—a law it passes, a budget it establishes, and even a decision not to act on an issue—is **public policy**. (See Table 1.1)
    2. Policy impacts are the effects that a policy has on people and on society's problems.

V. Democracy (pp. 14-23)
  A. Defining Democracy
    1. **Democracy** is a means of selecting policymakers and of organizing government so that policy reflects citizens preferences.
  B. Traditional Democratic Theory
    1. Equality in voting
    2. Effective participation
    3. Enlightened understanding
    4. Citizen control of the agenda
    5. Inclusion
    6. Democracies must practice **majority rule** and preserve **minority rights.**
    7. The relationship between the few leaders and the many followers is one of **representation.**
  C. Three Contemporary Theories of American Democracy
    1. **Pluralist theory** states that groups with shared interests influence public policy by pressing their concerns through organized efforts.
    2. **Elite and class theory** contends that societies are divided along class lines, and that an upper-class elite pulls the strings of government.
    3. **Hyperpluralism** contends that many groups are so strong that government is unable to act.
  D. Challenges to Democracy
    1. Increased Technical Expertise
    2. Limited Participation in Government
    3. Escalating Campaign Costs
    4. Diverse Political Interests (**policy gridlock**)
  E. American Political Culture and Democracy
    1. **Political culture** consists of the overall set of values widely shared within a society.
    2. Liberty
    3. Egalitarianism
    4. Individualism
    5. Laissez-faire
    6. Populism
  F. Preview Questions About Democracy

VI. The Scope of Government in America (pp. 23-26)
    A.   How Active Is American Government?
    B.   Preview Questions about the Scope of Government

VII. Summary (p. 26)

LEARNING OBJECTIVES

After studying Chapter 1, you should be able to:

1. Describe what government is and what governments do.

2. Understand how politics is the struggle over "who gets what, when, and how."

3. Identify the important features of the policymaking system and explain how public policies are the choices that government makes—and declines to make—in response to political issues.

4. Understand the nature of democratic government and traditional democratic theory, and the key questions concerning democracy.

5. Distinguish among the three contemporary theories of American democracy and politics (pluralist, elite and class, and hyperpluralist) and identify some of their strengths and weaknesses.

6. Understand the nature of American political culture and identify the elements of the American creed.

7. Understand the nature of the scope of government in America and the key questions concerning the scope of government.

The following exercises will help you meet these objectives:

Objective 1: Describe what government is and what governments do.

1. Define the term "government."

2. What are the two fundamental questions about governing that serve as themes throughout the textbook?

3

1.

2.

3. List the five functions that all national governments perform.

    1.

    2.

    3.

    4.

    5.

Objective 2: Understand that politics is the struggle over "who gets what, when, and how."

1. Define the term "politics."

2. Give examples of the "who," "what," "when," and "how" of politics.

    1. Who:

    2. What:

    3. When:

    4. How:

Objective 3: Identify the important features of the policy system and explain how public policies are the choices that government makes, and declines to make, in response to political issues.

1. Draw a diagram of how a policy system works.

2. List four key linkage institutions in a democratic society.

    1.

    2.

    3.

    4.

3. Define the term "policy agenda."

4. How does a government's policy agenda change?

5. List the four major policymaking institutions in the United States.

    1.

    2.

    3.

    4.

6. Define the term "policy impacts."

Objective 4: Understand the nature of democratic government, traditional democratic theory, and the key questions concerning democracy.

1. Define the term "democracy" as used in this text.

2.   List the five cornerstones of an ideal democracy.

    1.

    2.

    3.

    4.

    5.

3.   Explain what is meant by majority rule and minority rights.

Objective 5: Distinguish among the three contemporary theories of American democracy and politics (pluralist, elite and class, and hyperpluralist) and identify some of their strengths and weaknesses.

1.   Complete the following table comparing pluralist, elite and class, and hyperpluralist theories according to who holds the power and how policy is made.

Theory	Who Holds Power	How Policy is Made
Pluralist		
Elite and Class		
Hyperpluralist		

2.   List the major challenges facing American democracy.

        1.

        2.

        3.

        4.

Objective 6: Understand the nature of American political culture and identify the elements of the American creed.

    1.   What is "political culture" and why is it crucial to understanding American government?

    2.   List the five elements of the American creed according to Seymour Martin Lipset.

        1.

        2.

        3.

        4.

        5.

    3.   Explain what is meant by a "culture war."

Objective 7: Understand the nature of the scope of government in America and the key questions concerning the scope of government.

    1.   Make a list of items that illustrate the scope of American government.

2.   What is gross domestic product and how does the term illustrate the scope of American government?

KEY TERMS

Identify and describe:

government

public goods

politics

political participation

single-issue groups

policymaking system

linkage institutions

policy agenda

political issue

policymaking institutions

public policy

democracy

majority rule

minority rights

representation

pluralist theory

elite and class theory

hyperpluralism

policy gridlock

political culture

gross domestic product

Compare and contrast:

government and politics

policy agenda and public policy

policymaking system and linkage institutions

policymaking system and political issue

democracy and traditional democratic theory

majority rule and minority rights

democracy and representation

pluralist theory, elite and class theory, and hyperpluralism

Name that term:

1. Something in which any member of society can share without diminishing the supply to any other member of society.

    _____

2. It consists of subjects and problems getting the attention of government officials and their associates.

    _____

3. This is a choice that government makes in response to an issue on its agenda.

    _____

4. This arises when people disagree about a problem or about public policy choices made to combat a problem.

   _____

5. Political parties, elections, and interest groups are the main ones in the United States.

   _____

6. The effects a policy has on people and on society's problems.

   _____

7. The most fundamental aspect of democratic theory.

   _____

8. According to this theory of American government, many groups are so strong and numerous that the government is unable to act.

   _____

9. This problem is magnified when voters choose a president from one party and congressional majorities from the other party.

   _____

10. A key factor hat holds American democracy together.

    _____

11. The total value of all goods and services produced annually by the United States.

    _____

USING YOUR UNDERSTANDING

1. Identify and discuss, in your own words, the important features of the policymaking system. Take a problem (such as AIDS, racial discrimination, or crime) and describe how it might be dealt with in this system, from how it becomes a political issue to the policies that could be made in response to it and

their impact on people. Discuss different ways in which the problem could be dealt with based on beliefs about the appropriate role of government. State your own view as well.

2.   Collect some current examples of politics and policymaking that illustrate, support, or refute aspects of the three theories of American democracy. Use Internet news sources, newspapers, and/or news magazines in your search. Briefly describe what you discover. Based on your understanding of the three theories and the evidence you have collected make an initial judgment of the applicability of each theory to political and policy realities in America. As you continue to learn about American politics and policymaking, see how your perceptions change.

REVIEW QUESTIONS

Check ☑ the correct answer:

1.   According to Michael Delli Carpini and Scott Keeter, political knowledge is important because it
    ☐ a.   fosters civic virtues.
    ☐ b.   helps citizens identify policies that would benefit them.
    ☐ c.   promotes active participation in politics.
    ☐ d.   all of the above

2.   The age group with the lowest voter turnout rate is
    ☐ a.   25 years old or younger.
    ☐ b.   26 to 40 years old.
    ☐ c.   41 to 64 years old.
    ☐ d.   65 years old or older.

3.   The institutions that make authoritative decisions that apply to all of society are collectively known as
    ☐ a.   the political system.
    ☐ b.   government.
    ☐ c.   linkage institutions.
    ☐ d.   public goods.

4.   Which of the following is NOT an example of a public good?
    ☐ a.   college education
    ☐ b.   parks
    ☐ c.   national defense
    ☐ d.   clean air policies

5.   All national governments
      ☐ a.   provide services.
      ☐ b.   have written constitutions.
      ☐ c.   have a president.
      ☐ d.   have a legislature.

6.   One of the basic functions of government is to socialize young citizens into the political system through schooling.
      ☐ True
      ☐ False

7.   Harold Lasswell's definition of politics is
      ☐ a.   "who gets what, when, and how."
      ☐ b.   "what gets done, then and now."
      ☐ c.   the authoritative allocation of the GNP.
      ☐ d.   voting in a duly constituted election.

8.   The media usually focuses on the
      ☐ a.   "who" of politics.
      ☐ b.   "what" of politics.
      ☐ c.   "when" of politics.
      ☐ d.   "how" of politics.

9.   America has one of the highest voter turnout rates in the world.
      ☐ True
      ☐ False

10.   Single-issue groups
      ☐ a.   aid effective policymaking for the public interest.
      ☐ b.   are concerned with a wide range of problems.
      ☐ c.   have very little influence on voters or politicians.
      ☐ d.   have little taste for compromise.

11.   Political issues get government's attention through linkage institutions.
      ☐ True
      ☐ False

12.   One type of linkage institution is
      ☐ a.   an interest group.
      ☐ b.   a bureaucracy.
      ☐ c.   a government.
      ☐ d.   a legislature.

13.   Which of the following is NOT an example of a linkage institution?
        ☐ a.   the National Rifle Association
        ☐ b.   the Democratic party
        ☐ c.   a referendum
        ☐ d.   the Supreme Court

14.   A policy agenda is
        ☐ a.   ignored by public officials.
        ☐ b.   an electoral ballot.
        ☐ c.   a list of problems to which serious attention is paid.
        ☐ d.   a public opinion poll.

15.   A government's policy agenda changes infrequently.
        ☐ True
        ☐ False

16.   Which of the following policymaking institutions was NOT established by the Constitution?
        ☐ a.   Congress
        ☐ b.   the bureaucracy
        ☐ c.   the presidency
        ☐ d.   the courts

17.   Public policy
        ☐ a.   consists of laws passed by Congress.
        ☐ b.   is what government chooses not to do.
        ☐ c.   involves making decisions.
        ☐ d.   all of the above

18.   Public policies include
        ☐ a.   congressional statutes.
        ☐ b.   court decisions.
        ☐ c.   budgetary choices.
        ☐ d.   all of the above

19.   The last part of the policy system concerns
        ☐ a.   implementation.
        ☐ b.   the policy agenda.
        ☐ c.   policy impacts.
        ☐ d.   elections.

20.	(bonus) According to *The Communist Manifesto,* the specter haunting Europe was
☐ a.	democracy.
☐ b.	military dictatorship.
☐ c.	communism.
☐ d.	freedom.

21.	The writers of the U.S. Constitution
☐ a.	cherished the idea of democracy.
☐ b.	favored government by the people.
☐ c.	rejected democratic ideals.
☐ d.	had no fondness for democracy.

22.	(bonus) Who said the people "should have as little to do as may be with the government"?
☐ a.	Abraham Lincoln
☐ b.	Elbridge Gerry
☐ c.	Roger Sherman
☐ d.	Alexis de Tocqueville

23.	The basic principles of traditional democratic theory include all of the following EXCEPT
☐ a.	equality in voting.
☐ b.	effective participation.
☐ c.	government control of information.
☐ d.	inclusion.

24.	In democratic theory, the principle of minority rights accompanies the principle of
☐ a.	majority rule.
☐ b.	representation.
☐ c.	pluralism.
☐ d.	equality.

25.	The closer the correspondence between representatives and their electoral majority, the closer the approximation to democracy.
☐ True
☐ False

26.	Pluralists argue that
☐ a.	there are only a few influential groups that shape American policymaking.
☐ b.	the American political system is a competition among many groups.
☐ c.	the public interest rarely prevails.
☐ d.	many access points diminish group influence.

27. Critics of the pluralist theory contend that it
   - ☐ a. misses the larger question of how the pie is distributed by arguing that every group gets a piece of the pie.
   - ☐ b. is overly pessimistic.
   - ☐ c. places too much emphasis on class differences.
   - ☐ d. fails to explain bargains and compromises.

28. Elite and class theory holds that
   - ☐ a. power is dispersed among many institutions.
   - ☐ b. wealth is irrelevant to political power.
   - ☐ c. American society is divided along class lines.
   - ☐ d. elites influence policymakers but are distinct from them.

29. According to the theory of hyperpluralism, government has become more effective with time.
   - ☐ True
   - ☐ False

30. The idea of powerful groups and weak government is most closely associated with
   - ☐ a. democratic theory.
   - ☐ b. elite and class theory.
   - ☐ c. pluralism.
   - ☐ d. hyperpluralism.

31. Hyperpluralism can lead to
   - ☐ a. policy in the public interest.
   - ☐ b. muddled and inconsistent policy.
   - ☐ c. more effective and efficient government.
   - ☐ d. centralized power and authority.

32. Democratic theory requires citizens to become experts on most everything.
   - ☐ True
   - ☐ False

33. Winning a congressional seat these days requires a campaign war chest of at least
   - ☐ a. $100,000.
   - ☐ b. $250,000.
   - ☐ c. $500,000.
   - ☐ d. $1,000,000.

34. Political Action Committees usually care only about how members of Congress vote on issues that particularly affect them.
   - ☐ True
   - ☐ False

35. A situation that is magnified when different parties control the president and Congress is
   ☐ a.   policy compromise.
   ☐ b.   pluralism.
   ☐ c.   policy gridlock.
   ☐ d.   individualism.

36. What unites Americans more than anything else is
   ☐ a.   the president.
   ☐ b.   their political culture.
   ☐ c.   participation in elections.
   ☐ d.   a belief in group politics.

37. According to Seymour Martin Lipset, the American creed includes the idea of
   ☐ a.   individualism.
   ☐ b.   laissez-faire.
   ☐ c.   populism.
   ☐ d.   all of the above

38. A key aspect of American egalitarianism is economic equality.
   ☐ True
   ☐ False

39. An important result of American individualism has been a clear tendency to prefer
   ☐ a.   laissez-faire economic policies.
   ☐ b.   higher tax rates.
   ☐ c.   national welfare policies, such as health care.
   ☐ d.   big government.

40. Research clearly indicates that America is engaged in a bitter culture war.
   ☐ True
   ☐ False

41. The percentage of the gross domestic product currently spent by our governments is about
   ☐ a.   10%.
   ☐ b.   50%.
   ☐ c.   30%.
   ☐ d.   75%.

42. Which of the following statements about the scope of our national government is TRUE?
- ☐ a. It spends nearly $3 trillion annually.
- ☐ b. It employs nearly two million people.
- ☐ c. It owns one-third of the land in the United States.
- ☐ d. all of the above

43. The percentage of the federal budget devoted to national defense is about
- ☐ a. one-tenth.
- ☐ b. one-sixth.
- ☐ c. one-fourth.
- ☐ d. one-third.

ESSAY QUESTIONS

1. Define government and identify the functions that governments perform. What is the role of politics in government?

2. What are the principal choices that governments face when confronting policy problems? Illustrate your answer with an example of a policy that poses tough choices. Explain how government makes policy even when it chooses to do nothing.

3. What are the principle components of the policymaking system? Explain how a political issue travels through the policymaking system by using an example.

4. What is the definition of democracy? What are the basic principles of traditional democratic theory? What problems might emerge when the theory is put into practice?

5. Compare, contrast, and critically evaluate the three theories of American democracy: pluralist theory, elite and class theory, and hyperpluralism.

6. Summarize some of the major challenges facing American democracy today. Briefly state your opinion as to how serious these challenges are and how they might be met.

7. What is meant by political culture? What is the nature of the American political culture? In your opinion is America experiencing a "culture war"?

8. In what ways might it be said that American government is "big"? How active is American government and why does government grow?

CHAPTER 2

THE CONSTITUTION

CHAPTER OUTLINE

I. The Origins of the Constitution (pp. 32-37)
    A. The Road to Revolution
    B. Declaring Independence, the **Declaration of Independence**
    C. The English Heritage: The Power of Ideas
        1. **Natural rights** are the rights inherent in human beings, not dependent on governments.
        2. **Consent of the governed** means the people must agree on who their rulers will be.
        3. **Limited government** means there must be clear restrictions on what rulers may do.
    D. Jefferson's Handiwork: The American Creed
    E. Winning Independence
    F. The "Conservative" Revolution

II. The Government That Failed: 1776-1787 (pp. 37-40)
    A. The **Articles of Confederation**
    B. Changes in the States
    C. Economic Turmoil
    D. **Shays' Rebellion**
    E. The Aborted Annapolis Meeting

III. Making a Constitution: The Philadelphia Convention (pp. 40-42)
    A. Gentlemen in Philadelphia
    B. Philosophy into Action
        1. Human Nature
        2. Political Conflict (**Factions** arise from sources of conflict.)
        3. Objects of Government
        4. Nature of Government

IV. The Agenda in Philadelphia (pp. 43-48)
    A. The Equality Issues
        1. Equality and Representation of the States
            a. **New Jersey Plan** had each state equally represented in Congress.
            b. **Virginia Plan** made state representation in Congress based on population.
            c. **Connecticut Compromise** created two houses of Congress.
        2. Slavery: Congress could limit the future importation of slaves and the three-fifths compromise settled how slaves would be represented.

　　　　　3.　　　　Political Equality
　　B.　　The Economic Issues
　　C.　　The Individual Rights Issues
　　　　　1.　　　　The Constitution says little about personal freedoms.
　　　　　2.　　　　Article I prohibits suspension of the **writ of habeas corpus.**

V.　　The Madisonian Model (pp. 48-51)
　　A.　　Thwarting Tyranny of the Majority
　　　　　1.　　　　Limiting Majority Control
　　　　　2.　　　　Separating Power (Under **separation of powers**, the three branches of government are relatively independent of each other and share powers.)
　　　　　3.　　　　Creating Checks and Balances (Under **checks and balances**, each branch of government requires the consent of the others for many of its actions.)
　　　　　4.　　　　Establishing a Federal System
　　B.　　The Constitutional Republic
　　　　　1.　　　　A **republic** is a system based on the consent of the governed in which representatives of the public exercise power.
　　C.　　The End of the Beginning

VI.　　Ratifying the Constitution (pp. 51-55)
　　A.　　Federalists and Anti-Federalists
　　　　　1.　　　　**Federalists** supported the Constitution and **Anti-Federalists** opposed it.
　　　　　2.　　　　The *Federalist Papers* were a series of articles supporting the Constitution.
　　　　　3.　　　　The **Bill of Rights** is the first ten amendments to the Constitution that restrain the national government from limiting personal freedoms.
　　B.　　Ratification

VII.　　Constitutional Change (pp. 55-61)
　　A.　　The Formal Amending Process: consists of two stages, proposal and ratification.
　　B.　　The Informal Process of Constitutional Change
　　　　　1.　　　　Judicial Interpretation: In *Marbury* **v.** *Madison* (1803), the Supreme Court claimed the power of **judicial review**, giving courts the right to decide the constitutionality of government actions.
　　　　　2.　　　　Changing Political Practice: includes political parties and the electoral college.
　　　　　3.　　　　Technology
　　　　　4.　　　　Increasing Demands on Policymakers
　　C.　　The Importance of Flexibility

VIII.　　Understanding the Constitution (pp. 61-65)
　　A.　　The Constitution and Democracy
　　B.　　The Constitution and the Scope of Government

IX.　　Summary (p. 65)

LEARNING OBJECTIVES

After studying Chapter 2, you should be able to:

1. Discuss the importance of the English philosophical heritage, the colonial experience, the Articles of Confederation, and the character of the Founding Fathers in shaping the agenda of the Constitution writers.

2. Identify the important principles and issues debated at the Constitutional Convention and describe how they were resolved.

3. Explain the Madisonian model of limiting majority control, separating powers, creating checks and balances, and establishing a federal system.

4. Understand the conflict between the Federalists and Anti-Federalists over the ratification of the Constitution.

5. Describe the formal and informal processes by which the Constitution is changed in response to new items on the policy agenda.

6. Evaluate the Constitution in terms of democracy and its impact on policymaking.

The following exercises will help you meet these objectives:

Objective 1: Discuss the importance of the English philosophical heritage, the colonial experience, the Articles of Confederation, and the character of the Founding Fathers in shaping the agenda of the Constitution writers.

1. Make a list of the major grievances of the colonists under British rule.

2. What are the major components of John Locke's political philosophy and how did they influence Thomas Jefferson's writings?

3. Draw a schematic diagram of the American government under the Articles of Confederation.

4. Make a list of the reasons why the Articles of Confederation failed.

5. Briefly describe the general philosophical views of the founding fathers on the following issues:

    Human Nature:

    Political Conflict:

    Objects of Government:

    Nature of Government:

Objective 2: Identify the important principles and issues debated at the Constitutional Convention and describe how they were resolved.

1. What were the three major equality issues at the Constitutional Convention and how were they resolved?

    1.

    2.

    3.

2.   What were the major economic problems addressed at the Constitutional Convention and how were they resolved?

3.   Why did the Founding Fathers believe it was not necessary to address individual rights issues specifically in the Constitution?

Objective 3: Explain the Madisonian model of limiting majority control, separating powers, and creating checks and balances.

    1.   Draw a schematic diagram of the Madisonian model of government.

    2.   Define the term "constitutional republic."

Objective 4: Understand the conflict between the Federalists and Anti-Federalists over the ratification of the Constitution.

    1.   Complete the following table summarizing the major differences between the Federalists and the Anti-Federalists on the issues of civil liberties, power of the states, and the economy.

Issues	Federalists	Anti-Federalists
Civil Liberties		
Power of the States		
Economy		

2.   Why did the Anti-Federalists believe the new Constitution was a class-based document?

Objective 5: Describe the formal and informal processes by which the Constitution is changed in response to new items on the policy agenda.

1.   What is meant by the "unwritten constitution"?

2.   Describe the different ways in which a formal constitutional amendment might be adopted.

3.   The text examines four ways the Constitution changes informally. Complete the following table, listing these ways, defining them, and giving an example for each.

Informal Change	Definition	Example

Objective 6: Evaluate the Constitution in terms of democracy and its impact on policymaking.

1.   List and explain the five Constitutional amendments that expanded the right to vote.

      1.

      2.

      3.

      4.

      5.

2.   In what ways does the Constitution expand and diminish the scope of government?

KEY TERMS

Identify and describe:

Constitution

Declaration of Independence

natural rights

consent of the governed

limited government

Articles of Confederation

Shays' Rebellion

U.S. Constitution

factions

New Jersey Plan

Virginia Plan

Connecticut Compromise

writ of habeas corpus

separation of powers

checks and balances

republic

Federalists

Anti-Federalists

Federalist Papers

Bill of Rights

Equal Rights Amendment

Marbury v. *Madison*

judicial review

Compare and contrast:

natural rights and consent of the governed

Constitution, Articles of Confederation, and U.S. Constitution

New Jersey Plan, Virginia Plan, and Connecticut Compromise

separation of powers and checks and balances

limited government and republic

Federalists and Anti-Federalists

Marbury v. *Madison* and judicial review

Name that term:

1. The first constitution of the United States.

   _____

2. A view that contrasts sharply with the divine right of kings.

   _____

3. A series of armed attacks on courthouses in 1787 to protest farm foreclosures.

   _____

4. Today these would be called interest groups or parties.

   _____

5. This enables persons detained by authorities to secure an immediate inquiry into the causes of their detention.

   _____

6.   This is a system of government based on the consent of the governed in which representatives of the public exercise power.

     _____

7.   A series of articles published under the name "Publius."

     _____

8.   The first ten amendments to the Constitution.

     _____

9.   First introduced in 1923, this constitutional amendment was passed by Congress in 1972 but never ratified by the states.

     _____

10.   Not found in the Constitution, this power was given to the courts in the case of *Marbury* v. *Madison.*

     _____

USING YOUR UNDERSTANDING

1.   Try your hand at sketching out a new Constitution for the contemporary United States. Be sure to indicate key governmental institutions and their functions. Also, include a bill of rights in your constitution. Keep in mind today's high-tech politics and the current policy agenda. Briefly discuss how the twentieth-century constitution you envision is similar to or different from the eighteenth-century Constitution of the Founders. Evaluate how well the Founders did in terms of these similarities or differences.

2.   Locate the written constitution of your state or that of another modern democratic system, such as France, Germany, or Japan. In reading the document or parts of it, look for similarities or differences with the American Constitution. Take note of the governmental institutions it creates, the functions they perform, and whether or not something comparable to the Bill of Rights is included. Describe briefly what you have found. Use this exercise to write a term paper comparing different types of constitutions and their effectiveness.

REVIEW QUESTIONS

Check ☑ the correct answer:

1.   Which of the following statements is FALSE?
   ☐ a.   A constitution is a nation's basic law.
   ☐ b.   A constitution is an unwritten accumulation of traditions and precedents.
   ☐ c.   A constitution allocates power within government.
   ☐ d.   A constitution sets neutral rules of the game of politics.

2.   During the colonial period, the British king and Parliament
   ☐ a.   were involved in nearly every aspect of colonial life.
   ☐ b.   confined themselves to governing America's foreign policy and trade.
   ☐ c.   allowed the colonists a limited number of representatives in Parliament.
   ☐ d.   put strict limits on American freedom.

3.   (bonus) The motion for declaring the United States as free and independent was made by
   ☐ a.   Thomas Jefferson.
   ☐ b.   Benjamin Franklin.
   ☐ c.   Richard Henry Lee.
   ☐ d.   John Adams.

4.   Which of the following concepts is inconsistent with the political philosophy associated with John Locke?
   ☐ a.   natural rights
   ☐ b.   the divine right of kings
   ☐ c.   limited government
   ☐ d.   the sanctity of property

5.   John Locke held that people should revolt when
   ☐ a.   injustices become deeply felt.
   ☐ b.   transient issues emerge.
   ☐ c.   government no longer has their consent.
   ☐ d.   both a. and c.

6.   Which of the following Lockean concepts of government does not have a direct parallel in Thomas Jefferson's draft of the Declaration of Independence?
   ☐ a.   natural rights
   ☐ b.   limited government
   ☐ c.   the sanctity of property
   ☐ d.   the right to revolt

7. The American Revolution drastically altered the colonists' way of life.
   ☐ True
   ☐ False

8. Our first constitution was the Articles of Confederation.
   ☐ True
   ☐ False

9. Most governmental authority in the early American experience rested with
   ☐ a. state legislatures.
   ☐ b. local townships.
   ☐ c. the Continental Congress.
   ☐ d. voluntary alliances.

10. The Articles of Confederation established the
    ☐ a. presidency.
    ☐ b. Senate and the House of Representatives.
    ☐ c. Supreme Court.
    ☐ d. Continental Congress.

11. The Continental Congress did not have the power to
    ☐ a. tax.
    ☐ b. issue securities.
    ☐ c. maintain a military.
    ☐ d. print money.

12. Which of the following did NOT occur under the Articles of Confederation?
    ☐ a. Shays' Rebellion
    ☐ b. a power shift in the states away from the elite
    ☐ c. an aborted meeting at Annapolis
    ☐ d. sweeping policies favoring creditors over debtors

13. Shays' Rebellion was
    ☐ a. a battle in the Revolutionary War.
    ☐ b. an attack on courthouses to prevent foreclosure proceedings.
    ☐ c. a constitutional debate.
    ☐ d. a colonial newspaper.

14. Which of the following does NOT, in general, describe the "Gentlemen in Philadelphia"?
    ☐ a. college educated
    ☐ b. wealthy
    ☐ c. Western
    ☐ d. successful

15. James Madison believed that factions would check themselves.
    ☐ True
    ☐ False

16. The philosophy of the Founders was based in part on
    ☐ a. the faith that self-restraint was part of human nature.
    ☐ b. a belief that political conflict is unrelated to the distribution of wealth in society.
    ☐ c. a view that the principal object of government is the preservation of property.
    ☐ d. the idea that the separation of power is not needed in balanced government.

17. Which of the following was NOT one of the key equality issues debated at the Constitutional Convention?
    ☐ a. representation of the states in Congress
    ☐ b. equal opportunity for women
    ☐ c. slavery
    ☐ d. political equality

18. Representation of the states in Congress was settled at the Constitutional Convention with the
    ☐ a. Connecticut Compromise.
    ☐ b. three-fifths compromise.
    ☐ c. New Jersey Plan.
    ☐ d. Virginia Plan.

19. Regarding the issue of slavery, the delegates to the Constitutional Convention agreed
    ☐ a. to abolish slavery.
    ☐ b. not to count slaves in determining representation in Congress.
    ☐ c. to sanction slavery officially.
    ☐ d. to limit future importing of slaves.

20. Delegates to the Constitutional Convention left it up to the states to decide who could vote in national elections.
    ☐ True
    ☐ False

21. One of the major economic issues that the writers of the Constitution felt they needed to address was
    ☐ a. tariffs erected by the states.
    ☐ b. virtually worthless paper money forced on creditors in some states.
    ☐ c. the inability of the Continental Congress to raise needed money.
    ☐ d. all of the above

22. Which of the following statements is TRUE?
   - ☐ a. The writers of the Constitution believed that the national economy was in good shape.
   - ☐ b. Economic issues were nonexistent at the writing of the Constitution.
   - ☐ c. The power of Congress to make economic policy is carefully spelled out in the Constitution.
   - ☐ d. The Constitution writers were men of little wealth.

23. The original Constitution says very little about personal freedoms.
   - ☐ True
   - ☐ False

24. A writ of habeas corpus
   - ☐ a. enables persons detained by authorities to secure an immediate inquiry into the causes of their detention.
   - ☐ b. allows for the punishment of people without a judicial trial.
   - ☐ c. allows for people to be punished or have their penalties increased for acts that were not illegal or not punishable when committed.
   - ☐ d. narrowly defines and outlines strict rules of evidence for conviction of treason.

25. The principle of separation of powers resulted from the fact that the Constitution writers feared the possibility of a tyranny of the majority.
   - ☐ True
   - ☐ False

26. The Madisonian model of government is based on the idea that
   - ☐ a. as much of government as possible should be beyond the direct control of a majority.
   - ☐ b. the power of government's different institutions should be separated.
   - ☐ c. a system of checks and balances is needed in government.
   - ☐ d. all of the above

27. In the Madisonian model of government, majority rule is accomplished by the election of the
   - ☐ a. Senate.
   - ☐ b. House of Representatives.
   - ☐ c. president.
   - ☐ d. Supreme Court.

28. The president's veto power is an example of
   - ☐ a. checks and balances.
   - ☐ b. majority rule.
   - ☐ c. presidential supremacy.
   - ☐ d. judicial review.

29. The Madisonian system
☐ a. created a form of direct democracy.
☐ b. had a liberal bias toward change.
☐ c. created a republic based on the consent of the governed.
☐ d. made change virtually impossible.

30. The final version of the Constitution was read aloud at a public meeting in Philadelphia.
☐ True
☐ False

31. (bonus) Immediately after the Constitution was signed, the delegates to the convention
☐ a. returned to their rooms.
☐ b. adjourned to a tavern.
☐ c. attended religious services.
☐ d. composed the national anthem.

32. The Federalist Papers were published under the name
☐ a. Philadelphiensis.
☐ b. Monteczuma.
☐ c. Aggrippa.
☐ d. Publius.

33. The Anti-Federalists were an unpatriotic and un-American group.
☐ True
☐ False

34. Which of the following was NOT an Anti-Federalist argument against the ratification of the Constitution?
☐ a. a charge that it was a class-based document
☐ b. a claim that it would weaken the power of the states
☐ c. a claim that the Bill of Rights was unnecessary
☐ d. a charge that it would benefit creditors

35. The Constitution was ratified by
☐ a. state conventions.
☐ b. a general election.
☐ c. state legislatures.
☐ d. a referendum.

36. An unwritten constitution
    ☐ a. is a body of tradition, practice, and procedure.
    ☐ b. is represented by the Bill of Rights.
    ☐ c. does not affect the spirit of the Constitution.
    ☐ d. does not encompass political parties.

37. An amendment to the Constitution can be ratified either by the legislature of three-fourths of the states or by special conventions called in three-fourths of the states.
    ☐ True
    ☐ False

38. Taken as a whole, the amendments to the Constitution make it
    ☐ a. more democratic.
    ☐ b. elite- and class-oriented.
    ☐ c. less egalitarian.
    ☐ d. more focused on economic issues.

39. The Equal Rights Amendment failed in part because of the system of checks and balances.
    ☐ True
    ☐ False

40. The Constitution does not formally provide for
    ☐ a. the two-party system.
    ☐ b. the role of television in politics.
    ☐ c. binding members of the electoral college to the preference of voters.
    ☐ d. all of the above

41. The case of *Marbury* v. *Madison*
    ☐ a. firmly established the power of judicial review.
    ☐ b. forced the delivery of court commissions.
    ☐ c. gave Congress the right to review the judiciary.
    ☐ d. diminished the power of the Supreme Court.

42. The writers of the Constitution
    ☐ a. favored the formation of a two-party system.
    ☐ b. intended there to be no popular vote for the president.
    ☐ c. required presidential electors to pledge in advance to vote for the candidate that won their state's popular vote.
    ☐ d. established the electoral college as a rubber stamp for the popular vote.

43. The roles of political parties and members of the electoral college are examples of constitutional change through political practice.
☐ True
☐ False

44. Which of the following statements regarding the U.S. Constitution is FALSE?
☐ a. The U.S. Constitution is a very flexible document.
☐ b. The U.S. Constitution is the oldest functioning constitution.
☐ c. The U.S. Constitution is very long compared to other constitutions.
☐ d. The only court provided for by the U.S. Constitution is the Supreme Court.

45. The Constitution is in many ways an undemocratic, even anti-democratic, document.
☐ True
☐ False

46. Which of the following statements regarding the Constitution is FALSE?
☐ a. One of the central themes of American history has been the gradual democratization of the Constitution.
☐ b. The original Constitution was characterized by numerous restrictions on direct voter participation.
☐ c. The original Constitution offers numerous guidelines on voter eligibility.
☐ d. Five of the 17 constitutional amendments passed since the Bill of Rights have focused on the expansion of the electorate.

47. During the early years of the civil rights movement, African Americans had the most luck getting their interests on the political agenda through the
☐ a. Congress.
☐ b. president.
☐ c. Supreme Court.
☐ d. state legislatures.

48. The separation of powers and the system of checks and balances promote
☐ a. the politics of bargaining.
☐ b. compromise.
☐ c. playing one institution against another.
☐ d. all of the above

ESSAY QUESTIONS

1. What are the historical origins of the American national government? What is the English heritage? How was the Declaration of Independence shaped by the philosophy of John Locke?

2. What philosophical views did the delegates to the Constitutional Convention share? How did they influence the nature of the Constitution?

3. How did the colonial experience shape the policy agenda at the Constitutional Convention? What issues comprised the agenda and how were they resolved?

4. What is the Madisonian model of government? How is it reflected in the structure of American government? What issues or problems does it raise?

5. Explain the process by which the Constitution was ratified. What were the major arguments raised against its ratification? How were some of these issues resolved?

6. What are the formal and informal processes by which the Constitution is changed? Include a discussion of the formal amendment process and the unwritten constitution in your answer.

7. In what ways was the original Constitution both democratic and undemocratic? How has the Constitution become democratized throughout American history?

CHAPTER 3

FEDERALISM

CHAPTER OUTLINE

I. Defining Federalism (pp. 70-74)
    A. What Is Federalism?
        1. **Federalism** is a way of organizing a nation so that two or more levels of government have formal authority over the same area and people.
        2. **Unitary governments** place all power in the central government.
        3. Confederations place all or most power in the hands of the components while the national government is weak.
        4. **Intergovernmental relations** refers to the entire set of interactions among national, state, and local governments.
    B. Why Is Federalism So Important?
        1. Federalism decentralizes politics in America.
        2. Federalism decentralizes policies in America.

II. The Constitutional Basis of Federalism (pp. 74-81)
    A. The Division of Power
        1. The **supremacy clause** establishes the Constitution, laws of the national government, and treaties as the supreme law of the land.
        2. The **Tenth Amendment** states that "powers not delegated to the United States by the Constitution, nor prohibited by it to the states, are reserved to the states respectively, or to the people."
    B. Establishing National Supremacy
        1. Implied Powers: *McCulloch* v. *Maryland* established the principle of **implied powers**, powers that go beyond the **enumerated powers** of the Constitution, on the basis of the **elastic clause.**
        2. Commerce Power: *Gibbons* v. *Ogden* defined commerce very broadly.
        3. The Civil War
        4. The Struggle for Racial Equality
    C. States' Obligations to Each Other
        1. **Full Faith and Credit**
        2. **Extradition**
        3. **Privileges and Immunities**

III. Intergovernmental Relations Today (pp. 81-90)
    A. From Dual to Cooperative Federalism

1.   In **dual federalism** the states and the national government each remain supreme within their own spheres.
2.   In **cooperative federalism** powers and policy assignments are shared between states and the national government.
    a.   Shared costs
    b.   Federal guidelines
    c.   Shared administration
B.   **Fiscal Federalism** is the pattern of spending, taxing, and providing grants in the federal system.
    1.   The Grant System: Distributing the Federal Pie
        a.   **Categorical grants** are the main source of federal aid to state and local governments.
            (1)   **Project grants** are awarded on the basis of competitive applications.
            (2)   **Formula grants** are distributed according to a formula.
        b.   **Block grants** are given more or less automatically to states or communities that have discretion in deciding how to spend the money.
    2.   The Scramble for Federal Dollars
    3.   The Mandate Blues

IV.   Understanding Federalism (pp. 90-95)
    A.   Federalism and Democracy
        1.   Advantages for Democracy
        2.   Disadvantages for Democracy
    B.   Federalism and the Scope of the National Government

V.   Summary (pp. 95-96)

LEARNING OBJECTIVES

After studying Chapter 3, you should be able to:

1.   Define federalism and explain why it is important to American government and politics.

2.   Describe how the Constitution divides power between the national and state governments and understand why the supremacy of the national government is the central principle of American federalism.

3.   Explain the nature of the states' obligations to each other.

4. Explain how federalism in the United States has shifted from dual federalism to cooperative federalism.

5. Describe the nature of fiscal federalism and how states and cities compete for federal grants and aid.

6. Explain the relationship between federalism and democracy, and how federalism contributes to and detracts from democracy.

7. Understand how federalism has contributed to the scope of the national government.

The following exercises will help you meet these objectives:

Objective 1: Define federalism and explain why it is important to American government and politics.

   1. Define the three ways of organizing a nation that were discussed in the text.

      1.

      2.

      3.

   2. In what ways does federalism decentralize politics and policies?

Objective 2: Describe how the Constitution divides power between the national and state governments and understand why the supremacy of the national government is the central principle of American federalism.

   1. List the three items that are considered the supreme law of the land.

      1.

      2.

3.

2.   What is the significance of the Tenth Amendment?

3.   Explain the difference between enumerated powers and implied powers.

Objective 3: Explain the nature of the states' obligations to each other.

1.   Describe the three general obligations that each state has to every other state under the Constitution.

1.

2.

3.

Objective 4: Explain how federalism in the United States has shifted from dual federalism to cooperative federalism.

1.   How is dual federalism analogous to a layer cake and cooperative federalism analogous to a marble cake?

2.   Explain the three general standard operating procedures of cooperative federalism.

1.

2.

3.

Objective 5: Describe the nature of fiscal federalism and how states and cities compete for federal grants and aid.

1. What is meant by "cross-over sanctions" and "cross-cutting requirements"?

   Cross-over Sanctions:

   Cross-cutting Requirements:

2. Explain the two types of categorical grants.

   1.

   2.

3. For what reasons might a state or locality not want to receive federal aid?

Objective 6: Explain the relationship between federalism and democracy, and how federalism contributes to and detracts from democracy.

1. List four advantages of federalism for democracy.

   1.

   2.

   3.

   4.

2. List four disadvantages of federalism for democracy.

   1.

2.

3.

4.

Objective 7: Understand how federalism has contributed to the scope of the national government.

    1.   How did industrialization increase the role of the national government?

    2.   Why don't the states handle more issues?

KEY TERMS

Identify and describe:

federalism

unitary governments

intergovernmental relations

supremacy clause

Tenth Amendment

McCulloch v. *Maryland*

enumerated powers

implied powers

elastic clause

Gibbons v. *Ogden*

full faith and credit

extradition

privileges and immunities

dual federalism

cooperative federalism

fiscal federalism

categorical grants

project grants

formula grants

block grants

Compare and contrast:

federalism and unitary government

intergovernmental relations and fiscal federalism

supremacy clause and Tenth Amendment

enumerated powers and implied powers

McCulloch v. *Maryland* and *Gibbons* v. *Ogden*

full faith and credit, extradition, and privileges and immunities

dual federalism and cooperative federalism

categorical grants and block grants

project grants and formula grants

Name that term:

1. In this type of system, the national government can redraw the boundaries of local governments or change their form.

   _____

2. The supremacy of the national government over the states was established by this court case.

   _____

3. Examples of this include the power of Congress to coin money, regulate its value, and impose taxes.

   _____

4. In this case, the Supreme Court broadly defined commerce to include virtually every form of commercial activity.

   _____

5. When a state returns a person charged with a crime in another state to that state for trial or imprisonment, they are practicing this constitutional requirement.

   _____

6. This type of federalism has been likened to a "marble cake."

   _____

7. These grants are awarded on the basis of competitive applications.

   _____

8. This was a response to state and local governmental unhappiness with cumbersome and tedious categorical grants.

   _____

USING YOUR UNDERSTANDING

1. Try to identify all of the governments that have authority and policymaking responsibilities in your area, from the federal and state governments to the various types of local government. At the same time, identify the types of public policies for which they are responsible. Briefly discuss your impressions of the federal system from your own vantage point. Indicate whether or not you found what you expected, based on your understanding of the American federal system.

2. Contact your local Chamber of Commerce and find out what strategies your community is pursuing in order to compete with other communities, including its efforts to win federal aid. You may even be able to find some brochures that "sell" your community to prospective residents and industries. Describe what you found in terms of how well you think your community is doing in the economic growth game. Try devising some marketing strategies for your community based on its location and other advantages.

REVIEW QUESTIONS

Check ☑ the correct answer:

1. In federalism, governmental power and authority is
   ☐ a. concentrated with the federal government.
   ☐ b. concentrated with local governments.
   ☐ c. shared between governments.
   ☐ d. nonexistent.

2. The majority of the world's governments are federal systems.
   ☐ True
   ☐ False

3. An example of a unitary government is
   ☐ a. the United States.
   ☐ b. Canada.
   ☐ c. Mexico.
   ☐ d. France.

4. The American states are unitary with respect to their local governments.
   ☐ True
   ☐ False

47

5.   When it comes to presidential campaigns, the candidates can basically ignore the states.
       ☐ True
       ☐ False

6.   The federal system in America decentralizes
       ☐ a.   politics.
       ☐ b.   government.
       ☐ c.   policies.
       ☐ d.   all of the above

7.   In the U.S., the federal government is responsible for most social, family, and moral public policies.
       ☐ True
       ☐ False

8.   Sometimes social issues become national issues when groups try to use the power of the national government to influence the states.
       ☐ True
       ☐ False

9.   Which of the following statements regarding the states is FALSE?
       ☐ a.   The states constitute a national laboratory to develop and test public policies.
       ☐ b.   Almost every policy the national government has adopted had its beginnings in the states.
       ☐ c.   The states rarely produce policy innovations.
       ☐ d.   The states often share the results of new policy ideas with other states and the national government.

10.   The term federalism is found repeatedly in the Constitution.
       ☐ True
       ☐ False

11.   Which of the following statements about the Constitution is FALSE?
       ☐ a.   It forbids Congress to divide up individual states.
       ☐ b.   It makes the federal government responsible for elections.
       ☐ c.   It is unamendable as to the equal representation of the states in the Senate.
       ☐ d.   It requires the national government to protect states against violence and invasion.

12. According to the supremacy clause, the supreme law of the land consists of all of the following EXCEPT
   ☐ a.   the Constitution.
   ☐ b.   laws of the national government.
   ☐ c.   treaties.
   ☐ d.   state laws.

13. The Constitution grants the national government exclusive power to
   ☐ a.   coin money.
   ☐ b.   tax.
   ☐ c.   establish courts.
   ☐ d.   charter banks.

14. The Constitution specifically denies to states the power to
   ☐ a.   make and enforce laws.
   ☐ b.   conduct elections.
   ☐ c.   establish local governments.
   ☐ d.   tax imports and exports.

15. The Tenth Amendment provides for
   ☐ a.   universal suffrage.
   ☐ b.   civil liberties.
   ☐ c.   the delegation of power to the states and the people.
   ☐ d.   the abolition of slavery.

16. The question of how national and state powers are related was largely settled by
   ☐ a.   the civil rights movement.
   ☐ b.   the case of *McCulloch* v. *Maryland.*
   ☐ c.   the Civil War.
   ☐ d.   all of the above

17. In 1791, the newly created national bank was regarded favorably by
   ☐ a.   state legislatures.
   ☐ b.   farmers.
   ☐ c.   Federalists.
   ☐ d.   Thomas Jefferson.

18. (bonus) One of the country's ablest lawyers, who argued the case for Maryland before the Supreme Court in *McCulloch* v. *Maryland,* was
   ☐ a.   Daniel Webster.
   ☐ b.   Luther Martin.
   ☐ c.   Thomas Jefferson.
   ☐ d.   John Hancock.

19. In *McCulloch* v. *Maryland*, the Supreme Court stated that as long as the national government behaves in accordance with the Constitution, its policies take precedence over state policies.
☐ True
☐ False

20. *McCulloch* v. *Maryland* established the two constitutional principles of
☐ a. equality and freedom.
☐ b. national supremacy and implied powers.
☐ c. checks and balances.
☐ d. federalism and intergovernmental relations.

21. The implied powers of Congress
☐ a. mean that Congress has powers that go beyond those enumerated in the Constitution.
☐ b. mean that Congress can make laws that are unconstitutional.
☐ c. include its powers to coin money and impose taxes.
☐ d. were listed in the Tenth Amendment.

22. New Deal and civil rights legislation illustrate the powers of the national government as derived through its constitutional requirement to regulate
☐ a. foreign policy.
☐ b. interstate commerce.
☐ c. the military.
☐ d. elections.

23. Conflict over federalism was at the center of the
☐ a. Civil War.
☐ b. Revolutionary War.
☐ c. War of 1812.
☐ d. World War I.

24. The battle for racial equality
☐ a. has been fought exclusively at the state level.
☐ b. was resolved by the Thirteenth, Fifteenth, and Nineteenth Amendments.
☐ c. ended with the end of the Civil War.
☐ d. demonstrates national supremacy in the federal system.

25. The constitutional requirement that states must return a person charged with a crime in another state to that state for trial or imprisonment is called
☐ a. full faith and credit.
☐ b. extradition.
☐ c. privileges and immunities.
☐ d. dual federalism.

26. The goal of the principle of privileges and immunities is to
   - a. make the public acts, records, and civil proceedings of each state legal and binding in all states.
   - b. allow for a person charged with a crime in another state to be returned to that state for trial or imprisonment.
   - c. prohibit states from discriminating against citizens of other states.
   - d. require the national government to give each state an equivalent share of federal grant money.

27. The Supreme Court has clearly identified which privileges a state must make available to all Americans, and which privileges can be limited to its own citizens.
   - True
   - False

28. In dual federalism the
   - a. states are supreme over all policies.
   - b. national government is supreme over all policies.
   - c. powers and policy responsibilities of the government layers are distinct.
   - d. administration of programs is shared by governmental units.

29. (bonus) Cooperative federalism has been likened to a
   - a. layer cake.
   - b. marble cake.
   - c. upside-down cake.
   - d. fruit cake.

30. Education is a policy area that most exemplifies
   - a. dual federalism.
   - b. cooperative federalism.
   - c. federal supremacy.
   - d. state supremacy.

31. Which of the following is NOT a standard operating procedure of cooperative federalism?
   - a. exclusive control by state agencies
   - b. shared costs
   - c. federal guidelines
   - d. shared administration

32. The pattern of spending, taxing, and providing grants in the federal system is
   - a. cooperative federalism.
   - b. fiscal federalism.
   - c. extradition.
   - d. categorical federalism.

33. The federal grants-in-aid system gives the national government very little control over the states.
   ☐ True
   ☐ False

34. Categorical grants
   ☐ a. are the main source of federal aid to states and cities.
   ☐ b. are given more or less automatically.
   ☐ c. are designed to support broad programs.
   ☐ d. have very few strings attached.

35. Using federal dollars in one program to influence state and local policy in another is called
   ☐ a. cross-cutting requirements.
   ☐ b. cross-over sanctions.
   ☐ c. grantsmanship.
   ☐ d. fiscal federalism.

36. Categorical grants include all of the following EXCEPT
   ☐ a. project grants.
   ☐ b. grants with strings attached.
   ☐ c. block grants.
   ☐ d. formula grants.

37. A type of grant awarded on the basis of competitive applications is the
   ☐ a. project grant.
   ☐ b. formula grant.
   ☐ c. block grant.
   ☐ d. fiscal grant.

38. The federal aid programs that allow states some discretion in deciding how to spend the money are
   ☐ a. categorical grants.
   ☐ b. block grants.
   ☐ c. project grants.
   ☐ d. formula grants.

39. The National League of Cities, the United States Conference of Mayors, and the Council of State Governments are governmental interest groups.
   ☐ True
   ☐ False

40. A general rule of federalism is that, the more money at stake, the more people will argue about its distribution.
☐ True
☐ False

41. States and localities are always eager to receive increased aid from the federal government.
☐ True
☐ False

42. The Americans with Disabilities Act of 1990 is an example of
☐ a. the federal courts creating unfunded mandates for the states.
☐ b. the federal government unintentionally creating financial obligations for the states.
☐ c. a congressional law creating financial obligations for the states but providing no funds to meet these obligations.
☐ d. the federal government attaching conditions to federal grants-in-aid.

43. Federalism contributes to democracy by
☐ a. creating more opportunities for participation in democracy.
☐ b. increasing the opportunities for government to be responsive to demands for policies.
☐ c. ensuring that each state can establish a power base to promote its interests.
☐ d. all of the above

44. Federalism tends to increase the amount of decision making and conflict at the national level.
☐ True
☐ False

45. Which of the following statements is FALSE?
☐ a. States differ in the resources they can devote to services like public education.
☐ b. Diversity in policy tends to encourage states to provide services that would otherwise not be available, such as generous welfare benefits.
☐ c. Local interests may be able to thwart national majority support of certain policies.
☐ d. The number of governments in the United States makes it difficult to know which governments are doing what.

46. Voter turnout in local elections is often
☐ a. more than for presidential elections.
☐ b. over 50 percent.
☐ c. less than 20 percent.
☐ d. the same as for presidential elections.

47.   A major consequence of the United States changing from an agricultural to an industrial nation was
☐ a.   an increase in the role of state governments.
☐ b.   a decrease in cooperative federalism.
☐ c.   an increase in demands on the national government for new policies.
☐ d.   a decrease in the number of federal grants.

48.   Labor unions tend to channel their demands for public policies through state governments rather than through the national government.
☐ True
☐ False

49.   The proportion of our GDP spent by state and local governments
☐ a.   has grown less rapidly than the national government's share.
☐ b.   has declined since 1929.
☐ c.   is twice as much as the national government's share.
☐ d.   is about the same as the national government's share.

ESSAY QUESTIONS

1.   Define federalism. How is federalism different from unitary governments and confederations? Why is federalism important to understanding American government?

2.   What does the Constitution have to say about national versus state power? How was the supremacy of the national government established in the American federal system?

3.   Explain the obligations that states have to each other. Give examples to illustrate your answer.

4.   Why does cooperative federalism, as compared to dual federalism, best describe the American federal system today? Why is fiscal federalism important to intergovernmental relations?

5.   Compare and contrast the different types of federal aid and grants given to states and cities. What is the nature of the competition for federal grants? Under what conditions might states not want to receive federal aid?

6.   What are the advantages and disadvantages of federalism for democracy? Give examples to illustrate your answer.

7.   How and why has federalism contributed to the growth of the national government?

8.   Evaluate federalism as a way of organizing government in America. Could the American system have been a unitary system?

CHAPTER 4

CIVIL LIBERTIES AND PUBLIC POLICY

CHAPTER OUTLINE

I. Introduction (pp. 98-100)
    A. **Civil liberties** are individual legal and constitutional protections against the government.
    B. Americans' civil liberties are set down in the **Bill of Rights**, the first ten amendments to the Constitution.

II. The Bill of Rights - Then and Now (pp. 100-102)
    A. The **First Amendment** is the source of Americans' freedom of religion, speech, press, and assembly.
    B. The Bill of Rights and the States
        1. *Barron* **v.** *Baltimore*: The Bill of Rights restrained only the national government.
        2. *Gitlow* **v.** *New York* relied on the **due process clause** of the **Fourteenth Amendment** to rule that a state government must respect some First Amendment rights.
        3. The **incorporation doctrine** is a legal concept under which the Supreme Court has nationalized the Bill of Rights by making most of its provisions applicable to the states through the Fourteenth Amendment.

III. Freedom of Religion (pp. 102-109)
    A. The **Establishment Clause**: "Congress shall make no law respecting an establishment of religion."(*Lemon* **v.** *Kurtzman*, *Zelman* **v.** *Simmons-Harris*, *Engel* **v.** *Vitale*, and *School District of Abington Township, Pennsylvania* **v.** *Schempp*)
    B. The **Free Exercise Clause** prohibits the abridgment of the citizens' freedom to worship, or not to worship, as they please.

IV. Freedom of Expression (pp. 109-122)
    A. **Prior Restraint**, or governmental actions that prevent material from being published (censorship), has been consistently struck down by the Supreme Court (*Near* **v.** *Minnesota*).
    B. Free Speech and Public Order: the right to protest has been protected to varying extent depending on the political climate (*Schenck* **v.** *United States*).
    C. Free Press and Fair Trials
        1. Press coverage may interfere with a fair trial.

2.   Reporters do not always like to open their files to the courts; shield laws may protect reporters from revealing their sources. (***Zurcher* v. *Stanford Daily***)

D.   Obscenity has not been regarded as a fully constitutionally protected area of free speech and press, but remains controversial. (***Roth* v. *United States*** and ***Miller* v. *California***)

E.   **Libel** and Slander, the Supreme Court has held (***New York Times* v. *Sullivan***) that statements about public figures are libelous only if made with malice and reckless disregard for the truth.

F.   **Symbolic Speech** is an action that does not consist of speaking or writing but that expresses an opinion. (***Texas* v. *Johnson***)

G.   **Commercial Speech** is restricted far more extensively than other expressions of opinion.

H.   Regulation of the Public Airwaves, the Federal Communications Commission regulates the content, nature, and very existence of radio and television broadcasting. (***Miami Herald Publishing Co.* v. *Tornillo*** and ***Red Lion Broadcasting Co.* v. *Federal Communication Commission***)

I.   Freedom of Assembly
    1.   Right to Assemble, to gather together in order to make a statement.
    2.   Right to Associate, to associate with people who share a common interest, including an interest in political change. (***NAACP* v. *Alabama***)

V.   Defendants' Rights (pp. 122-130)
    A.   Interpreting Defendants' Rights
    B.   Searches and Seizures
        1.   Before making an arrest, police need **probable cause** to believe that someone is guilty of a crime.
        2.   The Fourth Amendment forbids **unreasonable searches and seizures.**
        3.   The Constitution requires that probable cause exist before issuing a **search warrant.**
        4.   The **exclusionary rule** prevents illegally seized evidence from being introduced in the courtroom (***Mapp* v. *Ohio***).
    C.   **Self-incrimination**: the **Fifth Amendment** forbids self-incrimination and *Miranda* v. *Arizona* set guidelines for police questioning.
    D.   The Right to Counsel: the **Sixth Amendment** ensures the right to counsel and *Gideon* v. *Wainwright* extended this right to those who can not afford counsel.
    E.   Trials: Most cases are settled through **plea bargaining.**
    F.   **Cruel and Unusual Punishment**
        1.   The **Eighth Amendment** forbids cruel and unusual punishment.
        2.   Almost all of the constitutional debate over cruel and unusual punishment has centered on the death penalty (***Gregg* v. *Georgia*** and ***McClesky* v. *Kemp***).

VI.   The Right To Privacy (pp. 130-135)
        A.   Is There a **Right to Privacy**?
        B.   Controversy over Abortion: ***Roe* v. *Wade*** defined the conditions under which abortions are allowed. ***Planned Parenthood* v. *Casey*** permitted more regulation of abortions.

VII.   Understanding Civil Liberties (pp. 135-136)
        A.   Civil Liberties and Democracy
        B.   Civil Liberties and the Scope of Government

VIII.   Summary (pp. 136-137)

LEARNING OBJECTIVES

After studying Chapter 4, you should be able to:

    1.   Understand the constitutional basis of civil liberties and the Supreme Court's role in defining them.

    2.   Discuss the religious liberties guaranteed in the First Amendment.

    3.   Explain the nature of and the issues involving freedom of expression in America.

    4.   Identify the rights of individuals accused of crimes.

    5.   Evaluate and discuss the issue of the right to privacy.

    6.   Understand the impact of civil liberties on democracy and the scope of government.

The following exercises will help you meet these objectives:

Objective 1: Understand the constitutional basis of civil liberties and the Supreme Court's role in defining them.

    1.   Define the term "civil liberties."

2.   What was the most important difference between the Supreme Court's decision in *Barron* v. *Baltimore* and *Gitlow* v. *New York*?

3.   Explain the importance of the Fourteenth Amendment.

4.   What is the incorporation doctrine?

Objective 2: Discuss the religious liberties guaranteed in the First Amendment.

1.   List four Supreme Court cases concerning the establishment clause and comment on their significance.

    1.

    2.

    3.

    4.

2. Compare and contrast the Supreme Court case of *Employment Division v. Smith* (1990) with the Religious Freedom Restoration Act of 1993.

Objective 3: Explain the nature of and the issues involving freedom of expression in America.

1.   Define the term "prior restraint."

2.   List and explain the significance of three Supreme Court cases concerning free speech and public order.

        1.

        2.

        3.

3.   What is a shield law?

4.   How did the Supreme Court define obscenity in the case of *Miller* v. *California*?

5.   How are the standards for winning libel lawsuits different for public figures and private individuals?

6.   Define the term "symbolic speech."

7.   Who regulates commercial speech?

8.   What is the function of the Federal Communications Commission (FCC)?

9.   Explain the two facets of the freedom of assembly.

        1.

        2.

Objective 4: Identify the rights of individuals accused of crimes.

    1.   Draw a diagram of the criminal justice system as a series of funnels.

    2.   How are the following terms interrelated: probable cause, unreasonable searches and seizures, search warrant, and exclusionary rule?

    3.   What are the three guidelines for police questioning of suspects as set forth in *Miranda* v. *Arizona* (1966)?

        1.

        2.

        3.

    4.   What is the significance of the Supreme Court case of *Gideon* v. *Wainwright* (1963)?

5.   What are the pros and cons of plea bargaining?

6.   List and explain the importance of three Supreme Court cases concerning the death penalty.

    1.

    2.

    3.

Objective 5: Evaluate and discuss the issue of the right to privacy.

1.   Explain how the Constitution implies a right to privacy.

2.   List and explain the importance of four Supreme Court cases concerning abortion.

    1.

    2.

    3.

    4.

Objective 6: Understand the impact of civil liberties on democracy and the scope of government.

1.   In your opinion are the rights guaranteed in the Fourth, Fifth, Sixth, Seventh, and Eighth Amendments more beneficial to criminals or society at large?

2.	In what ways do civil liberties limit the scope of government and in what ways do they expand the scope of government?

KEY TERMS AND CASES

Identify and describe: key terms

civil liberties

Bill of Rights

First Amendment

Fourteenth Amendment

incorporation doctrine

establishment clause

free exercise clause

prior restraint

libel

symbolic speech

commercial speech

probable cause

unreasonable searches and seizures

search warrant

exclusionary rule

Fifth Amendment

self-incrimination

Sixth Amendment

plea bargaining

Eighth Amendment

cruel and unusual punishment

right of privacy

Identify and describe: key cases

Barron v. *Baltimore* (1833)

Gitlow v. *New York* (1925)

Lemon v. *Kurtzman* (1971

Zelman v. *Simmons-Harris* (2002)

Engel v. *Vitale* (1962)

School District of Abington Township, Pennsylvania v. *Schempp* (1963)

Near v. *Minnesota* (1931)

Schenk v. *United States* (1919)

Zurcher v. *Stanford Daily* (1976)

Roth v. *United States* (1957)

Miller v. *California* (1973)

New York Times v. *Sullivan* (1964)

Texas v. *Johnson* (1989)

Miami Herald Publishing Co. v. *Tornillo* (1974)

Red Lion Broadcasting Co. v. *Federal Communications Commission* (1969)

NAACP v. *Alabama* (1958)

Mapp v. *Ohio* (1961)

Miranda v. *Arizona* (1966)

Gideon v. *Wainwright* (1963)

Gregg v. *Georgia* (1976)

McCleskey v. *Kemp* (1987)

Roe v. *Wade* (1973)

Planned Parenthood v. *Casey* (1992)

Compare and contrast:

civil liberties and Bill of Rights

First Amendment and Fourteenth Amendment

Barron v. *Baltimore* and *Gitlow* v. *New York*

Gitlow v. *New York* and Fourteenth Amendment

establishment clause and free exercise clause

Lemon v. *Kurtzman* and *Zelman* v. *Simmons-Harris*

Engel v. *Vitale* and *School District of Abington Township, Pennsylvania* v. *Schempp*

67

prior restraint and *Near* v. *Minnesota*

Roth v. *United States* and *Miller* v. *California*

libel and *New York Times* v. *Sullivan*

Texas v. *Johnson* and symbolic speech

Miami Herald Publishing Company v. *Tornillo* and *Red Lion Broadcasting Company* v. *Federal Communications Commission*

probable cause, unreasonable searches and seizures, and search warrant

unreasonable searches and seizures and *Mapp* v. *Ohio*

unreasonable searches and seizures and exclusionary rule

Fifth Amendment and self-incrimination

Fifth Amendment and *Miranda* v. *Arizona*

Sixth Amendment and *Gideon* v. *Wainwright*

Eighth Amendment and cruel and unusual punishment

Gregg v. *Georgia* and *McCleskey* v. *Kemp*

right of privacy and *Roe* v. *Wade*

Name that term:

1. The Supreme Court has one-by-one done this to the Bill of Rights.

    _____

2. This part of the First Amendment forbids the government from having an official church.

    _____

3. A government's actions that prevent material from being published in the first place.

    _____

4. This 1973 Supreme Court case attempted to clarify the meaning of obscenity by spelling out what would and would not be obscene.

    _____

5. The publication of knowingly false or malicious statements that damage someone's reputation.

    _____

6. Actions that do not consist of speaking or writing, but that express an opinion.

    _____

7.   This type of speech is restricted far more extensively than expressions of opinion on religious, political, or other matters.

_____

8.   This case established the principle of "clear and present danger."

_____

9.   This case upheld the right to associate.

_____

10.   The Constitution requires that no court may issue one of these unless probable cause exists to believe that a crime has occurred or is about to occur.

_____

11.   This case extended the exclusionary rule to the states.

_____

12.   This case set strict guidelines for police questioning of suspects.

_____

13.   Most criminal cases are settled through this process.

_____

14.   Undefined by the Eighth Amendment, this has been the basis of the controversy over the death penalty.

_____

15.   This right is implied, but not directly stated, in the Bill of Rights.

_____

USING YOUR UNDERSTANDING

1. Select one of the Supreme Court cases discussed in this chapter that is of interest to you. Find and read the opinions presented in the case, including any dissenting opinions, and briefly describe what you found. Identify the social values that were in conflict in the case. Based on your understanding, state whether or not you are persuaded by the arguments presented in justification of the decision.

2. How have the terrorist attacks of September 11, 2001 affected civil liberties in the United States? List and explain the various restrictions put in place and laws, such as the Patriot Act, passed by the government that have had an impact on our personal freedoms since September 11, 2001. In your opinion, are these restrictions worth the tradeoff? Does the reality of international terrorism require a reevaluation of an unconditional commitment to civil liberties? In your opinion, how far should we go?

REVIEW QUESTIONS

Check ☑ the correct answer:

1. Civil liberties are legal and constitutional protections against
   - ☐ a.   criminals.
   - ☐ b.   government.
   - ☐ c.   foreign invasions.
   - ☐ d.   private enterprise.

2. Civil liberties are formally set down in the
   - ☐ a.   Bill of Rights.
   - ☐ b.   preamble to the Constitution.
   - ☐ c.   Declaration of Independence.
   - ☐ d.   Articles of Confederation.

3. Most cases concerning civil liberties are easy and straightforward.
   - ☐ True
   - ☐ False

4. Which of the following statements about civil liberties is FALSE?
   - ☐ a.   The first Congress passed the Bill of Rights.
   - ☐ b.   All of the original states had their own bills of rights.
   - ☐ c.   The American people are entirely devoted to political rights in both theory and practice.
   - ☐ d.   Our civil liberties often conflict.

5. In literal terms, the First Amendment is directed toward
    - ☐ a. the states.
    - ☐ b. Congress.
    - ☐ c. the courts.
    - ☐ d. all units of government.

6. In the case of *Barron* v. *Baltimore* (1833), the Supreme Court held that the Bill of Rights restrained only the national government, not the states and cities.
    - ☐ True
    - ☐ False

7. Freedom of speech was incorporated into state laws by
    - ☐ a. *Barron* v. *Baltimore.*
    - ☐ b. the first Congress.
    - ☐ c. *Gitlow* v. *New York.*
    - ☐ d. the Tenth Amendment.

8. The Bill of Rights
    - ☐ a. applies only to the national government.
    - ☐ b. immediately applied to the states after ratification of the Fourteenth Amendment.
    - ☐ c. was gradually incorporated into state laws.
    - ☐ d. has always applied to the states as well as national government.

9. According to Thomas Jefferson, the First Amendment was designed to create
    - ☐ a. a national church.
    - ☐ b. federal support for religious pursuits.
    - ☐ c. a wall of separation between church and state.
    - ☐ d. government control of churches.

10. The "wall of separation" separates
    - ☐ a. assembly and association.
    - ☐ b. government and religion.
    - ☐ c. protected and unprotected speech.
    - ☐ d. civil liberties and civil rights.

11. According to the Supreme Court, school-sponsored prayers in public schools are acceptable only with certain restrictions.
    - ☐ True
    - ☐ False

12. Which of the following statements regarding religion in the United States in recent years is FALSE?
- ☐ a. Religious issues and controversies have assumed much greater importance in political debate.
- ☐ b. Fundamentalist religious groups have shied away from political action due to recent controversies.
- ☐ c. Some groups have advocated the teaching of "intelligent design" as an alternative to evolution in the public schools.
- ☐ d. Conservative Republicans have pushed for a constitutional amendment permitting school prayer.

13. The Supreme Court has been very tolerant of the right of people to believe what they want and less tolerant of their right to practice what they believe.
- ☐ True
- ☐ False

14. (bonus) Who said, "The most stringent protection of free speech would not protect a man in falsely shouting 'fire' in a theater and causing a panic"?
- ☐ a. Justice Oliver Wendell Holmes
- ☐ b. Justice Hugo Black
- ☐ c. Justice Thurgood Marshall
- ☐ d. Justice Potter Stewart

15. Prior restraint
- ☐ a. is frequently exercised by the United States government.
- ☐ b. was allowed in *Near* v. *Minnesota* (1931).
- ☐ c. means government prevention of publication.
- ☐ d. allows a newspaper to print libelous materials.

16. According to the Supreme Court in the case of *Schenck* v. *United States* (1919), free speech can be restricted by the government only on the basis of
- ☐ a. obscenity.
- ☐ b. community sentiment.
- ☐ c. symbolic protest.
- ☐ d. clear and present danger.

17. In the case of *Dennis* v. *United States* (1951), the Supreme Court permitted the government to
- ☐ a. exercise prior restraint over certain publications.
- ☐ b. jail some American Communist Party leaders.
- ☐ c. prohibit all forms of symbolic speech.
- ☐ d. use wiretaps to spy on American citizens.

18. Constitutional protections of free speech diminish once a person steps on private property.
☐ True
☐ False

19. Some states have passed shield laws that protect
☐ a. criminals from self-incrimination.
☐ b. publications from prior restraint.
☐ c. reporters' notes and information from being revealed in court.
☐ d. courts from holding trials in public.

20. In *Roth* v. *United States* (1957), the Supreme Court ruled that obscene material was not within the realm of constitutionally protected speech or press.
☐ True
☐ False

21. (bonus) "I know it when I see it" refers to
☐ a. obscenity.
☐ b. libel.
☐ c. crime.
☐ d. cruel and unusual punishment.

22. In *Miller* v. *California* (1973), defining obscenity was left up to
☐ a. private individuals.
☐ b. courts.
☐ c. Congress.
☐ d. state and local officials.

23. The newest issue in the obscenity controversy involves
☐ a. regulations aimed at keeping obscene material away from the young.
☐ b. the proliferation of pornography on the Internet.
☐ c. the proliferation of pornography in video stores.
☐ d. the use of obscene words in public places.

24. To be libelous, a statement must be knowingly false or malicious.
☐ True
☐ False

25. The Supreme Court case of *New York Times* v. *Sullivan* (1964)
☐ a. made it easier for public officials to win libel cases.
☐ b. held that statements about public officials are libelous only if made with malice and reckless disregard for the truth.
☐ c. held that statements about public officials are libelous if they are intended to damage severely the person's reputation.
☐ d. severely limited the ability of the press to express its opinions freely.

26. Private individuals have a lower standard to meet for winning lawsuits for libel than public figures.
☐ True
☐ False

27. The Supreme Court has dealt with questions of free speech by
☐ a. allowing the government to regulate the content of speech on the airwaves.
☐ b. distinguishing between pure and symbolic speech.
☐ c. using a "clear and present danger" test.
☐ d. all of the above

28. In 1989, the Supreme Court ruled that the burning of an American flag was a form of constitutionally protected speech.
☐ True
☐ False

29. Which of the following has received the greatest amount of regulation by the federal government?
☐ a. symbolic speech
☐ b. commercial speech
☐ c. television news
☐ d. newspapers

30. The Federal Communications Commission regulates the content, nature, and licensing of radio, television, and newspapers.
☐ True
☐ False

31. The Supreme Court has
☐ a. ruled that newspapers must provide space for political candidates to reply to newspaper criticisms.
☐ b. allowed the policy of barring certain words from radio or television when children might hear them.
☐ c. ruled that cable television is subject to the same regulations as commercial television.
☐ d. all of the above

75

32.   Freedom of assembly only concerns the literal right of people to gather in one place.
        ☐ True
        ☐ False

33.   The Supreme Court has ruled that spontaneous demonstrations at any time, anywhere, and in any way are protected by the First Amendment's freedom of assembly.
        ☐ True
        ☐ False

34.   Most of the words contained in the Bill of Rights pertain to the rights of persons accused of crime.
        ☐ True
        ☐ False

35.   The most infrequent event in the criminal justice system is a(n)
        ☐ a.   crime.
        ☐ b.   arrest.
        ☐ c.   prosecution.
        ☐ d.   trial.

36.   In *Mapp* v. *Ohio* (1961), the Supreme Court
        ☐ a.   extended the principle of unreasonable searches and seizures to the states.
        ☐ b.   established the exclusionary rule.
        ☐ c.   required probable cause to make an arrest.
        ☐ d.   protected individuals against self-incrimination.

37.   The exclusionary rule prohibits a court's use of
        ☐ a.   illegally seized evidence.
        ☐ b.   cruel and unusual punishment.
        ☐ c.   search warrants.
        ☐ d.   plea bargaining.

38.   Fifth Amendment protection against self-incrimination begins with
        ☐ a.   a trial.
        ☐ b.   prosecution.
        ☐ c.   an arrest.
        ☐ d.   criminal sentencing.

39. According to the Supreme Court's decision in *Miranda* v. *Arizona* (1966), police suspects must be told that
   ☐ a. they are constitutionally entitled to remain silent.
   ☐ b. anything they say can be used against them.
   ☐ c. they have a right to have a lawyer present during police questioning.
   ☐ d. all of the above

40. The Sixth Amendment's guarantee of a right to a lawyer was extended to state courts by the Supreme Court case of
   ☐ a. *Miranda* v. *Arizona* (1966).
   ☐ b. *Gideon* v. *Wainwright* (1963).
   ☐ c. *Mapp* v. *Ohio* (1961).
   ☐ d. *Gregg* v. *Georgia* (1976).

41. Most criminal cases are settled through plea bargaining.
   ☐ True
   ☐ False

42. Plea bargaining usually
   ☐ a. costs the state more money.
   ☐ b. results in fewer defendants going to prison.
   ☐ c. results in harsher punishment for defendants.
   ☐ d. can only be used by defendants accused of minor crimes.

43. The Constitution
   ☐ a. does not specify the size of a jury.
   ☐ b. sets jury size at twelve.
   ☐ c. sets jury size according to the type of crime.
   ☐ d. sets jury size according to the type of court.

44. The Supreme Court has ruled that the death penalty
   ☐ a. is suitable to the most extreme of crimes.
   ☐ b. is always unconstitutional.
   ☐ c. can be made mandatory for certain crimes.
   ☐ d. is the highest form of cruel and unusual punishment.

45. The Bill of Rights spells out the right of privacy in the Third Amendment.
   ☐ True
   ☐ False

46. In *Roe* v. *Wade* (1973), the Supreme Court
    ☐ a. forbade state regulation of abortion during the first trimester.
    ☐ b. permitted states to allow abortion in the second trimester only to protect a mother's health.
    ☐ c. permitted states to forbid abortions in the third trimester.
    ☐ d. all of the above

47. Which of the following statements about recent Supreme Court decisions concerning abortion is FALSE?
    ☐ a. It has upheld state laws forbidding the use of state funds to pay for abortions.
    ☐ b. It has upheld a ban on abortion counseling in federally supported family planning programs.
    ☐ c. It has upheld a law requiring a married woman to tell her husband of her intent to have an abortion.
    ☐ d. It has upheld a law requiring a 24-hour waiting period prior to an abortion.

48. Which of the following statements is FALSE?
    ☐ a. First Amendment rights are essential to a democracy.
    ☐ b. Ultimately, Congress decides what constitutional guarantees mean in practice.
    ☐ c. The courts enhance democracy by protecting liberty and equality from the excesses of majority rule.
    ☐ d. The Bill of Rights places strict limitations on governmental power.

49. In general, civil liberties limit the scope of government.
    ☐ True
    ☐ False

ESSAY QUESTIONS

1. What is the relationship between the national government and the states in the protection of civil liberties? How was the issue of protecting civil liberties at the state level resolved?

2. What would a literal interpretation of the First Amendment mean for the protection of civil liberties? What factors tend to prevent such a literal interpretation? Give examples to illustrate your answer.

3. Compare the First Amendment freedoms in terms of the restrictions placed on their application. Do you agree with these restrictions? Support your position with examples of actual or hypothetical cases.

4. What role has religion played in American politics? How has religious freedom been interpreted in the United States?

5. Identify the various types of speech. Categorize the different types of speech according to the extent to which they are protected by the Constitution. Give examples of court cases that have helped to establish these protections.

6. What are the constitutional protections of persons accused of crimes, and where are they found? How has the Supreme Court interpreted and shaped these protections?

7. What is meant by the "right to privacy"? Explain the controversies that have arisen over the right to privacy.

8. How do civil liberties affect the nature of democracy and the scope of government in the United States?

CHAPTER 5

CIVIL RIGHTS AND PUBLIC POLICY

CHAPTER OUTLINE

I.   Introduction (pp. 140-142)
    A.   **Civil rights** are policies that extend basic rights to groups historically subject to discrimination.
    B.   Debates on inequality in America center on racial discrimination, gender discrimination, and discrimination based on age, disability, sexual orientation, and other factors.

II.   Racial Equality: Two Centuries of Struggle (pp. 142-145)
    A.   Conceptions of Equality
        1.   Equality of opportunity: everyone should have the same chance.
        2.   Equal results or rewards: everyone should have the same rewards.
    B.   Early American Views of Equality
    C.   The Constitution and Inequality: The **Fourteenth Amendment** provides for **equal protection of the laws,** resulting in expansive constitutional interpretation.

III.   Race, the Constitution, and Public Policy (pp. 145-157)
    A.   The Era of Slavery
        1.   *Scott* v. *Sandford* (1857) upheld slavery.
        2.   The Civil War and the **Thirteenth Amendment** ended slavery.
    B.   The Era of Reconstruction and Resegregation
        1.   Jim Crow laws (segregation laws) established in the South.
        2.   *Plessy* v. *Ferguson* justified segregation through the "equal but separate" doctrine.
    C.   The Era of Civil Rights
        1.   *Brown* v. *Board of Education* (1954) overturned *Plessy* and ended legal segregation.
        2.   The civil rights movement organized to end the policies and practice of segregation.
        3.   The **Civil Rights Act of 1964** made racial discrimination illegal in places of public accommodation and in employment.
    D.   Getting and Using the Right to Vote
        1.   **Suffrage** was guaranteed to African Americans by the **Fifteenth Amendment** in 1870.
        2.   Southern practices to deny African American suffrage (literacy tests, grandfather clause, **poll taxes,** and the **White primary**) were gradually struck down by the Supreme Court and the **Twenty-fourth Amendment.**

3. The **Voting Rights Act of 1965** prohibited any government from using voting procedures that denied a person the vote on the basis of race or color.
E. Other Minority Groups
   1. Native Americans
   2. Hispanic Americans
   3. Asian Americans: *Korematsu* **v.** *United States,* 1944 upheld the internment of Japanese Americans during World War II.
   4. Other Groups

IV. Women, the Constitution, and Public Policy (pp. 157-165)
   A. The Battle for the Vote, the **Nineteenth Amendment** gave women the right to vote.
   B. The "Doldrums": 1920-1960
      1. Public policy toward women was dominated by protectionism.
      2. The **Equal Rights Amendment** was first introduced in Congress in 1923.
   C. The Second Feminist Wave
      1. *Reed* **v.** *Reed* (1971) ruled that any "arbitrary" sex-based classification violated the Fourteenth Amendment.
      2. *Craig* **v.** *Boren* (1976) established a "medium scrutiny" standard.
   D. Women in the Workplace: Congressional acts and Supreme Court decisions have reduced sex discrimination in employment and business activity.
   E. Wage Discrimination and Comparable Worth: Women should receive equal pay for jobs of "**comparable worth.**"
   F. Women in the Military
      1. Only men must register for the draft.
      2. Statutes and regulations prohibit women from serving in combat.
   G. Sexual Harassment: The Supreme Court has ruled that sexual harassment that is so pervasive as to create a hostile or abusive work environment is a form of sex discrimination.

V. Newly Active Groups Under the Civil Rights Umbrella (pp. 165-169)
   A. Civil Rights and the Graying of America
   B. Civil Rights and People with Disabilities: the **Americans with Disabilities Act of 1990** required employers and public facilities to make reasonable accommodations and prohibited employment discrimination against the disabled.
   C. Gay and Lesbian Rights

VI. Affirmative Action (pp. 169-172)
   A. **Affirmative action** involves efforts to bring about increased employment, promotion, or admission for members of groups that have suffered invidious discrimination.

B.   In ***Regents of the University of California* v. *Bakke*** (1978), the Court ruled against the practice of setting aside a quota of spots for particular groups.

C.   The Court has been more deferential to Congress than to local government in upholding affirmative action programs.

D.   In ***Adarand Constructors* v. *Peña*** (1995), the Court ruled that federal programs that classify people by race are constitutional only if they are "narrowly tailored" to accomplish a "compelling governmental interest."

E.   Opponents view affirmative action as reverse discrimination.

VII.   Understanding Civil Liberties and the Constitution (pp. 172-173)

A.   Civil Rights and Democracy, equality favors majority rule that may threaten minority rights.

B.   Civil Rights and the Scope of Government, civil rights laws increase the scope and power of government.

VIII. Summary (pp. 173-174)

LEARNING OBJECTIVES

After studying Chapter 5, you should be able to:

1.   Understand the historical and constitutional basis of the struggle for equal rights.

2.   Discuss the struggle for equality for African Americans in terms of three historical eras, the Constitution, and public policy.

3.   Explain how women have gained civil rights and what equality issues remain important for women today.

4.   Describe the new groups in the civil rights movement.

5.   Explain the controversy over the issue of affirmative action.

6.   Understand the impact of civil rights on democracy and the scope of government.

The following exercises will help you meet these objectives:

Objective 1: Understand the historical and constitutional basis of the struggle for equal rights.

1.   What are the three key types of inequality in America?

1.

2.

3.

2.   Explain the two major conceptions of equality.

1.

2.

3.   What is the only mention of the idea of equality in the Constitution?

4.   Explain the Supreme Court's three standards for classifications under the equal protection clause and give an example of each.

Objective 2: Discuss the struggle for equality for African Americans in terms of three historical eras, the Constitution, and public policy.

1.   Complete the following table listing the three eras of the struggle for African American equality, the major policy focus during each era, major court cases and their importance in each era, and any acts of Congress or constitutional amendments passed during each era.

Historical Era	Policy Focus	Court Cases	Acts/Amendments

2. Compare and contrast the significance of the Supreme Court cases of *Dred Scott v. Sandford* (1857), *Plessy v. Ferguson* (1896), and *Brown v. Board of Education* (1954).

3. What is the difference between *de jure* segregation and *de facto* segregation?

4. List the six major provisions of the Civil Rights Act of 1964.

1.

2.

3.

4.

5.

6.

5.   List and explain four ways in which the southern states denied African Americans the right to vote.

        1.

        2.

        3.

        4.

6.   What was the impact of the Voting Rights Act of 1965?

7.   List three other minority groups that have faced discrimination similar to that experienced by African Americans.

        1.

        2.

        3.

Objective 3: Explain how women have gained civil rights and what equality issues remain important for women today.

1.   Explain the policy of "protectionism."

2.   What was the Equal Rights Amendment?

3.   List and explain the significance of four Supreme Court cases dealing with sex-based discrimination.

        1.

        2.

        3.

        4.

4.   How has Congress attempted to end sex discrimination in the area of employment?

5.   What is meant by "comparable worth"?

6.   In what two ways are women legally treated differently in the military?

        1.

        2.

7.   How has the Supreme Court dealt with the issue of sexual harassment?

Objective 4: Describe the new groups in the civil rights movement.

1.   In what ways are the elderly discriminated against in American society?

2.   What are the main provisions of the Rehabilitation Act of 1973 and Americans with Disabilities Act of 1990?

3.   Why might gays and lesbians face the toughest battle for equality?

Objective 5: Explain the controversy over the issue of affirmative action.

1.   Define the term "affirmative action."

2.   List four cases in which the Supreme Court seems to support affirmative action and four cases in which it seems to oppose affirmative action.

Support	Oppose
1.	1.
2.	2.
3.	3.
4.	4.

Objective 6: Understand the impact of civil rights on democracy and the scope of government.

1.   How does equality threaten liberty?

2.   How do civil rights laws increase the scope and power of government?

KEY TERMS AND KEY CASES

Identify and describe: key terms

civil rights

Fourteenth Amendment

equal protection of the laws

Thirteenth Amendment

Civil Rights Act of 1964

suffrage

Fifteenth Amendment

poll taxes

White primary

Twenty-fourth Amendment

Voting Rights Act of 1965

Nineteenth Amendment

Equal Rights Amendment

comparable worth

Americans with Disabilities Act of 1990 (ADA)

affirmative action

Identify and describe: key cases

Scott v. *Sandford* (1857)

Plessy v. *Ferguson* (1896)

Brown v. *Board of Education* (1954)

Korematsu v. *United States* (1944)

Reed v. *Reed* (1971)

Craig v. *Boren* (1976)

Regents of the University of California v. *Bakke* (1978)

Adarand Constructors v. *Peña* (1995)

Compare and contrast:

Fourteenth Amendment and equal protection of the laws

Dred Scott v. *Sandford* and Thirteenth Amendment

Plessy v. *Ferguson* and *Brown* v. *Board of Education*

Civil Rights Act of 1964 and Voting Rights Act of 1965

suffrage and Fifteenth Amendment

poll taxes and White primary

Twenty-fourth Amendment and poll taxes

Nineteenth Amendment and Equal Rights Amendment

Reed v. *Reed* and *Craig* v. *Boren*

affirmative action and *Regents of the University of California* v. *Bakke*

affirmative action and *Adarand Constructors* v. *Peña*

Name that term:

1. Policies that extend basic rights to groups historically subject to discrimination.

   _____

2. The Fourteenth Amendment forbids the state from denying this to their citizens.

   _____

3. The Supreme Court case that justified segregation.

   _____

4. This law made racial discrimination illegal in hotels, motels, restaurants, and other places of public accommodations.

   _____

5. A device that permitted political parties in the heavily Democratic South to exclude blacks from primary elections.

   _____

6. This case upheld the internment of Japanese Americans in encampments during World War II.

   _____

7. "Equality of rights under the law shall not be denied or abridged by the United States or by any state on account of sex."

_____

8. This idea suggests that women should receive equal pay with men for jobs demanding similar skills.

_____

9. The law that requires employers and public facilities to make reasonable accommodations for disabled people.

_____

USING YOUR UNDERSTANDING

1. Investigate the policy that your college or university follows with regard to the admission of minority and women students. Also find out about its employment practices, and whether or not it has an affirmative action program. Collect statistics on the percentage of minorities enrolled and employed by the school. Does your college or university offer special academic programs for minorities and women? Evaluate whether or not you believe your school is doing too much or too little in addressing equality issues. Include a recommendation as to how you believe the school's policy might be improved, describing what consequences your recommendation would have.

2. The onslaught of the AIDS epidemic has raised new issues of equality in the United States. Examine this issue. Should AIDS victims receive the same protections as other handicapped people? How has AIDS affected the gay rights movement? Compile a list of state and local ordinances concerning homosexuals. Do most of these laws protect or discriminate against homosexuals? Also compile survey research results on public opinion towards gays and lesbians. Has the public become more or less tolerant of gays and lesbians? How has AIDS affected public attitudes? Compare the gay rights movement with the civil rights and women's movements. How are they similar and how are they different?

REVIEW QUESTIONS

Check ☑ the correct answer:

1. The rallying cry for groups demanding more equality has been
   - ☐ a. civil rights.
   - ☐ b. civil liberties.
   - ☐ c. civil disobedience.
   - ☐ d. civil war.

2. Policies that are designed to protect people against arbitrary or discriminatory treatment by government officials or individuals are called
   - ☐ a. social policies.
   - ☐ b. civil liberties.
   - ☐ c. civil rights.
   - ☐ d. civil equalities.

3. Today, debates about equality typically center on each of the following key types of inequality in America EXCEPT
   - ☐ a. discrimination based on income.
   - ☐ b. racial discrimination.
   - ☐ c. gender discrimination.
   - ☐ d. discrimination based on age, disability, and other factors.

4. American society tends to emphasize
   - ☐ a. equal results.
   - ☐ b. equal rewards.
   - ☐ c. equal opportunities.
   - ☐ d. equal distributions.

5. The word "equality" does not appear in the original Constitution.
   - ☐ True
   - ☐ False

6. The idea of equality in the Constitution first appeared in the
   - ☐ a. original Constitution.
   - ☐ b. Bill of Rights.
   - ☐ c. Fourteenth Amendment.
   - ☐ d. Nineteenth Amendment.

7. The five words in the Constitution that refer to equality are
   - ☐ a. "all men are created equal."
   - ☐ b. "equality and justice for all."
   - ☐ c. "equal protection of the laws."
   - ☐ d. "equal representation of the states."

8.   The Supreme Court has ruled that classifications based on gender are subject to a lower level of scrutiny than classifications based on race.
☐ True
☐ False

9.   In the case of *Dred Scott* v. *Sandford* (1857), the Supreme Court defended the idea of
☐ a.   slavery.
☐ b.   equality.
☐ c.   civil rights.
☐ d.   equal protection of the laws.

10.   The Thirteenth Amendment
☐ a.   promoted equal protection of the laws.
☐ b.   gave women the right to vote.
☐ c.   abolished slavery.
☐ d.   legalized segregation.

11.   During the first ten years after the Civil War, many African American men held both state and federal offices.
☐ True
☐ False

12.   In the case of *Plessy* v. *Ferguson* (1896), the Supreme Court upheld a Louisiana law providing for
☐ a.   slavery.
☐ b.   the civil rights movement.
☐ c.   equal opportunity.
☐ d.   segregated facilities.

13.   The case of *Brown* v. *Board of Education* (1954) ended the era of
☐ a.   slavery.
☐ b.   legal segregation.
☐ c.   civil rights.
☐ d.   equal opportunity.

14.   School busing was used as a tool for segregation after the passage of the Civil Rights Act of 1964.
☐ True
☐ False

15.   School busing was a practice upheld in the case of
☐ a.   *Dred Scott* v. *Sandford.*
☐ b.   *Plessy* v. *Ferguson.*
☐ c.   *Brown* v. *Board of Education.*
☐ d.   *Swann* v. *Charlotte-Mecklenberg County Schools.*

16. Children assigned to schools near their homes when those homes are in racially segregated neighborhoods is an example of
    ☐ a. separate but equal.
    ☐ b. *de jure* segregation.
    ☐ c. *de facto* segregation.
    ☐ d. all of the above

17. The civil rights movement organized both African Americans and Whites to end segregation.
    ☐ True
    ☐ False

18. Which of the following was NOT a key strategy of the civil rights movement?
    ☐ a. sit-ins
    ☐ b. marches
    ☐ c. quiet acceptance
    ☐ d. civil disobedience

19. The 1950s and 1960s saw a marked increase in public policies to foster racial equality primarily due to
    ☐ a. court decisions.
    ☐ b. the civil rights movement.
    ☐ c. increased African American voting.
    ☐ d. all of the above

20. Racial discrimination in public places became illegal by the
    ☐ a. Supreme Court case of *Brown* v. *Board of Education.*
    ☐ b. Civil Rights Act of 1964.
    ☐ c. Voting Rights Act of 1965.
    ☐ d. Equality in Employment Act of 1991.

21. By the 1980s, few, if any, forms of racial discrimination were left to legislate against.
    ☐ True
    ☐ False

22. Suffrage is the legal right to
    ☐ a. free speech.
    ☐ b. vote.
    ☐ c. equal opportunities.
    ☐ d. suffer.

23. The Fifteenth Amendment extended suffrage to
☐ a. African Americans.
☐ b. women.
☐ c. Native Americans.
☐ d. naturalized citizens.

24. Implementation of the Fifteenth Amendment proceeded swiftly and with the total support of the states.
☐ True
☐ False

25. Southern states attempted to deny African Americans the right to vote through the use of the
☐ a. literacy test.
☐ b. poll tax.
☐ c. White primary.
☐ d. all of the above

26. Poll taxes were declared void by the
☐ a. Thirteenth Amendment.
☐ b. Fifteenth Amendment.
☐ c. Nineteenth Amendment.
☐ d. Twenty-fourth Amendment.

27. Which of the following was NOT a consequence of the Voting Rights Act of 1965?
☐ a. the registration of many southern black voters
☐ b. the use of White primaries
☐ c. the election of more black officials
☐ d. the intervention of federal election registrars

28. Which of the following statements is FALSE?
☐ a. Native Americans comprise the oldest American minority.
☐ b. African Americans achieved citizenship before Native Americans.
☐ c. The Indian Claims Act was passed by Congress to settle disputes arising from lands taken from Indians.
☐ d. Native Americans are not protected by policy protections against discrimination.

29. Hispanic Americans are the largest minority group in the United States.
☐ True
☐ False

30. In the case of *Korematsu* v. *United States* (1944), the Supreme Court upheld
 ☐ a. affirmative action programs for Asian Americans.
 ☐ b. the tribal system of government for Native Americans.
 ☐ c. the internment of Americans of Japanese descent.
 ☐ d. the enforcement of immigration policies.

31. Equality for women did not appear on the nation's political agenda until the middle of the twentieth century.
 ☐ True
 ☐ False

32. Suffrage for women was achieved with the passage of the
 ☐ a. Tenth Amendment.
 ☐ b. Fifteenth Amendment.
 ☐ c. Nineteenth Amendment.
 ☐ d. Twenty-fourth Amendment.

33. Winning the right to vote gave the women's movement great momentum in the fight for equality.
 ☐ True
 ☐ False

34. After women received the right to vote, public policy toward women was dominated by the idea of
 ☐ a. protectionism.
 ☐ b. equality.
 ☐ c. coverture.
 ☐ d. autonomy.

35. The Equal Rights Amendment was first introduced in Congress as an Amendment in 1923.
 ☐ True
 ☐ False

36. The Supreme Court ruled in *Reed* v. *Reed* (1971) that
 ☐ a. any arbitrary sex-based classification under state law violated the equal protection clause.
 ☐ b. people should be paid comparable wages for comparable jobs.
 ☐ c. women should be allowed to hold combat positions in the military.
 ☐ d. sexual harassment violates federal policies against sexual discrimination in the workplace.

37. The Supreme Court has voided laws that
- ☐ a. provide for alimony payments to women only.
- ☐ b. close nursing schools to men.
- ☐ c. set a higher age for drinking for men than for women.
- ☐ d. all of the above

38. Most American mothers who have children below school age are in the labor force. ☐ True
☐ False

39. The Civil Rights and Women's Equity in Employment Act of 1991
- ☐ a. banned sex discrimination in employment.
- ☐ b. forbade sex discrimination in federally subsidized education programs.
- ☐ c. shifted the burden of proof in justifying hiring and promotion practices to employers.
- ☐ d. made it illegal for employers to exclude pregnancy and childbirth from their health-benefits plans.

40. Comparable worth is based on the idea that comparable wages should be paid to
- ☐ a. blacks and whites.
- ☐ b. men and women.
- ☐ c. people performing jobs requiring comparable skill.
- ☐ d. people holding comparable job titles.

41. (bonus) The subject referred to by the head of the U.S. Civil Rights Commission in the Reagan administration as "the craziest idea since Looney Tunes" was
- ☐ a. suffrage for women.
- ☐ b. comparable worth.
- ☐ c. the Equal Rights Amendment.
- ☐ d. affirmative action.

42. Statutes and regulations prohibit women from serving in combat.
☐ True
☐ False

43. The Supreme Court has made it very difficult to prove sexual harassment.
☐ True
☐ False

44. Age discrimination is one area that has received very little attention from the U.S. Congress.
☐ True
☐ False

45. The Americans with Disabilities Act of 1990
   ☐ a. strengthened previous protections against discrimination against the disabled.
   ☐ b. required employers and public facilities to make reasonable accommodations.
   ☐ c. prohibited employment discrimination against the disabled.
   ☐ d. all of the above

46. The one group that probably faces the toughest battle for equality is
   ☐ a. the handicapped.
   ☐ b. the elderly.
   ☐ c. young people.
   ☐ d. gays and lesbians.

47. Members of the armed services who declare their homosexuality face discharge unless they can prove they will remain celibate.
   ☐ True
   ☐ False

48. The women's movement and the civil rights movement converged when it came to the debate over
   ☐ a. comparable worth.
   ☐ b. the Equal Rights Amendment.
   ☐ c. affirmative action.
   ☐ d. protectionism.

49. Affirmative action emphasizes equal opportunities over equal results.
   ☐ True
   ☐ False

50. The Supreme Court held that an admissions quota for particular groups was illegal in
   ☐ a. *United Steelworkers of America, AFL-CIO* v. *Weber.*
   ☐ b. *Fullilove* v. *Klutznick.*
   ☐ c. *Regents of the University of California* v. *Bakke.*
   ☐ d. *Wygart* v. *Jackson Board of Education.*

51. Opposition to affirmative action is especially strong when people view it as
   ☐ a. affecting only African Americans.
   ☐ b. a form of separate-but-equal.
   ☐ c. reverse discrimination.
   ☐ d. discriminating against women.

52.   Which of the following statements is FALSE?
- a.   Equality is a basic principle of democracy.
- b.   The principle of equality can invite the denial of minority rights.
- c.   Civil rights laws and court decisions tell groups and individuals that there are certain things they may and may not do.
- d.   Current civil rights policies conform to the eighteenth-century idea of limited government.

ESSAY QUESTIONS

1.   How would you define the term "equality"? What does the U.S. Constitution say about equality?

2.   What have been the different eras in the struggle for racial equality? What public policy achievements were made in each era?

3.   Explain how the right to vote has been extended in the United States to include both African Americans and women. How was the struggle for suffrage among these two groups similar and different?

4.   Explain the nature of the feminist movement in the United States. What policies have resulted from the struggle for equal rights for women? Explain the controversy over the issue of comparable worth.

5.   Who are the new groups under the civil rights umbrella and what issues are they concerned about? What equality issues might arise in the near future?

6.   What is meant by affirmative action? What are the pros and cons of affirmative action? How has the Supreme Court dealt with the issue of affirmative action?

7.   How do civil rights affect the nature of democracy and the scope of government in the United States?

CHAPTER 6

PUBLIC OPINION AND POLITICAL ACTION

CHAPTER OUTLINE

I.   The American People (pp. 178-184)
    A.   The study of American **public opinion** aims to understand the distribution of the population's belief about politics and policy issues.
    B.   **Demography** is the science of human populations. The Constitution requires a **census**, "an actual enumeration" of the population, every ten years.
    C.   The Immigrant Society: there have been three great waves of immigration.
    D.   The American Melting Pot
        1.   A **melting pot** refers to a mixture of cultures, ideas, and peoples.
        2.   The United States will soon experience a **minority majority**, where white Anglo-Saxons will no longer be a majority.
        3.   The Simpson-Mazzoli Act required employers to document the citizenship of their employees.
        4.   Americans share a common **political culture**—an overall set of values widely shared within a society.
    E.   The Regional Shift
        1.   Over the last 60 years, the Sunbelt has had the greatest population growth.
        2.   **Reapportionment** occurs after every census. House seats are reallocated to the states based on population changes.
    F.   The Graying of America: Citizens over 65 compose the fastest growing age group.

II.   How Americans Learn About Politics: Political Socialization (pp. 184-188)
    A.   **Political socialization** is "the process through which an individual acquires his or her particular political orientations."
    B.   The Process of Political Socialization
        1.   The Family
        2.   The Mass Media
        3.   School
    C.   Political Learning over a Lifetime

III.   Measuring Public Opinion and Political Information (pp. 189-195)
    A.   How Polls are Conducted
        1.   A **sample** of the population is a relatively small proportion of people who are chosen as representative of the whole.
        2.   **Random sampling** operates on the principle that everyone should have an equal probability of being selected.

3.   **Sampling error** depends on the size of the sample.
4.   Most polling is done on the telephone with samples selected through **random-digit dialing.**

B.   The Role of Polls in American Democracy
1.   Polls help political candidates detect public preferences.
2.   Polls may make politicians followers rather than leaders.
3.   Polls can distort the election process.
4.   **Exit polls** may discourage people from voting.
5.   Polls can be manipulated by altering the wording of questions.

C.   What Polls Reveal About Americans' Political Information: Americans are not well informed about politics.

D.   The Decline of Trust in Government

IV.   What Americans Value: Political Ideologies (pp. 196-200)

A.   A **political ideology** is a coherent set of values and beliefs about public policy.

B.   Who are the Liberals and Conservatives?
1.   More Americans consistently choose the ideological label of conservative over liberal.
2.   Liberals generally like to see the government do more.
3.   Groups with political clout tend to be more conservative than groups whose members have often been shut out from political power.
4.   Ideological differences between men and women have led to the **gender gap**, where women are more likely to support Democratic candidates.
5.   The role of religion in influencing political ideology has changed greatly in recent years.

C.   Do People Think in Ideological Terms? For most people, the terms liberal and conservative are not as important as they are for the political elite.

V.   How Americans Participate in Politics (pp. 200-206)

A.   **Political participation** encompasses the many activities used by citizens to influence the selection of political leaders or the policies they pursue.

B.   Conventional Participation: The majority of Americans participate only by voting in presidential elections.

C.   Protest as Participation
1.   **Protest** is designed to achieve policy change through dramatic and unconventional tactics.
2.   **Civil disobedience** is consciously breaking a law thought to be unjust.

D.   Class, Inequality, and Participation: Lower rates of political participation among minority groups are linked with lower socioeconomic status.

VI.   Understanding Public Opinion and Political Action (pp. 206-207)

A.   Public Attitudes toward the Scope of Government

B.   Democracy, Public Opinion, and Political Action

VII.   Summary (pp. 207-208)

LEARNING OBJECTIVES

After studying Chapter 6, you should be able to:

1. Describe how demographic factors shape who we are politically.

2. Identify the processes through which people learn about politics.

3. Define public opinion, identify how it is measured, explain its role in shaping public policy, and discuss the nature of political information in America.

4. Understand the concept of political ideology in American politics and government.

5. Explain the ways in which people participate in politics and in the policymaking process, and discuss the implications of unequal political participation.

6. Understand the relationship between the scope of government, democracy, public opinion, and political action.

The following exercises will help you meet these objectives:

Objective 1: Describe how demographic factors shape who we are politically.

1. What were the three great waves of immigration to the United States?

    1.

    2.

    3.

2. What is meant by the term "minority majority"?

3.   What was the goal of the Simpson-Mazzoli Act?

4.   How have the following demographic changes affected political changes?

    1. Immigration

    2. Regional Shifts

    3. Aging Population

Objective 2: Identify the processes through which people learn about politics.

    1.   Explain the significance of each of the following as sources for political learning:

        1. Family

        2. Mass media

        3. Schools

    2.   Name two ways in which aging affects political behavior.

        1.

        2.

Objective 3: Define public opinion, identify how it is measured, explain its role in shaping public policy, and discuss the nature of political information in America.

1. What is the key to the accuracy of opinion polls?

2. Explain the technique of random-digit dialing.

3. List three criticisms of public opinion polling.

    1.

    2.

    3.

4. What is the "paradox of mass politics," according to Russell Neuman?

5. What is the largest impact of declining trust in government since the 1960s?

Objective 4: Understand the concept of political ideology in the context of American politics and government.

1. Fill in the following table concerning political ideology.

Ideology	General Beliefs	Typical Demographic Characteristics
Liberals		
Conservatives		

2.   Explain how the role of religion influences political ideology in the United States.

3.   Fill in the following table on the classification of the ideological sophistication of American voters according to the study *The American Voter*.

Ideological Classification	Definition	Percent

Objective 5: Explain the ways in which people participate in politics and in the policymaking process, and discuss the implications of unequal political participation.

1.   List five activities of conventional political participation, placing a star next to the most common activity.

       1.

       2.

       3.

       4.

       5.

2.   Define civil disobedience and give an example.

3.   How does minority group status affect political participation?

Objective 6: Understand the relationship between the scope of government, democracy, public opinion, and political action.

1.   What is the public's general attitude about the scope of government?

2.   Comment on how Americans' lack of political knowledge and low participation rate affects democracy.

KEY TERMS

Identify and describe:

public opinion

demography

census

melting pot

minority majority

political culture

reapportionment

political socialization

sample

random sampling

sampling error

random-digit dialing

exit poll

political ideology

gender gap

political participation

protest

civil disobedience

Compare and contrast:
demography and census

melting pot and minority majority

public opinion and political ideology

sample, random sampling, and sampling error

random-digit dialing and exit poll

protest and civil disobedience

Name that term:

1. The mixing of cultures, ideas, and peoples.

    _____

2. An overall set of values widely shared within a society.

    _____

3. This occurs when the 435 seats in the House of Representatives are reallocated to the states based on population changes.

    _____

4. The process through which an individual acquires his or her particular political orientations.

    _____

5. The distribution of the population's beliefs about politics and policy issues.

    _____

6. This technique is the key to the accuracy of public opinion polls.

    _____

7. This is the most criticized type of poll.

    _____

8. In American politics, this is usually characterized by the liberal-conservative dimension.

_____

9. Ideological differences between men and women have led to this.

_____

10. Voting, running for office, and even violent protest are examples of this.

_____

USING YOUR UNDERSTANDING

1. Locate the published results of an opinion poll by Gallup, Harris, or one of the news organizations on a topic that is of interest to you. You may want to use polls that focused on the 2006 congressional election, the war on terrorism, or the war on Iraq. Assess the results in terms of the demographic distributions, if any, that are reflected in the results. See if males differed from females, whites from non-whites, and so on. If the results are compared with the findings of an earlier poll, see if public opinion on the topic is changing. Briefly describe what you found and what its implications are for policymaking. Alternatively, design a small questionnaire for your class dealing with questions of information, ideology, and political participation. Have the respondents to your survey provide demographic information. Summarize your findings in a table or two presenting the overall responses and those for particular demographic groups. Keep in mind that you will probably face the problems of a limited sample size and a lack of representativeness for the general population.

2. Conduct a study on the role of unconventional political participation in the United States. Compare and contrast the different types of unconventional political participation. Identify examples of historical events in the United States that exemplify unconventional political participation. Present an analysis of these events in terms of the number of people involved, the type of activity, the target of the activity, and the short-term and long-term results of the activity. In particular, you might want to analyze the protest movements against the war on Iraq. Critically evaluate the effectiveness of unconventional political participation as compared to conventional political participation.

111

REVIEW QUESTIONS

Check ☑ the correct answer:

1. Most Americans view cultural diversity as one of the most appealing aspects of their society.
   ☐ True
   ☐ False

2. Demography is the
   ☐ a. historical analysis of political participation.
   ☐ b. study of public opinion.
   ☐ c. science of human populations.
   ☐ d. enumeration of a population.

3. The enumeration of a population is called
   ☐ a. an opinion poll.
   ☐ b. demography.
   ☐ c. a census.
   ☐ d. cartography.

4. The Constitution requires an actual enumeration of the population
   ☐ a. annually.
   ☐ b. every ten years.
   ☐ c. every 25 years.
   ☐ d. never.

5. The census is basically a procedural requirement that creates very little controversy.
   ☐ True
   ☐ False

6. The third great wave of immigration, after World War II, consisted primarily of
   ☐ a. northwestern Europeans.
   ☐ b. southern and eastern Europeans.
   ☐ c. Africans.
   ☐ d. Hispanics and Asians.

7. The American "melting pot" refers to the mix of
   ☐ a. cultures.
   ☐ b. ideas.
   ☐ c. people.
   ☐ d. all of the above

8. The largest minority group in the United States today is
   ☐ a. African Americans.
   ☐ b. Hispanics.
   ☐ c. Asians.
   ☐ d. American Indians.

9. The Hispanics in the United States tend to be concentrated in the cities.
   ☐ True
   ☐ False

10. The Simpson-Mazzoli Act
   ☐ a. allowed employers to employ illegal immigrants.
   ☐ b. required documentation of the citizenship of all employees.
   ☐ c. provided for legal discrimination against minority workers.
   ☐ d. put an end to all immigration from Mexico.

11. The most highly skilled immigrant group in American history is
   ☐ a. African Americans.
   ☐ b. Hispanic Americans.
   ☐ c. Asian Americans.
   ☐ d. Eastern European Americans.

12. Over the last 50 years, much of America's population growth has been concentrated
   ☐ a. north of the Mason-Dixon line.
   ☐ b. east of the Mississippi River.
   ☐ c. in the West and South.
   ☐ d. in the Midwest.

13. Reapportionment can lead to
   ☐ a. an increase in the number of members of the House of Representatives.
   ☐ b. power shifts among the states.
   ☐ c. an increase or decrease in the number of senators from each state.
   ☐ d. none of the above

14. The biggest reapportionment winner in the most recent census has been
   ☐ a. California.
   ☐ b. New York.
   ☐ c. Florida.
   ☐ d. Ohio.

15. The fastest-growing age group in America is composed of citizens
   ☐ a. over the age of 65.
   ☐ b. under the age of 18.
   ☐ c. between the ages of 19 and 35.
   ☐ b. between the ages of 36 and 55.

16. By the year 2040, the Social Security system will be solvent and self-sufficient.
   ☐ True
   ☐ False

17. The process of acquiring political orientations is called political socialization.
   ☐ True
   ☐ False

18. Which of the following statements regarding political socialization is FALSE?
   ☐ a. Only a small portion of Americans' political learning is formal.
   ☐ b. Most of what Americans learn about politics is acquired from high school civics courses.
   ☐ c. As one becomes more socialized with age, one's political orientations grow firmer.
   ☐ d. Governments largely aim their socialization efforts at the young.

19. Formal learning about politics is far more important than informal learning.
   ☐ True
   ☐ False

20. Which of the following statements about political socialization and the family is FALSE?
   ☐ a. The influence of families is central to socialization because of time and emotional commitment.
   ☐ b. One can predict how the majority of young people will vote simply by knowing the political leanings of their parents.
   ☐ c. Family influence on socialization is mostly informal.
   ☐ d. The generation gap is a well-proven phenomenon.

21. According to many observers, the "new parents" are
   ☐ a. the mass media.
   ☐ b. peer groups.
   ☐ c. schools.
   ☐ d. government agencies.

22. One of the most obvious intrusions of the government into Americans' socialization is
☐ a.　political parties.
☐ b.　schools.
☐ c.　television.
☐ d.　the military.

23. As people grow older,
☐ a.　political party attachment declines.
☐ b.　political participation rises steadily.
☐ c.　voting declines.
☐ d.　political learning ends.

24. (bonus) The public opinion poll was perfected by
☐ a.　Abraham Lincoln.
☐ b.　the *Literary Digest*.
☐ c.　George Gallup.
☐ d.　Alf Landon.

25. Which of the following statements is FALSE?
☐ a.　As long as a survey is large enough, representativeness is not important.
☐ b.　All surveys have sampling error.
☐ c.　A sample of about 1,000 to 1,500 people can represent faithfully the "universe" of potential voters.
☐ d.　Random-digit dialing costs about a fifth of the cost of person-to-person interviewing.

26. The key to the accuracy of opinion polls is the
☐ a.　number of people interviewed.
☐ b.　technique of random sampling.
☐ c.　use of telephones for interviewing.
☐ d.　use of computers.

27. The *Literary Digest* poll of 1936 wrongly predicted the results of the presidential election because
☐ a.　they did not interview enough people.
☐ b.　they used exit polls to predict the election results.
☐ c.　most of the people they interviewed did not vote.
☐ d.　they did not interview a random sample of voters.

28.   Most polling today is done through
☐ a.   random-digit dialing.
☐ b.   door-to-door interviews.
☐ c.   exit polls.
☐ d.   mail surveys.

29.   Public opinion polling is almost exclusively an American phenomenon.
☐ True
☐ False

30.   Exit polls allow television networks to project all but very close races before the polls close.
☐ True
☐ False

31.   Which of the following statements is NOT a criticism of public opinion polling?
☐ a.   Public opinion polling makes politicians more concerned with following than leading.
☐ b.   Polls can weaken democracy by distorting the election process.
☐ c.   Polling is a fad that should not be taken seriously.
☐ d.   Pollsters can often get the results they want by altering the wording of questions.

32.   Thomas Jefferson believed that
☐ a.   education is irrelevant to good citizenship.
☐ b.   the people are "a great beast."
☐ c.   a majority of people will exercise good sense.
☐ d.   people lack a capacity for self-government.

33.   (bonus) Who said, "Your people, sir, are a great beast"?
☐ a.   Abraham Lincoln
☐ b.   Thomas Jefferson
☐ c.   Alexander Hamilton
☐ d.   Winston Churchill

34.   One thing that public opinion polls have shown is that the
☐ a.   United States is becoming more liberal.
☐ b.   level of public knowledge about politics is dismally low.
☐ c.   American people have strong opinions about political issues.
☐ d.   American people are becoming more ideologically oriented.

35. Public opinion polls have shown that the majority of Americans
☐ a.   can name the chief justice of the Supreme Court.
☐ b.   can explain their opinion on major political issues.
☐ c.   can locate Bosnia on a map.
☐ d.   recognize commercial slogans better than the names of political figures.

36. According to Russell Neuman, the paradox of mass politics is that the American political system works as well as it does given the
☐ a.   discomforting lack of public knowledge about politics.
☐ b.   high degree of ideologically oriented people in the United States.
☐ c.   lack of opinions on major issues in American politics.
☐ d.   none of the above

37. Political ideology consists of views that are simply "gut reactions."
☐ True
☐ False

38. A liberal ideology favors
☐ a.   a strong central government.
☐ b.   greater reliance on the private sector.
☐ c.   smaller government.
☐ d.   passive government.

39. Conservatives would tend to support all of the following EXCEPT
☐ a.   a strong military.
☐ b.   school prayer.
☐ c.   low taxes.
☐ d.   affirmative action.

40. No significant difference has ever been found between the ideological orientations of men and women.
☐ True
☐ False

41. Which of the following statements regarding religion and ideology is FALSE?
☐ a.   Most Jews tend to be more conservative than liberal.
☐ b.   The ideological gap between Catholics and Protestants is smaller than the gender gap.
☐ c.   Born-again Christians are the most conservative demographic group.
☐ d.   People who have no religious affiliation are more liberal than conservative.

42. Researchers in the 1950s found that the largest share of the electorate consisted of
☐ a. no-issue-content voters.
☐ b. nature-of-the-times voters
☐ c. highly ideological voters.
☐ d. group-benefits voters.

43. When identical methods were used to update the analysis of the 1956 study *The American Voter* in 1988, researchers found
☐ a. a majority of the people identified as ideologues in 1988.
☐ b. a huge increase in the no-issue-content group in 1988.
☐ c. just six percent more ideologues in 1988 than in 1956.
☐ d. a disappearance of the nature-of-the-times voters in 1988.

44. Election results often indicate the movement of the public either to the left or right.
☐ True
☐ False

45. Political participation
☐ a. is aimed at influencing the selection of political leaders and the policies they pursue.
☐ b. is higher in the U.S. than anywhere in the world.
☐ c. consists exclusively of voting and campaigning.
☐ d. excludes unconventional political actions such as protest.

46. When it comes to political participation, the common denominator among political activists is
☐ a. campaigning.
☐ b. protesting.
☐ c. voting.
☐ d. contacting.

47. Protest is a form of political participation that loses its effectiveness because the media are unwilling to cover unusual activities.
☐ True
☐ False

48. The conscious decision to break a law believed to be immoral and suffer the consequences is called
☐ a. protest.
☐ b. civil disobedience.
☐ c. political participation.
☐ d. activation.

49. Nearly every study of participation in America has concluded that citizens of higher social and economic status participate more in politics.
☐ True
☐ False

50. Income and education being equal, African Americans and Hispanics participate in politics
☐ a. the same as whites.
☐ b. more than whites.
☐ c. less than whites.
☐ d. none of the time.

51. For most of the population, questions about the scope of government
☐ a. elicit no or little opinion.
☐ b. guide their ideological leanings.
☐ c. are consistent with their policy choices.
☐ d. produce strong emotional responses.

52. Even if people only vote according to the nature of the times with no knowledge of the issues, they are holding public officials accountable for their actions.
☐ True
☐ False

ESSAY QUESTIONS

1. What is demography, and why is it important to understanding political changes? What demographic changes have occurred in the United States and what are their political and public policy consequences?

2. What is political socialization? What is the difference between formal and informal learning? Which do you think is most important and why? Give examples to support your answer.

3. Explain how public opinion is measured. What scientific techniques are used to measure public opinion? What are the arguments against public opinion polling?

4. Contrast the views of Thomas Jefferson and Alexander Hamilton on the political sophistication of the American electorate. Be sure to include a discussion of political information and ideology in your answer. Based on the available evidence, defend one view over the other.

5.   To what extent is ideology important in the United States? Explain the main differences between liberals and conservatives. What are the public's attitudes on the scope of government?

6.   What are some of the ways in which people participate in politics? Compare conventional and unconventional participation. How do they affect policy in different ways?

7.   Why is participation in America unequal? What are the political and policy implications of unequal participation?

CHAPTER 7

The Mass Media and the Political Agenda

CHAPTER OUTLINE

I.   Introduction (pp. 210-212)
    A.   **High-tech politics** is a politics in which technology increasingly shapes the behavior of citizens and policymakers, as well as the political agenda itself.
    B.   The **mass media** consist of television, radio, newspapers, magazines, and other means of popular communication that reach, and profoundly influence, not only the elites but also the masses.

II.   The Mass Media Today (pp. 212-213)
    A.   A **media event** is staged primarily for the purpose of being covered.
    B.   Image making is critical to campaigning and day-to-day governing.

III.   The Development of Media Politics (pp. 213-225)
    A.   Introduction
         1.   Franklin D. Roosevelt practically invented media politics, holding two **press conferences** (presidential meetings with reporters) a week.
         2.   The Vietnam War and the Watergate scandal soured the press on government.
         3.   **Investigative journalism** is the use of detective-like reporting methods to unearth scandals.
    B.   The **Print Media**
         1.   "Yellow journalism" characterized the early history of newspapers in the United States.
         2.   The press has a pecking order.
         3.   The political content of leading magazines is slim.
    C.   The **Broadcast Media**
         1.   During World War II, radio went into the news business in earnest.
         2.   Since the 1960s, television has had a profound impact on politics.
    D.   Government Regulation of the Broadcast Media
         1.   The Federal Communications Commission (FCC) regulates communications via radio, television, telephone, cable, and satellite.
         2.   The FCC regulates airwaves to prevent near-monopolies, license stations, and insure fair treatment.
    E.   From Broadcasting to **Narrowcasting**: The Rise of Cable News Channels
         1.   Rather than appealing to a general audience, cable news channels focus on a narrow particular interest.

2. Many scholars feel that cable news has reduced the overall quality of political journalism.
F. The Impact of the Internet
G. Private Control of the Media
1. Unlike many other countries, virtually all of American media outlets are in private hands, allowing freedom in journalistic content.
2. Major metropolitan newspapers are mostly owned by **chains**.

IV. Reporting the News (pp. 225-233)
A. News is what is timely and different.
B. Finding News
1. Most news organizations assign reporters to **beats,** specific locations where news frequently happens.
2. **Trial balloons** consist of information leaked to discover the political reaction.
C. Presenting the News: as technology has enabled the media to pass along information with greater speed, news coverage has become less complete and **sound bites** are more common.
D. Bias in the News
1. News reporting is not systematically biased toward a particular ideology or party.
2. Television is biased toward stories that generate good pictures. The **talking head** is considered boring.

V. The News and Public Opinion (pp. 233-234)
A. Although studies show that the media do not affect how people vote, they do affect what they think about and the priorities they attach to problems.
B. People's opinions shift with the tone of news coverage.

VI. The Media's Agenda-Setting Function (pp. 234-235)
A. The **policy agenda** is "the list of subjects or problems to which government officials, and people outside of government closely associated with those officials, are paying some serious attention at any given time."
B. **Policy entrepreneurs** are people who invest their political "capital" in an issue.
C. The media can be used by the poor and downtrodden as well as the elite.

VII. Understanding the Mass Media (pp. 235-237)
A. The Media and the Scope of Government
B. Individualism and the Media
C. Democracy and the Media

VIII. Summary (p. 237)

LEARNING OBJECTIVES

After studying Chapter 7, you should be able to:

1.   Describe the characteristics of the mass media today.

2.   Explain the development of the print and broadcast media from a historical perspective.

3.   Understand how news is found and reported by the media.

4.   Describe how the news media affect public opinion.

5.   Discuss what is meant by the concepts of policy agenda and policy entrepreneur and the media's importance to them.

6.   Understand how the media affect the scope of government and the democratic process.

The following exercises will help you meet these objectives:

Objective 1: Describe the characteristics of the mass media today.

1.   Explain the purpose of a media event.

2.   List the seven principles of news management as practiced in the Reagan White House.

                1.

                2.

                3.

                4.

                5.

                6.

                7.

Objective 2: Explain the development of the print media and the broadcast media from a historical perspective.

1. Explain two media techniques used most effectively by President Franklin Roosevelt.

    1.

    2.

2. What is meant by investigative journalism?

3. Explain the significance of the era of "yellow journalism," as it relates to the print media.

4. Explain how television affected the political career of Richard Nixon.

5. What effect did television have on the war in Vietnam?

6. Explain the three ways in which the Federal Communications Commission has regulated the airwaves.

    1.

    2.

    3.

7.   What impact has cable TV had on news reporting?

8.   List four findings of the Columbia University's Project for Excellence in Journalism on cable news programming.

        1.

        2.

        3.

        4.

9.   What makes news reporting on the Internet particularly different than news reporting on television?

10.   Explain two consequences of private control of the media in the United States.

        1.

        2.

Objective 3: Understand how news is found and reported by the media.

        1.   Where does most news come from?

        2.   What is meant by a "sound bite" and what does it tell us about news coverage?

        3.   Explain how the news media tend to be biased.

Objective 4: Describe how the news media affect public opinion.

    1.   In the experiments by Shanto Iyengar and Donald Kinder, what effect did manipulating TV stories have on viewers?

    2.   Give examples of how the media have had an effect on how the public evaluates specific events.

Objective 5: Discuss what is meant by the concepts of policy agenda and policy entrepreneur, and the media's importance to them.

    1.   Define the term "policy agenda."

    2.   List five items in the policy entrepreneurs' "arsenal of weapons."

            1.

            2.

            3.

            4.

            5.

Objective 6: Understand how the media affect the scope of government and the democratic process.

    1.   How do the media act as a "watchdog"?

    2.   What is the difference between the "information society" and the "informed society"?

KEY TERMS

Identify and describe:

high-tech politics

mass media

media event

press conferences

investigative journalism

print media

broadcast media

narrowcasting

chains

beats

trial balloons

sound bites

talking head

policy agenda

policy entrepreneurs

Compare and contrast:

high-tech politics and mass media

media event and press conferences

print media and broadcast media

sound bites and talking head

policy agenda and policy entrepreneur

Name that term:

1. It reaches the elite as well as the masses.

   _____

2. These are staged primarily for the purpose of being covered.

   _____

3. This tends to pit reporters against political leaders.

   _____

4. These control newspapers with most of the nation's circulation.

   _____

5. The primary mission of cable and Internet news.

   _____

6. Specific locations from where news frequently emanates.

   _____

7. Information leaked to see what the political reaction would be.

   _____

USING YOUR UNDERSTANDING

1. Choose one of the three major networks, CBS, NBC, or ABC, and watch the evening news every day for a week. While watching, write down the topic of each news story, the amount of time spent on the story, and an assessment of the story's content and the issues it raises. Read a daily newspaper (preferably the *New York Times* or another major paper) for the same days. Compare the television and newspaper coverage of the same news stories. Analyze the differences between these media in terms of how the stories were presented, depth of coverage, and issue orientation. Evaluate how the print media and the broadcast media might differ in their influence on public opinion.

129

2. Based on your understanding of the role of the media in the agenda-building process, critique a news item or article that concerns a policy issue. Your critique should begin by asking how well the item identified the policy issue, the policy entrepreneurs, and people in government concerned about the issue. Assess the news item as both a source of information and a source of influence on your perceptions of politics, government, and policy. Consider how policymakers might use the news item as well. Put yourself in the position of the reporter and consider how the story might have been improved. In light of your critique, discuss your impressions of the media as unofficial but important sources of influence on public opinion and the policy agenda.

REVIEW QUESTIONS

Check ☑ the correct answer:

1. The American political system has entered a new period of high-tech politics.
   ☐ True
   ☐ False

2. Television, radio, newspapers, and other means of popular communication are called
   ☐ a.   chains.
   ☐ b.   high-tech politics.
   ☐ c.   mass media.
   ☐ d.   public relations.

3. The influence of the mass media is limited to the elites in the United States.
   ☐ True
   ☐ False

4. Media events are spontaneous circumstances that get the media's attention.
   ☐ True
   ☐ False

5. A president who was particularly successful in playing to the media was
   ☐ a.   George H.W. Bush.
   ☐ b.   Ronald Reagan.
   ☐ c.   Richard Nixon.
   ☐ d.   Jimmy Carter.

6.   News management in the Reagan White House operated on each of the following
       principles EXCEPT
       ☐ a.   staying on the offensive.
       ☐ b.   controlling the flow of information.
       ☐ c.   speaking in one voice.
       ☐ d.   spontaneity.

7.   Today, for a president to ignore the power of image and the media would be
       perilous.
       ☐ True
       ☐ False

8.   (bonus) Who said, "The President of the United States will not stand and be
       questioned like a chicken thief by men whose names he does not even know"?
       ☐ a.   Herbert Hoover
       ☐ b.   Franklin D. Roosevelt
       ☐ c.   Lyndon Johnson
       ☐ d.   Richard Nixon

9.   The president who held numerous press conferences and practically created media
       politics was
       ☐ a.   Herbert Hoover.
       ☐ b.   Franklin Roosevelt.
       ☐ c.   John F. Kennedy.
       ☐ d.   Ronald Reagan.

10.   Prior to the 1960s, the relationship between politicians and the press was one of
       skepticism and distrust.
       ☐ True
       ☐ False

11.   The press soured on government as a result of the events of the
       ☐ a.   Vietnam War.
       ☐ b.   Watergate scandal.
       ☐ c.   Korean War.
       ☐ d.   Both a. and b.

12.   News coverage of presidential candidates has become increasingly
       ☐ a.   focused on the issues.
       ☐ b.   limited.
       ☐ c.   favorable.
       ☐ d.   less favorable.

13. Joseph Pulitzer and William Randolph Hearst were
☐ a. inventors of the printing press.
☐ b. strong opponents of yellow journalism.
☐ c. turn-of-the-century newspaper magnates.
☐ d. presidential candidates.

14. (bonus) Who said, "The essence of American journalism is vulgarity divested of truth"?
☐ a. Joseph Pulitzer
☐ b. Horace Greeley
☐ c. William Randolph Hearst
☐ d. Winston Churchill

15. Gradually, the broadcast media have replaced the print media as our principal source of news and information.
☐ True
☐ False

16. The political career of Richard Nixon was made and unmade by television.
☐ True
☐ False

17. Richard Nixon's experiences during the 1960 presidential campaign illustrate the
☐ a. power of television in American politics.
☐ b. insignificance of presidential debates.
☐ c. greater importance of print media.
☐ d. friendly relationship between the media and political candidates.

18. Using the broadcast media, Lyndon Johnson was successful in persuading the public that America was winning the war in Vietnam.
☐ True
☐ False

19. Which of the following statements is TRUE?
☐ a. Newspapers are the main source of news for Americans.
☐ b. Most of the news originates from correspondents.
☐ c. In-depth analyses of policy issues are common in the media.
☐ d. Cable news and the Internet have supplanted the nightly news shows.

20. The use of the airwaves is regulated by the
☐ a. states.
☐ b. Federal Trade Commission.
☐ c. Federal Communication Commission.
☐ d. Federal Broadcasting System.

21. News on cable TV and the Internet
 ☐ a. is not available to most people.
 ☐ b. focuses on a narrow particular interest.
 ☐ c. appeals to a general audience.
 ☐ d. is rarely used by most young adults.

22. Which of the following statements regarding the impact of the Internet is FALSE?
 ☐ a. The impact of the Internet on politics has thus far been revolutionary.
 ☐ b. Most Americans utilize the Internet widely for detailed information on politics.
 ☐ c. The Internet is limited to sound bites and summaries of political events.
 ☐ d. The Internet has not been found to be useful for political campaigns.

23. Newspaper chains
 ☐ a. are organizations loosely linked by the wire services.
 ☐ b. are controlled by conglomerates that often control broadcast media as well.
 ☐ c. began to disappear with the advent of television.
 ☐ d. are local papers owned by fearless local editors.

24. The news media avoid odd events in favor of reporting only objective conditions.
 ☐ True
 ☐ False

25. The bottom line that shapes how journalists define news, where they get news, and how they present news is
 ☐ a. objectivity.
 ☐ b. truth.
 ☐ c. profits.
 ☐ d. comprehensiveness.

26. Most news organizations assign their best reporters to particular beats.
 ☐ True
 ☐ False

27. Trial balloons are used by politicians to
 ☐ a. put issues on the policy agenda.
 ☐ b. see their constituents.
 ☐ c. test political reactions.
 ☐ d. take public polls.

28. If you had to pick a single word to describe news coverage by the print and broadcast media, it would be
☐ a. comprehensive.
☐ b. biased.
☐ c. misleading.
☐ d. superficial.

29. Which of the following statements is FALSE?
☐ a. Television analysis of news events rarely lasts more than a minute.
☐ b. In-depth attention to the issues is given only during presidential campaigns.
☐ c. Newspapers rarely reprint the entire text of important political speeches.
☐ d. Snappy soundbites of 10 seconds or less are more common than full speeches on television.

30. Studies on bias in the news have found that the news media tend to
☐ a. favor the Democratic Party.
☐ b. be politically conservative.
☐ c. be politically neutral.
☐ d. favor the Republican Party.

31. Which of the following statements is FALSE?
☐ a. Most reporters strongly believe in journalistic objectivity.
☐ b. Most news stories are presented in a "point/counterpoint" format.
☐ c. The news media do not want to lose their audience by appearing biased.
☐ d. Most studies have shown that the media are systematically biased toward a conservative ideology.

32. The news media tend to do all of the following EXCEPT
☐ a. mirror reality.
☐ b. show more bad news than good news.
☐ c. focus on stories that generate good pictures.
☐ d. overemphasize dramatic events.

33. To which of the following news stories did Americans pay closest attention?
☐ a. arrest of O.J. Simpson
☐ b. terrorist attacks on the World Trade Center and Pentagon
☐ c. 2000 presidential election outcome
☐ d. congressional debate over NAFTA

34. A "talking head" is a media term referring to a shot of a person's face talking directly to the camera.
☐ True
☐ False

35. Studies have shown that the news media
   - [ ] a. have only a marginal effect on public opinion.
   - [ ] b. directly affect how people vote.
   - [ ] c. affect what Americans think about.
   - [ ] d. can conceal problems that actually exist.

36. By increasing public attention to specific problems, television news can influence the criteria by which the public evaluates political leaders.
   - [ ] True
   - [ ] False

37. Research indicates that public opinions remain constant even when news coverage changes.
   - [ ] True
   - [ ] False

38. Issues on the policy agenda are always defined by government officials, but not by people outside of government.
   - [ ] True
   - [ ] False

39. Which of the following characteristics is NOT common among policy entrepreneurs?
   - [ ] a. commitment to a single policy issue
   - [ ] b. investment of personal political capital
   - [ ] c. avoidance of the media
   - [ ] d. concern about government's priorities

40. Which of the following people would NOT qualify to be a policy entrepreneur?
   - [ ] a. an elected official
   - [ ] b. an interest group leader
   - [ ] c. an academic researcher
   - [ ] d. none of the above

41. The media act as key linkage institutions between the people and the policymakers, having a profound impact on the policy agenda.
   - [ ] True
   - [ ] False

42. The watchdog function of the media
   ☐ a. contributes to the growth of government.
   ☐ b. can be characterized as reformist.
   ☐ c. has a liberal political orientation.
   ☐ d. is no longer a central concern of the media.

43. When the media focus on injustice in society, they inevitably help keep government small.
   ☐ True
   ☐ False

44. The American institutional agenda has changed dramatically because television finds it easier to focus on groups than on individuals.
   ☐ True
   ☐ False

45. Which of the following statements is TRUE?
   ☐ a. The media are at their best when reporting stories about complex, high-tech issues.
   ☐ b. The amount of information available through the news media has decreased.
   ☐ c. The rise of the information society has brought about a rise in the informed society.
   ☐ d. The media attempts to appeal to the maximum number of people.

45. The news media's defense for being superficial is to say that this is what the people want.
   ☐ True
   ☐ False

ESSAY QUESTIONS

1. Using examples from presidential politics, explain why image and the use of the media are so important in the American political system.

2. Explain the historical development of the print and broadcast media in the United States. Use examples to illustrate your answer.

3. How has cable news channels and the Internet changed the nature of the mass media and news reporting? Give examples to illustrate your answer.

4. How does television define what is newsworthy? Explain where television finds its news stories and how they are presented to the American public.

5. Describe how the media shape public opinion. What are the consequences of the media's influence on public opinion?

6. What is the policy agenda? Who are the policy entrepreneurs and how do they utilize the media to get their issues on the policy agenda?

7. Explain how the news media affect the scope of government and American individualism. How have they helped and hindered the growth of democracy in the United States?

CHAPTER 8

POLITICAL PARTIES

CHAPTER OUTLINE

I.   The Meaning of Party (pp. 242-245)
   A.   Introduction
      1.   **Party competition** is the battle between Democrats and Republicans for the control of public offices.
      2.   A **political party** is a "team of men and women seeking to control the governing apparatus by gaining office in a duly constituted election."
      3.   Political parties are viewed as "three-headed political giants."
         a.   The *party-in-the-electorate*
         b.   The *party as an organization*
         c.   The *party-in-government*
   B.   Tasks of the Parties: parties act as **linkage institutions**, translating inputs from the public into outputs from the policymakers.
      1.   Parties pick candidates.
      2.   Parties run campaigns.
      3.   Parties give cues to voters.
      4.   Parties articulate policies.
      5.   Parties coordinate policymaking.
   C.   Parties, Voters, and Policy: The Downs Model
      1.   **Rational-choice theory** "seeks to explain political processes and outcomes as consequences of purposive behavior."
      2.   The wise party selects policies that are widely favored.

II.   The Party in the Electorate (pp. 245-247)
   A.   **Party images** help shape people's **party identification,** the self-proclaimed preference for one party or the other.
   B.   **Ticket-splitting,** voting with one party for one office and another for other offices is near an all-time high.

III.   The Party Organizations: From the Grassroots to Washington (pp. 247-251)
   A.   Local Parties
      1.   Urban political parties were once dominated by **party machines**.
      2.   **Patronage** is one of the key inducements used by party machines.
   B.   The 50 State Party Systems
      1.   American national parties are a loose aggregation of state parties.
      2.   States limit who can participate in their nomination contests by using **closed primaries**, **open primaries**, or **blanket primaries**.
   C.   The National Party Organizations

1. The supreme power within each of the parties is the **national convention**.
2. The **national committee** keeps the party operating between conventions.
3. The **national chairperson** is responsible for the day-to-day activities of the national party.

IV. The Party in Government: Promises and Policy (pp. 251-253)
    A. The party in control ultimately determines who gets what, where, when, and how.
    B. A **coalition** is a set of individuals and groups supporting a party.
    C. Parties have done a fairly good job of translating their platform promises into public policy.

V. Party Eras in American History (pp. 254-259)
    A. Introduction
        1. **Party eras** are long periods of time when one party has been the dominant majority party.
        2. Party eras are punctuated by a **critical election.**
        3. **Party realignment** is a rare event when the party system is transformed.
    B. 1796-1824: The First Party System
    C. 1828-1856: Jackson and the Democrats versus the Whigs
    D. 1860-1928: The Two Republican Eras
        1. 1850s-1896, Republican Party as the antislavery party.
        2. 1896-1928, Republican Party as the party of the new working class and moneyed interests.
    E. 1932-1964: The **New Deal Coalition**: following the Great Depression, a new Democratic coalition remained dominant for decades.
    F. 1968-Present: Southern Realignment and The Era of Divided Government
        1. Since 1968 the South has gradually realigned with the Republican Party.
        2. **Party dealignment** means that people are moving away from both parties.
        3. Recent dealignment has been characterized by growing **party neutrality**.

VI. **Third Parties:** Their Impact on American Politics (pp. 260-261)
    A. Parties that promote certain causes.
    B. Splinter parties.
    C. Parties that are an extension of a popular individual with presidential hopes.

VII. Understanding Political Parties (pp. 261-265)
    A. Democracy and Responsible Party Government: the **responsible party model** would make it easier to convert party promises into governmental policy.
    B. American Political Parties and the Scope of Government
    C. Is the Party Over?

VIII. Summary (p. 265)

LEARNING OBJECTIVES

After studying Chapter 8, you should be able to:

1. Discuss the meaning and functions of a political party.

2. Discuss the nature of the party-in-the-electorate, party organizations, and the party-in-government.

3. Describe the party eras in American history and how parties realign and dealign.

4. Evaluate the two-party system, its consequences, and the place of third parties in the system.

5. Identify the challenges facing the American political parties and explain their relationship to American democracy and the scope of government.

The following exercises will help you meet these objectives:

Objective 1: Discuss the meaning and functions of a political party.

1. Define the term "political party."

2. Explain the three heads of the political party as a "three-headed political giant."

   1.

   2.

   3.

3. What are the five tasks political parties should perform if they are to serve as effective linkage institutions?

   1.

2.

3.

4.

5.

4.   Draw a graph or diagram depicting Anthony Downs' rational-choice model of political parties.

Objective 2: Discuss the nature of the party-in-the-electorate, party organizations, and the party-in-government.

1.   What has been the most prominent trend in party identification in recent years?

2.   What is meant by "ticket-splitting"?

3.   Draw an organizational chart of an American political party and then mark where most of the power actually exists.

4.   What is meant by a "party machine"?

5.   What are the differences among the following types of party primaries?

    1. closed primaries

    2. open primaries

    3. blanket primaries

6.   What is the function of each of the following national party organizations?

    1. National Convention:

    2. National Committee:

    3. National Chairperson:

7.   What is the relationship between party promises and party performance?

Objective 3: Describe the party eras in American history and how parties realign and dealign.

1.   List four elections which might be considered "critical" or "realigning" and explain why.

    1.

    2.

3.

4.

2.   Complete the following table on party eras.

Party Era	Major Party	Major Party Coalition	Minor Party	Minor Party Coalition	Prominent President(s)
1796-1824					
1828-1856					
1860-1892					
1896-1928					
1932-1964					

3.List the six presidents since 1968 and complete the following table on divided government.

President and Party Affiliation	Number Of Years With Republican Congress	Number Of Years With Democratic Congress

4.   What is meant by "party neutrality"?

Objective 4: Evaluate the two-party system, its consequences, and the place of third parties in the system.

1.   What are the three basic varieties of third parties?

    1.

    2.

    3.

2.   What are two ways in which third parties can have an impact on American politics?

    1.

    2.

3.   What is the most important consequence of two-party governance in the United States?

Objective 5: Identify the challenges facing the American political parties, and explain their relationship to American democracy, individualism, and the scope of government.

1.   List the four conditions that advocates of the responsible party model believe the parties should meet.

1.

2.

3.

4.

2.   How does the American party system affect the scope of government?

3.   What is the key problem of the American political parties today?

KEY TERMS

Identify and describe:

party competition

political party

linkage institutions

rational-choice theory

party image

party identification

ticket-splitting

party machines

patronage

closed primaries

open primaries

blanket primaries

national convention

national committee

national chairperson

coalition

party eras

critical election

party realignment

New Deal Coalition

party dealignment

third parties

winner-take-all system

proportional representation

coalition government

responsible party model

Compare and contrast:

political party and linkage institutions

party identification and ticket-splitting

party machines and patronage

closed primaries, open primaries, and blanket primaries

national convention, national committee, and national chairperson

party eras and critical election

party realignment and party dealignment

party realignment and New Deal Coalition

winner-take-all system and proportional representation

Name that term:

1.   The battle between the parties for the control of public offices.

_____

2.   The perception of what the Republicans and Democrats stand for.

     _____

3.   This seeks to explain political processes and outcomes as consequences of purposive behavior.

     _____

4.   Voting with one party for one office and another for other offices.

     _____

5.   One of the key inducements used by political machines.

     _____

6.   A set of individuals and groups who support a political party.

     _____

7.   Political party eras are punctuated by these.

     _____

8.   Often a consequence of proportional representation; many European governments are ruled by these.

     _____

9.   Examples of these include the Free Soil party, the Jobless party, and the American Independent party.

     _____

10.   Advocates of this reform believe that it would make it easier for party promises to be turned into governmental policy.

     _____

USING YOUR UNDERSTANDING

1. Investigate the party system of another Western democratic political system that is of interest to you, such as Great Britain. Try to identify the major features of the political parties in the system in terms of the party-in-the-electorate, the party as organization, and the party-in-government. Briefly describe what you found in comparison to the two-party system in the United States. Include a discussion of whether the party system is experiencing realignment, dealignment, or another form of change.

2. Gerald Pomper's study of party platforms covered the years 1944-1976. Follow up on this study by examining the Republican Party platforms for 1980, 1984, 1988, 2000, and 2004, and the Democratic Party platforms for 1992 and 1996. Make a list of the promises made in the Republican platforms and compare them to the accomplishments of the Reagan, George H.W. Bush, and George W. Bush administrations. Make a list of the promises of the 1992 and 1996 Democratic platform and compare them to the policy initiatives of the Clinton administration. For the party not occupying the presidency, you might compare legislative initiatives by that party in Congress with their party platform. Evaluate the degree to which the parties keep the policy promises they set forth. If possible, look at public opinion polls to see if public opinion supports platform positions on key issues. Develop an analysis of the importance of party platforms in the electoral process and in making public policy.

REVIEW QUESTIONS

Check ☑ the correct answer:

1. The framers of the U.S. Constitution approved of the formation of political parties.
    ☐ True
    ☐ False

2. Which of the following statements regarding political parties is FALSE?
    ☐ a.   The main goal of political parties is to try to win elections.
    ☐ b.   Party teams are well disciplined and single-minded.
    ☐ c.   Party leaders often disagree about policy.
    ☐ d.   Between elections the parties seem to all but disappear.

3. The largest component of the political party is the
   ☐ a. party-in-the-electorate.
   ☐ b. party as an organization.
   ☐ c. party-in-government.
   ☐ d. local party machine.

4. The people who keep the party running between elections and make its rules are members of the
   ☐ a. party-in-the-electorate.
   ☐ b. party as an organization.
   ☐ c. party-in-government.
   ☐ d. local party machine.

5. Which of the following is NOT one of the four key linkage institutions?
   ☐ a. parties
   ☐ b. elections
   ☐ c. interest groups
   ☐ d. policymakers

6. According to Kay Lawson, the key tasks that parties perform, or should perform, include
   ☐ a. articulating policies.
   ☐ b. picking policymakers.
   ☐ c. running campaigns.
   ☐ d. all of the above

7. The concept of party image would be most important for parties to
   ☐ a. pick policymakers.
   ☐ b. run campaigns.
   ☐ c. give cues to voters.
   ☐ d. articulate party policies.

8. According to Anthony Downs, political parties and voters are both irrational.
   ☐ True
   ☐ False

9. According to the Downsian model, the most successful political parties would be
   ☐ a. extremely conservative.
   ☐ b. liberal.
   ☐ c. moderate.
   ☐ d. slightly conservative.

10.   More than half of the population currently feels that important differences exist between the parties.
☐ True
☐ False

11.   Party identification
☐ a.   requires formal membership with one of the parties.
☐ b.   is strongest for young Americans.
☐ c.   has declined while there has been an upsurge of people identifying as independents.
☐ d.   can always predict voting behavior.

12.   In America, ticket-splitting is
☐ a.   rare.
☐ b.   illegal.
☐ c.   near an all-time high.
☐ d.   a sign of party renewal.

13.   Power in the American political parties is highly centralized.
☐ True
☐ False

14.   Urban political machines depended on
☐ a.   specific inducements.
☐ b.   material inducements.
☐ c.   patronage.
☐ d.   all of the above

15.   The national parties are actually a loose aggregation of state parties.
☐ True
☐ False

16.   The 50 state party systems are all well organized, have sizable staffs, and spend a lot of money.
☐ True
☐ False

17.   Primaries that allow voters to decide on election day whether they want to participate in the Democratic or Republican contests are called
☐ a.   closed primaries.
☐ b.   open primaries.
☐ c.   blanket primaries.
☐ d.   political primaries.

18.   The supreme power within each of the parties is the
- ☐ a.   national chairperson.
- ☐ b.   national convention.
- ☐ c.   local party organization.
- ☐ d.   president.

19.   The day-to-day activities of the national party are the responsibility of the
- ☐ a.   president.
- ☐ b.   national committee.
- ☐ c.   national chairperson.
- ☐ d.   national convention.

20.   (bonus) Which of the following presidents failed to keep his campaign promise to balance the budget?
- ☐ a.   Lyndon Johnson
- ☐ b.   Richard Nixon
- ☐ c.   Jimmy Carter
- ☐ d.   Ronald Reagan

21.   Most promises by presidential candidates are kept once they take office.
- ☐ True
- ☐ False

22.   Gerald Pomper found that party platforms
- ☐ a.   do not predict party performance.
- ☐ b.   are ignored after elections.
- ☐ c.   consist of promises that are kept more often than not.
- ☐ d.   are very similar for the two major parties.

23.   Most democratic nations have a
- ☐ a.   one-party system.
- ☐ b.   two-party system.
- ☐ c.   multi-party system.
- ☐ d.   regional party system.

24.   During party eras, one party is the dominant majority party for long periods of time.
- ☐ True
- ☐ False

25. Party eras are punctuated by
☐ a. critical elections.
☐ b. party reforms.
☐ c. national party conventions.
☐ d. political coalitions.

26. Party realignment occurs with great frequency in American party politics.
☐ True
☐ False

27. The coalition behind the Democratic-Republican Party included
☐ a. Federalists.
☐ b. capitalists.
☐ c. farmers.
☐ d. silver interests.

28. More than anyone else, the person who founded the modern American political party was
☐ a. Alexander Hamilton.
☐ b. Andrew Jackson.
☐ c. Martin Van Buren.
☐ d. Abraham Lincoln.

29. Which of the following was NOT a part of the Republican era from 1860 to 1928?
☐ a. the battle to outlaw slavery
☐ b. the fight to establish the gold standard
☐ c. a shifting of party coalitions
☐ d. the New Deal

30. The New Deal was a political response to the
☐ a. Great Depression.
☐ b. Civil War.
☐ c. rise of agrarian interests.
☐ d. resurgence of capitalism.

31. Which of the following groups were NOT associated with the New Deal coalition?
☐ a. Catholics and Jews
☐ b. urban working classes
☐ c. Republicans
☐ d. intellectuals

32.   Lyndon Johnson's programs to help the poor, dispossessed, and minorities are
        known as the
        ☐ a.   New Deal.
        ☐ b.   Fair Deal.
        ☐ c.   New Frontier.
        ☐ d.   Great Society.

33.   The Democratic Party was torn apart in 1968 by
        ☐ a.   Johnson's War on Poverty.
        ☐ b.   Johnson's Vietnam War policies.
        ☐ c.   economic depression.
        ☐ d.   the Watergate scandal.

34.   The 1968 election was important because
        ☐ a.   it solidified Democratic control of the South.
        ☐ b.   it was the first time a newly elected president did not have his party in
               control of both houses of Congress.
        ☐ c.   it was the first time a third party won electoral college votes.
        ☐ d.   none of the above

35.   Most people say they vote for the person rather than the party.
        ☐ True
        ☐ False

36.   The recent party dealignment has been characterized by a
        ☐ a.   growing party neutrality.
        ☐ b.   dramatic decline in voter participation.
        ☐ c.   decline in party organization.
        ☐ d.   growth in the strength of third parties.

37.   Throughout American history, third parties have
        ☐ a.   developed as offshoots of a major party.
        ☐ b.   promoted specific causes.
        ☐ c.   developed as an extension of a popular presidential aspirant.
        ☐ d.   all of the above

38.   Which of the following consequences is LEAST associated with third parties in
        America?
        ☐ a.   serving as safety valves for popular discontent
        ☐ b.   bringing new groups into the electorate
        ☐ c.   consistent victories in federal offices
        ☐ d.   "sending a message" to Washington

39. Consequences of the two-party system include
☐ a. increased political conflict.
☐ b. moderation of conflict and policy ambiguity.
☐ c. more distinct policy choices.
☐ d. representation of extreme ideologies.

40. The founding of the world's first party system in the United States was seen as a risky adventure in the uncharted waters of democracy.
☐ True
☐ False

41. The system in which whoever gets the most votes wins the election is called the
☐ a. winner-take-all system.
☐ b. proportional representation system.
☐ c. coalition system.
☐ d. multi-party system.

42. In a system that employs proportional representation,
☐ a. whoever gets the most votes wins the election.
☐ b. parties are awarded legislative seats in proportion to their votes.
☐ c. every party gets represented in the legislature.
☐ d. there is very little difference between the political parties.

43. According to the responsible party model, which of the following is NOT one of the functions of the parties?
☐ a. They should present distinct, comprehensive programs.
☐ b. They should implement their programs once in office.
☐ c. They should create a fragmented decisional system.
☐ d. They should accept responsibility for the performance of government.

44. (bonus) The 1991 Republican nominee for Governor of Louisiana who was denounced by Republican President George H.W. Bush was
☐ a. George Wallace.
☐ b. David Duke.
☐ c. Ross Perot.
☐ d. David Mayhew.

45. Which of the following statements is FALSE?
   □ a. American parties are too decentralized to take a single national position and then enforce it.
   □ b. Party discipline in America has resulted in members of Congress voting with their party over 90 percent of the time.
   □ c. Most candidates are self-selected, gaining their nomination by their own efforts and not the party's.
   □ d. Parties do not have control over those who run under their labels.

46. The lack of disciplined and cohesive parties in America explains much of why the scope of governmental activity is less in the United States compared to other established democracies.
   □ True
   □ False

47. Which of the following is NOT one of the contemporary rivals of the political parties?
   □ a. the media
   □ b. urban machines
   □ c. interest groups
   □ d. campaign technology

ESSAY QUESTIONS

1. What is the meaning of a political party? What functions do parties in America perform? How well do you think they perform them, especially in comparison to other linkage institutions?

2. What is the Downsian model of party government? What are its limitations as a normative model for the American party system?

3. How has party identification changed over the years and what affect has it had on elections?

4. Describe the organization of the American political parties. How do party politics at the local, state, and national levels differ? Which level is most important and why?

5. How did the American two-party system evolve? How were coalitions important to this evolution? Include in your answer a discussion of party eras and critical elections.

6.	What are the political and policy consequences of having a two-party system? How have third parties made a difference?

7.	What is the responsible party model and what are its consequences for democracy?

8.	In what ways have the American political parties declined? What are the principal rivals of the political parties? Speculate on the future of political parties in America.

CHAPTER 9

NOMINATIONS AND CAMPAIGNS

CHAPTER OUTLINE

I.   The Nomination Game (pp. 270-279)
    A.   Introduction
        1.   A **nomination** is a party's official endorsement of a candidate for office.
        2.   **Campaign strategy** is the way in which candidates attempt to manipulate each of these elements to achieve the nomination.
    B.   Deciding to Run
    C.   Competing for Delegates: the goal of the nomination game is to win the majority of delegates' support at the **national party convention.**
        1.   The Caucus Road
            a.   A **caucus** is a meeting of state party leaders.
            b.   Caucuses usually are organized like a pyramid.
        2.   The Primary Road
            a.   In **presidential primaries**, voters in a state go to the polls and vote for a candidate or delegates pledged to one.
            b.   The **McGovern-Fraser Commission** had a mandate to make Democratic Party conventions more representative.
            c.   The proliferation of presidential primaries has transformed politics.
            d.   Politicians who are awarded convention seats on the basis of their position are known as **superdelegates**.
            e.   More states have moved their primaries up in the calendar in order to capitalize on media attention (**frontloading**).
        3.   Evaluating the Primary and Caucus System
            a.   Disproportionate attention goes to the early caucuses and primaries.
            b.   Prominent politicians find it difficult to take time out from their duties to run.
            c.   Money plays too big a role in the caucuses and primaries.
            d.   Participation in primaries and caucuses is low and unrepresentative.
            e.   The system gives too much power to the media.
    D.   The Convention Send-off
        1.   Conventions are no longer dramatic; the winner is a foregone conclusion.
        2.   Conventions orchestrate a massive send-off for the candidates.
        3.   Conventions develop the party's policy positions (**party platform**) and promote representation.

II.   The Campaign Game (pp. 279-283)
        A.   The High-Tech Media Campaign
                1.   The technique of **direct mail** helps identify potential supporters and contributions.
                2.   Candidates use their advertising budget.
                3.   Candidates get free attention as newsmakers.
        B.   Organizing the Campaign
                1.   Get a campaign manager.
                2.   Get a fund-raiser.
                3.   Get a campaign counsel.
                4.   Hire media and campaign consultants.
                5.   Assemble a campaign staff.
                6.   Plan the logistics.
                7.   Get a research staff and policy advisors.
                8.   Hire a pollster.
                9.   Get a good press secretary.
                10.   Establish a Web site.

III.   Money and Campaigning (pp. 283-291)
        A.   The Maze of Campaign Finance Reforms (**Federal Election Campaign Act**, 1974)
                1.   It created the **Federal Election Commission (FEC)**.
                2.   It created the **Presidential Election Campaign Fund.**
                3.   It provided partial public financing for presidential primaries (**matching funds**).
                4.   It provided full public financing for major party candidates in the general election.
                5.   It required full disclosure.
                6.   It limited contributions.
                7.   1979 amendments placed no limits on **soft money**.
                8.   The McCain-Feingold Act (2002) banned soft money, increased the amounts individuals could contribute, and barred certain "issue ads."
                9.   527 groups are not subject to contribution restrictions because they do not directly seek the election of particular candidates.
        B.   The Proliferation of **political action committees (PACs)**
        C.   Are Campaigns Too Expensive?

IV.   The Impact of Campaigns (p. 291)
        A.   Campaigns have three potential effects: reinforcement, activation, and conversion.
        B.   Factors that weaken campaigns' impact on voters include: **selective perception**, party identification, and incumbency.

V.   Understanding Nominations and Campaigns (pp. 292-293)
        A.   Are Nominations and Campaigns Too Democratic?

B.   Do Big Campaigns Lead to an Increase in the Scope of Government?

VI.   Summary (pp. 293-294)

LEARNING OBJECTIVES

After studying Chapter 9, you should be able to:

1.   Explain the nomination process and the role of the national party conventions.

2.   Discuss the role of campaign organizations and the importance of the media in campaigns.

3.   Understand the role of money in campaigns, campaign finance reform, and the impact of political action committees.

4.   Explain the impact of campaigns on the voters.

5.   Understand how campaigns affect democracy, public policy, and the scope of government.

The following exercises will help you meet these objectives:

Objective 1: Explain the nomination process and the role of the national party conventions.

1.   List the three elements needed for success in the nomination game.

1.

2.

3.

2.   Draw a diagram depicting the pyramid structure of the typical state party caucus.

3.   What reforms did the McGovern-Fraser Commission bring to the Democratic Party?

4.   List five criticisms of the primary and caucus system.

       1.

       2.

       3.

       4.

       5.

5.   What are the primary functions of the national party conventions?

Objective 2: Discuss the role of campaign organizations and the importance of the media in campaigns.

    1.   What are the two factors that determine media coverage of a campaign?

       1.

       2.

2. Using a rating system of strong, medium, and weak, rate campaign advertisements and campaign news coverage in terms of their attention to candidate image, issues, and the campaign itself.

	Campaign Advertisements	Campaign News Coverage
Image		
Issues		
Campaign		

3. List ten things candidates must do to effectively organize their campaigns.

1.

2.

3.

4.

5.

6.

7.

8.

9.

10.

Objective 3: Understand the role of money in campaigns, campaign finance reform, and the impact of political action committees.

1. What were the main features of the Federal Election Campaign Act of 1974?

1.

2.

163

3.

4.

5.

6.

2. What were the three main provisions of the McCain-Feingold Act (2002)?

1.

2.

3.

3. Present an argument that political action committees are essential to a successful campaign.

Objective 4: Explain the impact of campaigns on the voters.

1. What are the three effects campaigns can have on voters?

1.

2.

3.

2. What three factors tend to weaken campaigns' impacts on voters?

1.

2.

3.

Objective 5: Understand how campaigns affect democracy, public policy, and the scope of government.

    1.   What is meant by the "permanent campaign"?

    2.   How might campaigns affect the scope of government?

KEY TERMS

Identify and describe:

nomination

campaign strategy

national party convention

caucus

presidential primaries

McGovern-Fraser Commission

superdelegates

frontloading

national primary

regional primaries

party platform

direct mail

Federal Election Campaign Act

Federal Election Commission (FEC)

Presidential Election Campaign Fund

matching funds

soft money

527 groups

political action committees (PACs)

selective perception

Compare and contrast:

nomination and national party convention

caucus and presidential primaries

McGovern-Fraser Commission and superdelegates

national primary and regional primaries

Federal Election Campaign Act and Federal Election Commission

Presidential Election Campaign Fund and matching funds

Name that term:

1. The way in which candidates attempt to manipulate resources to achieve their party's nomination.

   _____

2. A meeting of state party leaders.

   _____

3. Moving a state primary earlier in the calendar year to take advantage of media attention.

   _____

4.   A bipartisan body that administers the campaign finance laws.

_____

5.   These party contributions include money raised for voter registration drives and the distribution of campaign material.

_____

6.   Independent groups that seek to influence the political process but are not subject to contribution restrictions.

_____

7.   These organizations must register with the FEC and make meticulous reports about their expenditures.

_____

8.   When people pay most attention to things they already agree with and interpret events according to their own predispositions.

_____

USING YOUR UNDERSTANDING

1.   Present an analysis of the 2004 presidential campaign in terms of what you have learned in this chapter. In particular, compare the candidates in terms of their campaign organization, their access to and use of money, their use of the media, and their attention to the issues. Did PAC money make a difference in the campaign? Which candidate received the most PAC money? Did the media treat the candidates differently? Which candidate do you believe was able to use the media most effectively and why? How did the campaign of independent candidate Ralph Nader compare to that of John Kerry and George W. Bush, who had political party organizations behind them?

2.   Find out which political action committees contribute to the member of Congress from your district and the two senators from your state and how much they contribute. Which PACs contributed to the member's campaign in the 2006 congressional election? Determine what issues these PACs are most concerned with and investigate how your representative and senators voted on policies that would be relevant to the PACs' interests. Make a table or graph to illustrate your findings and use your results as the basis for a discussion of the relationship between members of Congress and Political Action Committees.

REVIEW QUESTIONS

Check ☑ the correct answer:

1. A political party's official endorsement of a candidacy for office is called
   - ☐ a. a campaign.
   - ☐ b. an election.
   - ☐ c. a platform.
   - ☐ d. a nomination.

2. Which of the following is NOT a key element of campaign strategy?
   - ☐ a. momentum
   - ☐ b. money
   - ☐ c. mediocrity
   - ☐ d. media attention

3. The presidential campaign game
   - ☐ a. lasts only a few weeks.
   - ☐ b. is limited to two contenders.
   - ☐ c. is not played by every politician.
   - ☐ d. is given scant media attention.

4. (bonus) Who said "The question is not whether I can get elected. The question is whether I can be elected and not be nuts when I get there"?
   - ☐ a. George Romney
   - ☐ b. Walter Mondale
   - ☐ c. Richard Nixon
   - ☐ d. John Kerry

5. In most industrialized countries, campaigns last longer than in the United States.
   - ☐ True
   - ☐ False

6. The number of roads to the national party convention is about
   - ☐ a. two.
   - ☐ b. 50.
   - ☐ c. 100.
   - ☐ d. 2,000.

7. Delegates to the national party convention are determined by
   - ☐ a. a general election.
   - ☐ b. presidential primaries.
   - ☐ c. state party caucuses.
   - ☐ d. both b. and c.

8. Once, all state parties selected their delegates to the national party convention in caucuses.
   ☐ True
   ☐ False

9. Which of the following characteristics is most associated with today's state caucuses?
   ☐ a. a private meeting of party elites
   ☐ b. widespread participation
   ☐ c. little to no media attention
   ☐ d. a pyramid selection process

10. In selecting delegates to the national party convention, most states use
    ☐ a. party bosses.
    ☐ b. caucuses.
    ☐ c. debates.
    ☐ d. presidential primaries.

11. The purpose of the McGovern-Fraser Commission was to
    ☐ a. regenerate the Republican party organization.
    ☐ b. conduct an investigation of the 1968 convention riots in Chicago.
    ☐ c. draft reforms to increase the representativeness of the Democratic National Convention.
    ☐ d. choose superdelegates from among national party leaders.

12. Superdelegates to the Democratic National Convention
    ☐ a. consist of minority groups previously not represented.
    ☐ b. help restore an element of peer review to the process.
    ☐ c. were established by the McGovern-Fraser Commission.
    ☐ d. are observers only, without a formal vote.

13. The early caucuses and primaries get very little media attention relative to those later in the campaign.
    ☐ True
    ☐ False

14. Congress makes the laws determining the way in which primaries are set up and the delegates are allocated.
    ☐ True
    ☐ False

15. The first presidential primary takes place in
    ☐ a. Delaware.
    ☐ b. New Hampshire.
    ☐ c. Maine.
    ☐ d. Virginia.

16. The Iowa caucus and the New Hampshire primary play a disproportionate role in
    ☐ a. building momentum.
    ☐ b. generating money.
    ☐ c. generating media attention.
    ☐ d. all of the above

17. Running for the presidency is a full-time job.
    ☐ True
    ☐ False

18. The percentage of voters who turn out for the presidential primaries is about
    ☐ a. 10 percent.
    ☐ b. 20 percent.
    ☐ c. 50 percent.
    ☐ d. 60 percent.

19. Voters in primaries and caucuses are highly representative of the electorate at large.
    ☐ True
    ☐ False

20. Presidential primaries are largely ignored by the media.
    ☐ True
    ☐ False

21. Each of the following is an important function of the national party convention EXCEPT to
    ☐ a. nominate a candidate for president.
    ☐ b. develop the party's policy positions.
    ☐ c. select members of the electoral college.
    ☐ d. get the campaign rolling.

22. Most delegates to the national party convention are not committed to vote for a particular candidate.
    ☐ True
    ☐ False

23.   Television networks have substantially scaled back their coverage of national party conventions.
☐ True
☐ False

24.   Which of the following is central to the success of a campaign?
☐ a.   a campaign organization
☐ b.   money
☐ c.   media attention
☐ d.   all of the above

25.   Which of the following statements is FALSE?
☐ a.   Advertising and news coverage are central to media attention to campaigns.
☐ b.   Most television advertising has little to do with salient campaign issues.
☐ c.   Candidates have less control over news coverage than advertising.
☐ d.   More political news has to do with campaign details than the policy positions of candidates.

26.   Newspapers and newsmagazines pay little attention to the campaign itself in favor of comprehensive coverage of the issues.
☐ True
☐ False

27.   The political candidate can handle most of the tasks of a campaign without assistance.
☐ True
☐ False

28.   Which of the following is NOT a part of the Federal Election Campaign Act, as amended?
☐ a.   partial public financing for candidates
☐ b.   disclosure of contributions
☐ c.   limits on contributions
☐ d.   elimination of Political Action Committees (PACs)

29.   The Supreme Court case of *Buckley* v. *Valeo* (1976)
☐ a.   struck down limits on the amount individuals could contribute to their own campaigns.
☐ b.   eliminated PACs.
☐ c.   required PACs to register with the FEC.
☐ d.   declared the Federal Election Campaign Act unconstitutional.

30. Which of the following is NOT part of the McCain-Feingold Act?
   - ☐ a. a ban on Political Action Committees
   - ☐ b. a ban on soft money contributions
   - ☐ c. an increase in the amount that individuals could give to candidates
   - ☐ d. a ban on groups running "issue ads" within 60 days of the general election

31. Independent groups that seek to influence the political process but are not subject to contribution restrictions because they do not directly seek he election of particular candidates are called
   - ☐ a. Political Action Committees.
   - ☐ b. 527 groups.
   - ☐ c. Grass Roots Committees.
   - ☐ d. Issue Groups.

32. The formation of a Political Action Committee (PAC) makes it possible to avoid reporting expenditures to the Federal Election Commission (FEC).
   - ☐ True
   - ☐ False

33. In return for contributions, Political Action Committees (PACs) hope to gain
   - ☐ a. campaign finance reform.
   - ☐ b. access to officeholders.
   - ☐ c. bribes.
   - ☐ d. recognition for public service.

34. Which of the following statements about Political Action Committees is FALSE?
   - ☐ a. There is no data to support the contention that PACs can "buy" Congress.
   - ☐ b. Most PACs support those who agree with them in the first place.
   - ☐ c. Presidents are particularly vulnerable to PAC influence.
   - ☐ d. Candidates need PACs because high-tech campaigning is expensive.

35. (bonus) American elections cost, per person, about as much as a
   - ☐ a. DVD movie.
   - ☐ b. candy bar.
   - ☐ c. new car.
   - ☐ d. new house.

36. The most important ingredient of electoral success is
   - ☐ a. having enough money to get a message across.
   - ☐ b. outspending opponents.
   - ☐ c. getting interest group endorsements.
   - ☐ d. kissing babies.

37. The LEAST frequent consequence of campaigns for voters is
☐ a. reinforcement.
☐ b. activation.
☐ c. conversion.
☐ d. both a. and b.

38. Which of the following does NOT weaken the impact of campaigns?
☐ a. selective perception
☐ b. the advantage of incumbents
☐ c. party identification
☐ d. close elections

39. Party outsiders have virtually no chance of being elected in the United States.
☐ True
☐ False

40. Campaigns today tend to promote individualism in American politics.
☐ True
☐ False

41. To secure votes from each region and state of the country, candidates
☐ a. promise to reduce government programs and spending.
☐ b. develop a national policy platform.
☐ c. end up supporting a variety of local interests.
☐ d. avoid talking about local issues.

ESSAY QUESTIONS

1. How is a candidate nominated for the presidency? What functions do national party conventions perform? What criticisms have been raised about the nomination process? Is it a representative process?

2. What are the elements of a successful political campaign? What impacts do campaigns have on voters? What factors tend to weaken these impacts?

3. What is the role of money in campaigns? What campaign finance reforms have been adopted? What effects have they had?

4. What are the positive and negative features of Political Action Committees? How might they affect politicians and policymaking?

5. How do campaign images and issues conflict; or do they? What is the role of the media in shaping both?

6. How do campaigns affect democracy, public policy, and the scope of government?

CHAPTER 10

ELECTIONS AND VOTING BEHAVIOR

CHAPTER OUTLINE

I.   How American Elections Work (pp. 298-299)
 A.   Elections socialize and institutionalize political activity and provide regular access to political power, thus establishing **legitimacy**.
 B.   A **referendum** gives voters the chance to approve or disapprove some legislative act or constitutional amendment.
 C.   **Initiative petitions** enable voters to put proposed legislation on the ballot.

II. A Tale of Three Elections (pp. 299-304)
 A.   1800: The First Electoral Transition of Power
 B.   1896: A Bitter Fight over Economic Interests
 C.   2004: The Ratification of a Polarizing Presidency

III. Whether To Vote: A Citizen's First Choice (pp. 304-309)
 A.   Deciding Whether to Vote
  1.   The costs of voting may rationally outweigh the benefits.
  2.   People who see policy differences in the parties are more likely to vote.
  3.   People with a high sense of **political efficacy** are more likely to vote.
  4.   People with a high sense of **civic duty** are more likely to vote.
 B.   Registering to Vote
  1.   **Voter registration** procedures currently differ greatly from state to state.
  2.   The 1993 **Motor Voter Act** requires states to permit people to register at the same time they apply for driver's licenses.
 C.   Who Votes?
  1.   People with a higher education vote more regularly.
  2.   Older people vote more regularly than younger people.
  3.   African Americans and Hispanics vote less regularly.
  4.   Women vote slightly more regularly than men.
  5.   Married people are more likely to vote than nonmarried.
  6.   Government employees vote more regularly.

IV. How Americans Vote: Explaining Citizens' Decisions (pp. 310-315)
 A.   The **mandate theory of elections** suggests that the winner has a mandate to carry out promised policies.
 B.   Party Identification provides a perspective through which voters can view the political world.

176

      C.   Candidate Evaluations: How Americans see the Candidates
      D.   **Policy Voting** occurs when people base their choices in an election on their own issue preferences.

V.   The Last Battle: The **Electoral College** (pp. 315-316)

VI.   Understanding Elections and Voting Behavior (pp. 316-319)
      A.   Democracy and Elections
          1.   The greater the policy differences between the candidates, the more likely voters will be able to steer government policies by their choices.
          2.   People who feel better off than before will vote for candidates who pledge to continue the status quo; those who feel worse off will vote for the opposition (**retrospective voting**).
      B.   Elections and the Scope of Government

VII.   Summary (p. 319)

LEARNING OBJECTIVES

After studying Chapter 10, you should be able to:

    1.   Explain the functions and unique features of American elections.

    2.   Describe how American elections have evolved using the presidential elections of 1800, 1896, and 2004 as examples.

    3.   Discuss the factors that affect a citizen's choice of whether to vote.

    4.   Explain how Americans vote and what factors influence how they vote.

    5.   Explain how the electoral college works and what biases it can introduce.

    6.   Understand how elections affect democracy, public policy, and the scope of government.

The following exercises will help you meet these objectives:

Objective 1: Explain the functions and unique features of American elections.

    1.   List the three kinds of elections found in the United States and their purpose.

        1.

2.

3.

2.   What is the difference between an initiative petition and a referendum?

Objective 2: Describe how American elections have evolved using the presidential elections of 1800, 1896, and 2004.

1.   Complete the following table on the elections of 1800, 1896, and 2004.

Year	Candidates and Party	Winner	Major Issues	Campaign Style	Significance of Election
1800					
1896					
2004					

2. What were the major reasons why people voted for either George W. Bush or John Kerry in the 2004 presidential election?

George W. Bush:

John Kerry:

Objective 3: Discuss the factors that affect a citizen's choice of whether to vote.

1. List and explain three major reasons why people might vote.

   1.

   2.
   3.

2. What is the major provision of the 1993 Motor Voter Act?

3. List and explain six demographic factors that are related to voter turnout.

   1.

   2.

   3.

   4.

   5.

   6.

Objective 4: Explain how Americans vote and what factors influence how they vote.

1.   What is meant by the "mandate theory of elections"?

2.   How has the influence of party identification on voting changed since the 1950s?

3.   What are the three most important dimensions of candidate image?

   1.

   2.

   3.

4.   What are the four conditions necessary for true policy voting to take place?
   1.

   2.

   3.

   4.

Objective 5: Explain how the electoral college works and what biases it can introduce.

1.   Briefly explain how the electoral college works.

2.   What are the two reasons why the electoral college is important to presidential elections?

1.

2.

Objective 6: Understand how elections affect democracy, public policy, and the scope of government.

    1.   What are the two tasks that elections accomplish, according to democratic theory?

           1.

           2.

    2.   According to the text, what is the clearest way in which elections broadly affect public policy?

    3.   What does retrospective voting mean?

KEY TERMS

Identify and describe:

legitimacy

referendum

initiative petition

suffrage

political efficacy

civic duty

voter registration

Motor Voter Act

mandate theory of elections

policy voting

electoral college

retrospective voting

Compare and contrast:

initiative petition and referendum

suffrage and voter registration

voter registration and Motor Voter Act

policy differences and civic duty

mandate theory of elections and policy voting

Name that term:

1. A term used to describe elections that are almost universally accepted as a fair and free method to select political leaders.

   _____

2. This enables voters in 23 states to put proposed legislation on the ballot.

   _____

3. It varies among the states and tends to dampen voter turnout.

   _____

4. This reflects the belief that one's vote can make a difference.

   _____

5. Politicians are more attracted to this idea than are political scientists.

   _____

6. A unique American institution created by the Constitution.

   _____

7. When voters essentially ask the simple question, "What have you done for me lately?"

   _____

USING YOUR UNDERSTANDING

1. The text points out that the United States has one of the lowest voter turnout rates among all democratic nations. Examine the reasons why voter turnout is so low and outline a comprehensive plan that would increase voter turnout in the United States. What policies need to be changed to increase voter turnout? How might incentives be used to get people to vote? You might want to look at voting laws in other countries with high turnout rates to get ideas. Also include an examination of the Motor Voter Act. Speculate on how the Motor Voter Act might increase participation. What are the main criticisms of the Motor Voter Act? Comment on how your suggestions might be implemented.

2. Find out about electoral turnout in your state for the 2004 and 2006 elections. How did the participation rates for various population groups (based on race, income, region, etc.) differ? Compare your state's voting rate to the national turnout rate and to that of other states. How well does your state fare? See if you can identify some of the demographic features of your state that might help explain its rate of turnout, such as its size, urbanization, or population composition. How did participation rates differ between 2004 and 2006 and why? How might the voter registration system in your state affect turnout? Briefly describe what you found and suggest ways to improve electoral participation.

REVIEW QUESTION

Check ☑ the correct answer:

1. Elections serve the purpose of
   - ☐ a.   socializing and institutionalizing political activity.
   - ☐ b.   providing regular access to political power.
   - ☐ c.   providing a legitimate means to replace leaders.
   - ☐ d.   all of the above

2. In the United States, elections are used to
   - ☐ a.   select party nominees.
   - ☐ b.   select officeholders.
   - ☐ c.   make or ratify legislation.
   - ☐ d.   all of the above

3. Voters in some states can put a proposed law on the ballot with
   - ☐ a.   an initiative petition.
   - ☐ b.   an opinion poll.
   - ☐ c.   a referendum.
   - ☐ d.   a three-fifths vote.

4.   A referendum is used to give voters a chance to approve a proposed legislative act or constitutional amendment.
     ☐ True
     ☐ False

5.   In the election of 1800,
     ☐ a.   candidates were nominated at national conventions.
     ☐ b.   the focus of the campaign was on the voters.
     ☐ c.   the candidate with the second-highest number of electoral votes became vice president.
     ☐ d.   media coverage was extensive.

6.   In the election of 1896, the Republicans supported
     ☐ a.   low tariffs.
     ☐ b.   the gold standard.
     ☐ c.   rural farmers in debt.
     ☐ d.   unlimited coinage of silver.

7.   (bonus) Which candidate traveled through 26 states and logged 18,000 miles?
     ☐ a.   William McKinley
     ☐ b.   Grover Cleveland
     ☐ c.   John Adams
     ☐ d.   William Jennings Bryan

8.   Voter turnout in 1896 approached
     ☐ a.   20 percent.
     ☐ b.   60 percent.
     ☐ c.   50 percent.
     ☐ d.   80 percent.

9.   The election of 2000 boiled down to who would win the state of
     ☐ a.   California.
     ☐ b.   Pennsylvania.
     ☐ c.   Florida.
     ☐ d.   New York.

10. The U.S. Supreme Court ultimately determined the winner of the 2000 presidential election.
     ☐ True
     ☐ False

11. In 2004, George W. Bush successfully portrayed John Kerry as a "flip flopper."
     ☐ True
     ☐ False

12. One of the main reasons people voted for George W. Bush in 2004 was
   ☐ a. his stand on the economy.
   ☐ b. the war in Iraq.
   ☐ c. strong leadership in the war on terrorism.
   ☐ d. his stand on health care.

13. A paradox in American electoral history is that while suffrage has expanded,
   ☐ a. fewer Americans exercise the right to vote.
   ☐ b. participation in elections has increased.
   ☐ c. people place greater value on their right to vote.
   ☐ d. fewer people are eligible to vote.

14. Rational people might decide that the costs of voting outweigh the benefits.
   ☐ True
   ☐ False

15. Which of the following factors is NOT central to the decision of whether or not to vote?
   ☐ a. perceived policy differences between the parties
   ☐ b. the knowledge that most elections are extremely close
   ☐ c. a sense of political efficacy
   ☐ d. a sense of civic duty

16. The belief that ordinary people can influence the government is known as
   ☐ a. political efficacy.
   ☐ b. rational behavior.
   ☐ c. civic duty.
   ☐ d. class-based voting.

17. The voter registration system is
   ☐ a. implemented by federal authorities.
   ☐ b. more restrictive in northern states.
   ☐ c. an important factor in low voter turnout.
   ☐ d. the same in every state.

18. The Motor Voter Act made voter registration easier.
   ☐ True
   ☐ False

19. All other things being equal, who of the following individuals is most likely to vote?
   ☐ a. a single person
   ☐ b. a married government employee
   ☐ c. a high school drop-out
   ☐ d. a southern black

20. African Americans and other minorities with high income and education levels vote with greater frequency than whites with high income and education levels.
    ☐ True
    ☐ False

21. Politicians and political scientists agree on the relevance of the mandate theory of elections.
    ☐ True
    ☐ False

22. Which of the following factors is NOT central to the decision of how to vote?
    ☐ a. simplified registration procedures
    ☐ b. party identification
    ☐ c. candidate evaluation
    ☐ d. policy voting

23. In the 1950s, the single best predictor of a voter's decision of how to vote was
    ☐ a. political efficacy.
    ☐ b. policy voting.
    ☐ c. party identification.
    ☐ d. candidate evaluation.

24. A study by Rosenberg and McCafferty concluded that
    ☐ a. a candidate's appearance and image has no real effect on voters.
    ☐ b. policy voting has become the single most important determinant of how to vote.
    ☐ c. it is possible to manipulate a candidate's appearance in a way that affects voters' choices.
    ☐ d. party identification has all but disappeared as a determinant of how to vote.

25. Studies have shown that the most important dimension of candidate image is
    ☐ a. integrity.
    ☐ b. reliability.
    ☐ c. competence.
    ☐ d. all of the above

26. Which of the following conditions is NOT central to policy voting?
    ☐ a. a voter's clear view of his or her policy preferences
    ☐ b. a voter's knowledge of where the candidates stand
    ☐ c. a voter's party identification
    ☐ d. a vote for the candidate whose positions match those of the voter

27.   No longer can a candidate get a party's nomination without taking stands on the major issues of the day.
☐ True
☐ False

28.   The electoral college system was created by
☐ a.   political practice.
☐ b.   political parties.
☐ c.   an act of Congress.
☐ d.   the Constitution.

29.   Which of the following statements about the electoral college is FALSE?
☐ a.   It is used in many countries of the world.
☐ b.   Each state has as many electors as it has senators and representatives.
☐ c.   In most states, there is a winner-take-all system.
☐ d.   Electoral college votes are counted when the new congressional session opens in January.

30.   Electoral college votes are cast in proportion to the popular vote for each candidate.
☐ True
☐ False

31.   The electoral college is important to the presidential election because it
☐ a.   introduces a bias into the campaign and electoral process.
☐ b.   overrepresents the less populated states.
☐ c.   may result in the election of a president who did not receive the most popular votes.
☐ d.   all of the above

32.   The electoral college system can introduce bias in the electoral process because it overrepresents
☐ a.   urban states.
☐ b.   small states.
☐ c.   big states.
☐ d.   states without big cities.

33.   It is possible for the electoral college to choose a president who did not win a majority of the popular vote.
☐ True
☐ False

34.   The greater the policy differences between the candidates, the more likely voters will be able to steer government policies by their choices.
☐ True
☐ False

35.   Parties and candidates
☐ a.   are skilled in the art of ambiguity.
☐ b.   prefer to tackle the controversial issues.
☐ c.   use the media for comprehensive issue coverage.
☐ d.   always provide voters with sharp choices.

36.   (bonus) Who said that candidates should offer "a choice, not an echo"?
☐ a.   Jimmy Carter
☐ b.   Barry Goldwater
☐ c.   Benjamin Page
☐ d.   Ronald Reagan

37.   Retrospective voting refers to voting
☐ a.   by absentee ballot.
☐ b.   for an incumbent because the perception that his or her policies have made you better off.
☐ c.   according to party identification.
☐ d.   the same way year after year.

38.   Because of retrospective voting, nothing makes incumbent politicians more nervous than the state of
☐ a.   foreign affairs.
☐ b.   the environment.
☐ c.   the economy.
☐ d.   all of the above

39.   Individuals who believe they can influence the government's actions are also more likely to believe, in turn, that the government should have more power.
☐ True
☐ False

ESSAY QUESTIONS

1.   What are the functions of elections in American society? What are some of the electoral features that are unique to the United States?

2.   How has the American electoral system evolved? How did the election of 2004 contrast with elections of the past, particularly the elections of 1800 and 1896?

3. What is the electoral paradox of more suffrage and less participation? Why would we expect people to vote more today and why do they not do so? How does the voter registration system affect the decision to vote?

4. What factors determine why people choose to vote? What groups are most likely to vote and what groups are least likely to vote? What are the implications of these differences in electoral participation?

5. Why do people vote the way they do? Which reason do you believe is most important and why?

6. What is the electoral college and how does it work? What biases in the electoral process does it introduce? Should the electoral college system be preserved or abolished?

7. How do elections affect democracy, public policy, and the scope of government?

CHAPTER 11

INTEREST GROUPS

CHAPTER OUTLINE

I.   The Role of Interest Groups (pp. 324-326)
    A.   An **interest group** is an organization of people with similar policy goals who enter the political process to try to achieve those aims.
    B.   Interest groups are often policy specialists, whereas parties are policy generalists.

II.   Theories of Interest Group Politics (pp. 326-329)
    A.   Pluralism and Group Theory
        1.   **Pluralist theory** argues that interest group activity brings representation to all.
        2.   The group theory of politics contains several arguments.
            a.   Groups provide a key link between people and government.
            b.   Groups compete.
            c.   No one group is likely to become too dominant.
            d.   Groups usually play by the "rules of the game."
            e.   Groups weak in one resource can use another.
    B.   Elites and the Denial of Pluralism
        1.   **Elite theory** argues that a few groups, primarily the wealthy, have most of the power.
        2.   Groups are extremely unequal in power.
        3.   Awesome power is controlled by the largest corporations.
        4.   The power of a few is fortified by a system of interlocking directorates.
        5.   Corporate elites prevail when it comes to the big decisions.
    C.   Hyperpluralism and Interest Group Liberalism
        1.   **Hyperpluralist theory** asserts that too many groups are getting too much of what they want, resulting in a government policy that is often contradictory and lacking in direction.
        2.   Interest group liberalism refers to government's excessive deference to groups.
            a.   Groups have become too powerful in the political process as government tries to aid every conceivable interest.
            b.   Interest group liberalism is aggravated by numerous **subgovernments**.
            c.   Trying to please every group results in contradictory and confusing policy.

III. What Makes an Interest Group Successful? (pp. 329-333)
    A. The Surprising Ineffectiveness of Large Groups
        1. A **potential group** is composed of all people who might be group members because they share some common interest.
        2. An **actual group** is composed of those in the potential group who choose to join.
        3. A **collective good** is something of value that cannot be withheld from a potential group member.
        4. The **free-rider problem** occurs when members of the potential group share in benefits that members of the actual group work to secure.
        5. **Olson's law of large groups** states that the larger the group, the further it will fall short of providing an optimal amount of a collective good.
        6. **Selective benefits** are goods that a group can restrict to those who pay their yearly dues.
    B. Intensity
        1. Intensity is a psychological advantage that can be enjoyed by small and large groups alike.
        2. A **single-issue group** is a group that has a narrow interest, dislikes compromise, and single-mindedly pursues its goal.
    C. Financial Resources

IV. The Interest Group Explosion (pp. 333-334)

V. How Groups Try To Shape Policy (pp. 335-340)
    A. Lobbying
        1. **Lobbying** is a communication, by someone other than a citizen acting on his or her own behalf, directed to a governmental decision-maker with the hope of influencing his or her decision.
        2. Lobbyists can help a member of Congress
            a. They are an important source of information.
            b. They can help politicians with political strategy.
            c. They can help formulate campaign strategy.
            d. They are a source of ideas and innovations.
    B. Electioneering
        1. **Electioneering** consists of aiding candidates financially and getting group members out to support them.
        2. **Political Action Committees (PACs)** provide a means for groups to participate in electioneering.
    C. Litigation
        1. *Amicus curiae* **briefs** consist of written arguments submitted to the courts in support of one side of a case.
        2. **Class action lawsuits** enable a group of similarly situated plaintiffs to combine similar grievances into a single suit.
    D. Going Public

VI. Types of Interest Groups (pp. 341-347)
    A. Economic Interests
        1. Labor
            a. The **union shop** requires new employees to join the union representing them.
            b. **Right-to-work laws** outlaw union membership as a condition of employment.
        2. Business
    B. Environmental Interests
    C. Equality Interests
    D. Consumers and Public Interest Lobbies
        1. **Public interest lobbies** are organizations that seek a collective good.
        2. The consumer movement was spurred by the efforts of Ralph Nader.

VII. Understanding Interest Groups (pp. 347-349)
    A. Interest Groups and Democracy
    B. Interest Groups and the Scope of Government

VIII. Summary (pp. 349-350)

LEARNING OBJECTIVES

After studying Chapter 11, you should be able to:

1. Define interest groups and distinguish them from political parties.

2. Compare and contrast the pluralist, elite, and hyperpluralist theories of interest groups.

3. Explain what makes an interest group successful and why small groups have an advantage over large groups.

4. Identify and describe the strategies that groups use to shape public policy.

5. Describe some of the many types of groups in the American political system.

6. Evaluate interest groups in terms of their influence on democracy and the scope of government.

The following exercises will help you meet these objectives:

Objective 1: Define interest groups and distinguish them from political parties.

    1.   Provide a definition of the term "interest group."

    2.   Name two factors that distinguish interest groups from political parties.

        1.

        2.

Objective 2: Compare and contrast the pluralist, elite, and hyperpluralist theories of interest groups.

    1.   Complete the following table on the theories of interest group politics.

Theory	Definition	Role of Groups	Who Holds Power	Group Impact on Public Policy
Pluralist Theory				
Elite Theory				
Hyper-pluralist Theory				

2. List five essential arguments of the group theory of politics.

1.

2.

3.

4.

5.

3. List four major points made by the elitist view of the interest group system.

1.

2.

3.

4.

4. List the three major points of the hyperpluralist position on group politics.

1.

2.

3.

Objective 3: Explain what makes a group successful and why small groups have an advantage over large groups.

    1.   What is the difference between a potential group and an actual group?

    2.   What is Olson's law of large groups?

    3.   Define the term single-issue group and give an example.

Objective 4: Identify and describe the strategies that groups use to shape public policy.

    1.   List the four general strategies used by interest groups to shape public policy.

        1.

        2.

        3.

        4.

    2.   What are the two basic types of lobbyists?

        1.

        2.

    3.   List four important ways lobbyists can help a member of Congress.

        1.

        2.

3.

4.

4.   Why does PAC money go so overwhelmingly to incumbents?

5.   What is an *amicus curiae* brief?

Objective 5:   Describe some of the many types of groups in the American political system.

1.   What was the main purpose of the Taft-Hartley Act?

2.   List three issues that trade and product associations seek when lobbying Capitol Hill.

    1.

    2.

    3.

3.   List three items environmental groups have promoted and three items they have opposed.

Promoted:

    1.

    2.

3.

Opposed:

1.

2.

3.

4.   Name two important organizations involved in promoting equality and summarize their major goals.

1.

2.

5.   What is meant by a public interest lobby?

Objective 6: Evaluate interest groups in terms of their influence on democracy and the scope of government.

1.   Summarize the pluralist, elitist, and hyperpluralist perspectives on interest groups and democracy.

1. Pluralist:

2. Elitist:

3. Hyperpluralist:

2.   How do interest groups affect the scope of government?

KEY TERMS

Identify and describe:

interest group

pluralist theory

elite theory

hyperpluralist theory

subgovernments

potential group

actual group

collective good

free-rider problem

Olson's law of large groups

selective benefits

single-issue group

lobbying

electioneering

Political Action Committees (PACs)

amicus curiae briefs

class action lawsuits

union shop

right-to-work laws

public interest lobbies

Compare and contrast:

pluralist theory, elite theory, and hyperpluralist theory

hyperpluralist theory and subgovernments

potential group and actual group

collective good and free-rider problem

Olson's law of large groups and selective benefits

lobbying and electioneering

electioneering and Political Action Committees

amicus curiae briefs and class action lawsuits

union shop and right-to-work laws

Name that term:

1.   An organization of people with similar policy goals entering the political process to try to achieve those goals.

      _____

2.   These are also known as iron triangles.

      _____

3.   There are usually more members in this group than in the actual group.

      _____

201

4. When it is easier to not join a group because you will receive the benefits anyway.

   _____

5. "The larger the group, the further it will fall short of providing an optimal amount of a collective good."

   _____

6. People in this group tend to dislike compromise and single-mindedly pursue their goal.

   _____

7. In recent years, these have provided a means for groups to participate in electioneering more than ever before.

   _____

8. This enables a group of similarly situated plaintiffs to combine similar grievances into a single suit.

   _____

9. These organizations seek a collective good that will not selectively benefit the membership of the organization.

   _____

USING YOUR UNDERSTANDING

1. Investigate an interest group that is of interest to you. Contact the group to see if they can provide information on the group and its policy goals. Find out how the group's actual membership compares to its potential membership. Try to identify the strategies that the group uses in trying to achieve its policy goals. Briefly describe what you found in terms of how well the group is achieving its goals and forging a link between people and policy.

2. Using newspapers or newsmagazines, collect some current examples of group involvement in the policy process. Try to find examples of various types of groups — groups in different policy arenas, public interest lobbies, and single-issue groups. Analyze each example in terms of the policymaking area in which group activity was focused (e.g., electoral, legislative, administrative, or

judicial), strategies used by the group to affect policy, and the degree to which the group was successful in achieving its policy goals. Discuss whether or not your findings support the interpretation of groups provided by pluralist theory, elite theory, and hyperpluralist theory.

REVIEW QUESTIONS

Check ☑ the correct answer:

1. Participation in both elections and interest groups has declined dramatically since 1960.
   ☐ True
   ☐ False

2. Interest groups have no formal Constitutional protections.
   ☐ True
   ☐ False

3. Interest groups differ from political parties because
   ☐ a. parties use technology more effectively.
   ☐ b. groups tend to be policy specialists while parties tend to be policy generalists.
   ☐ c. the group's main arena is the electoral system.
   ☐ d. parties seek many access points in government.

4. The theory that argues that just a few groups have most of the power is the
   ☐ a. pluralist theory.
   ☐ b. elite theory.
   ☐ c. group theory of politics.
   ☐ d. hyperpluralist theory.

5. The group theory of politics
   ☐ a. is a part of traditional democratic theory.
   ☐ b. supports the idea that elites run the government.
   ☐ c. sees groups as an important linkage institution.
   ☐ d. states that groups have become too powerful.

6. Which of the following is NOT an essential part of the group theory of politics?
   ☐ a. Groups are extremely unequal in power.
   ☐ b. Groups usually play by the rules of the game.
   ☐ c. Groups weak in one resource can use another.
   ☐ d. Groups compete.

7.	Public opinion polls have shown that most people believe that government is pretty much run by a few big interests looking out for themselves.
☐ True
☐ False

8.	Which of the following statements about the elite theory perspective on groups is FALSE?
☐ a.	Real power is held by relatively few key groups.
☐ b.	The power of a few is fortified by an extensive system of interlocking directorates.
☐ c.	The real game of group politics is the one played by the corporate elites.
☐ d.	Groups provide an effective check on elite power.

9.	According to elite theorists, interest group lobbying is a problem because
☐ a.	it is open to too many groups.
☐ b.	it benefits the few at the expense of the many.
☐ c.	it disperses power among a wide range of groups.
☐ d.	legislators have become immune to group pressures.

10.	Interest-group liberalism is characterized by the philosophy that all interests are almost equally legitimate and the job of government is to advance them all.
☐ True
☐ False

11.	Which of the following is NOT a part of subgovernments?
☐ a.	interest group leaders
☐ b.	interlocking directorates
☐ c.	administrative agencies
☐ d.	congressional committees and subcommittees

12.	The Tobacco Institute, the Department of Agriculture, and the House Tobacco Subcommittee working together to protect the interest of tobacco farmers is a classic example of
☐ a.	interlocking directorates.
☐ b.	the group theory of politics.
☐ c.	a subgovernment.
☐ d.	elite control of government.

13.	The hyperpluralist position on groups is that
☐ a.	groups have become too powerful in the political process.
☐ b.	interest group liberalism is aggravated by numerous subgovernments.
☐ c.	the result of group conflict is contradictory and confusing policy.
☐ d.	all of the above

14.   The larger the group, the
      ☐ a.   more government support it receives.
      ☐ b.   more it behaves like a party.
      ☐ c.   less effective it is.
      ☐ d.   more specialized it becomes.

15.   Large groups have organizational advantages over small groups.
      ☐ True
      ☐ False

16.   A potential group
      ☐ a.   is composed of people who share a common interest.
      ☐ b.   is usually smaller than an actual group.
      ☐ c.   is composed of only active group members.
      ☐ d.   always consists of all consumers.

17.   Collective goods
      ☐ a.   can be packaged and sold separately.
      ☐ b.   can be withheld from any group member.
      ☐ c.   are available only to members of the actual group who secure them.
      ☐ d.   are shared by members of the potential group.

18.   Free-riders
      ☐ a.   are actual group members.
      ☐ b.   avoid collective goods.
      ☐ c.   aggravate large groups more than small groups.
      ☐ d.   automatically share in selective benefits.

19.   Which of the following matters could NOT be explained by Mancur Olson's law of large groups?
      ☐ a.   the problems of public interest lobbies
      ☐ b.   why small groups are easier to organize
      ☐ c.   why large groups are less effective
      ☐ d.   the successes of the Consumers Union

20.   (bonus) Which of the following organizations has the largest potential membership?
      ☐ a.   National Association for the Advancement of Colored People
      ☐ b.   National Organization for Women
      ☐ c.   Consumers Union
      ☐ d.   American Medical Association

21.   Goods that a group can restrict to those who pay their yearly dues are called
☐ a.   free-rider goods.
☐ b.   selective benefits.
☐ c.   collective goods.
☐ d.   actual benefits.

22.   Which of the following is NOT true of single-issue groups?
☐ a.   They are the same as public interest lobbies.
☐ b.   They have narrow interests.
☐ c.   They dislike compromise.
☐ d.   They single-mindedly pursue their goal.

23.   One of the most emotional issues to generate single-issue groups has been that of abortion.
☐ True
☐ False

24.   Critics charge that PACs make the interest group system biased toward the wealthy.
☐ True
☐ False

25.   Which of the following statements regarding the Tax Reform Act of 1986 is FALSE?
☐ a.   The Tax Reform Act eliminated all but a very few loopholes.
☐ b.   The Tax Reform Act is a classic example of how PACs can influence votes.
☐ c.   The Chairman of the Senate Finance Committee was Congress's top PAC recipient during the tax reform struggle.
☐ d.   Senator Packwood turned against lobbyists trying to get his ear on behalf of various tax loopholes.

26.   Technology has facilitated the explosion in the number of interest groups in the United States.
☐ True
☐ False

27.   Which of the following is NOT among the strategies used by interest groups to shape public policy?
☐ a.   lobbying
☐ b.   litigation
☐ c.   electioneering
☐ d.   avoiding publicity

28. Lobbying
☐ a. is aimed at influencing decision making.
☐ b. is confined solely to the legislative branch.
☐ c. was made illegal with the Federal Regulation of Lobbying Act.
☐ d. is most effective in converting legislators.

29. Which of the following is NOT one of the ways that lobbyists can help a member of Congress?
☐ a. helping to formulate campaign strategy
☐ b. writing and introducing bills
☐ c. providing important information
☐ d. providing ideas and innovations

30. Lobbyists are relatively ineffective in winning over legislators who are opposed to their goals.
☐ True
☐ False

31. Which of the following statements regarding lobbying is FALSE?
☐ a. Studies have shown that lobbyists are particularly effective as information sources.
☐ b. There is plenty of evidence to suggest that sometimes lobbying can persuade legislators to support a certain policy.
☐ c. It is hard to isolate the effects of lobbying from other influences.
☐ d. Unlike campaigning, lobbying is directed primarily toward conversion activities.

32. Which of the following is generally NOT a major part of electioneering?
☐ a. providing financial aid to candidates, frequently through PACs
☐ b. encouraging group members to campaign for a favorite candidate
☐ c. running an interest group leader as a political candidate
☐ d. activating group members to vote for a favorite candidate

33. Most PAC contributions are given to challengers rather than incumbents.
☐ True
☐ False

34. (bonus) Congressional candidate Steve Sovern organized a PAC called LASTPAC in order to
☐ a. get PAC money since no other PAC would support him.
☐ b. urge candidates to shun PAC-backing.
☐ c. unite the PACs under one political organization.
☐ d. get other candidates to support the goals of the Legal Assistance Support Team (LAST).

35. Which of the following types of groups has NOT resorted to litigation as a strategy for affecting policy?
☐ a. groups interested in equality
☐ b. groups interested in the environment
☐ c. public interest lobbies
☐ d. none of the above

36. *Amicus curiae* briefs
☐ a. enable a group of similarly situated plaintiffs to combine similar grievances into a single suit.
☐ b. consist of written arguments submitted to the courts in support of one side of a case.
☐ c. are required before an interest group can sue for enforcement of a particular piece of legislation.
☐ d. are most often used by Political Action Committees.

37. Most interest groups are not concerned with the opinions of people outside of their membership.
☐ True
☐ False

38. Public policy in America has economic effects through
☐ a. regulations.
☐ b. tax advantages.
☐ c. subsidies and contracts.
☐ d. all of the above

39. Right-to-work laws are generally supported by
☐ a. business groups.
☐ b. labor unions.
☐ c. public interest groups.
☐ d. all of the above

40. The concept of the "union shop" illustrates the seriousness of the free-rider problem for labor organizations.
☐ True
☐ False

41. The influence of business groups would best illustrate
☐ a. pluralist theory.
☐ b. elite theory.
☐ c. hyperpluralist theory.
☐ d. democratic theory.

42. Business PACs have increased more dramatically than any other category of PACs.
☐ True
☐ False

43. Which of the following issues is NOT on the hit list of environmentalist groups?
☐ a. alternative energy sources
☐ b. strip mining
☐ c. offshore oil drilling
☐ d. supersonic aircraft

44. When the two public interests of environmental protection and an ensured supply of energy clash,
☐ a. group conflict intensifies.
☐ b. compromise is achieved.
☐ c. the need for energy always wins.
☐ d. groups play a secondary role to elite interests.

45. Today, civil rights groups are particularly concerned with affirmative action programs to ensure equal educational and employment opportunities.
☐ True
☐ False

46. Most recently, the National Organization for Women has been most active in
☐ a. getting the Equal Rights Amendment ratified.
☐ b. the enactment of individual statutes on equal rights for women.
☐ c. achieving equal voting rights.
☐ d. all of the above

47. Organizations that seek a collective good, the achievement of which will not selectively and materially benefit the membership or activists of the organization, are called
☐ a. single-issue groups.
☐ b. public interest lobbies.
☐ c. Political Action Committees.
☐ d. pluralistic groups.

48. Which of the following would NOT be considered a public interest lobby?
☐ a. Common Cause
☐ b. the Sierra Club
☐ c. the Chamber of Commerce
☐ d. the Christian Coalition

49.   James Madison
        ☐ a.   favored a wide-open system in which many groups would be able to participate to counterbalance one another.
        ☐ b.   wanted the Constitution to forbid the growth of groups and factions.
        ☐ c.   believed American society would be best served by a relatively small number of powerful groups.
        ☐ d.   believed that public interest groups were dangerous because the common man was not qualified to speak for the public interest.

50.   Presidents Carter and Reagan both felt that interest groups were beneficial to their administrations and helped with policy formation.
        ☐ True
        ☐ False

ESSAY QUESTIONS

1.   What are interest groups? How do groups differ from political parties?

2.   Compare and contrast the pluralist, elite, and hyperpluralist theories of interest groups. In your opinion, which theory best describes reality and why?

3.   What is the difference between a potential group and an actual group? Why is this difference important to understanding the free-rider problem? Be sure to include a discussion of collective goods in your answer.

4.   Why are small groups generally more effective than large groups? Explain Olson's law of large groups.

5.   How do intensity and financial resources affect interest group success? What are single-issue groups and how effective have they been in American politics?

6.   What are the principal strategies that groups use to affect policymaking? Which strategy seems to be the most effective, and why? Are certain strategies better suited for different types of interest groups?

7.   What impact do Political Action Committees have on interest group behavior? Evaluate the role of Political Action Committees.

8.   What are the different types of interest groups? What are their primary goals, what strategies do they use, and how successful have they been?

9.   How do interest groups affect democracy and the scope of government in the United States?

CHAPTER 12

CONGRESS

CHAPTER OUTLINE

I.   The Representatives and Senators (pp. 354-358)
  A.   The Job
  B.   The Members

II. Congressional Elections (pp. 358-365)
  A.   Who Wins Elections?
    1.   **Incumbents** are individuals who already hold office.
    2.   Incumbents usually win.
  B.   The Advantages of Incumbents
    1.   Advertising
    2.   Credit Claiming
      a.   **Casework** is helping constituents as individuals.
      b.   **Pork barrel** is the mighty list of federal projects, grants, and contracts available to cities, businesses, colleges, and institutions.
    3.   Position-Taking
    4.   Weak Opponents
    5.   Campaign Spending
  C.   The Role of Party Identification
  D.   Defeating Incumbents
  E.   Open Seats
  F.   Stability and Change

III. How Congress Is Organized to Make Policy (pp. 365-376)
  A.   American Bicameralism
    1.   A **bicameral legislature** is a legislature divided into two houses.
    2.   The House
      a.   The House is more institutionalized and less anarchic than the Senate.
      b.   The **House Rules Committee** reviews most bills coming from a House committee before they go to the full House.
    3.   The Senate
      a.   The Senate is less disciplined and centralized than the House.
      b.   **Filibusters** allow unlimited debate in the Senate until a vote for cloture halts a filibuster.

B. Congressional Leadership
   1. The House
      a. The **Speaker of the House** is the most important leadership position in the House.
      b. The **majority leader** is responsible for scheduling bills and rounding up votes on behalf of the party.
      c. The party **whips** carry the word to party troops and help round up votes on behalf of the party.
      d. The **minority leader** is responsible for party cohesion among the minority party members.
   2. The Senate
      a. The vice president of the United States is the president of the Senate.
      b. Power is widely dispersed in the Senate.
   3. Congressional Leadership in Perspective
C. The Committees and Subcommittees
   1. Types of committees
      a. **Standing committees** are formed to handle bills in different policy areas.
      b. **Joint committees** exist in a few policy areas and are composed of both House and Senate members.
      c. **Conference committees** are formed when the Senate and House pass a particular bill in different forms.
      d. **Select committees** are appointed for a specific purpose.
   2. The Committees at Work: Legislation and Oversight
      a. All bills go though a committee that has considerable power over the fate of the bill.
      b. **Legislative oversight** is the process of monitoring the bureaucracy and its administration of policy.
   3. Getting on a Committee
   4. Getting Ahead on the Committee: Chairs and the Seniority System
      a. **Committee chairs** are the most important influencers of the committee agenda.
      b. The **seniority system** is the general rule for selecting chairs, but there are exceptions.
D. Caucuses: The Informal Organization of Congress
   1. A **caucus** is a grouping of members of Congress who share some interest or characteristic.
   2. The explosion of caucuses has made the representation of interests in Congress a more direct process.

E. Congressional Staff
    1. Personal Staff
    2. Committee Staff
    3. Staff Agencies (Congressional Research Service, General Accounting Office, and Congressional Budget Office)

IV. The Congressional Process (pp. 376-383)
  A. Introduction
    1. A **bill** is a proposed law, drafted in precise, legal language.
    2. Congress has many rules and procedures for passing bills.
  B. Presidents and Congress: Partners and Protagonists
    1. The president is often called the chief legislator.
    2. Presidential leadership in Congress is at the margins as a facilitator.
  C. Party, Constituency, and Ideology
    1. Party Influence
    2. Constituency versus Ideology
  D. Lobbyists and Interest Groups

V. Understanding Congress (pp. 383-386)
  A. Congress and Democracy
    1. Representativeness versus Effectiveness
  B. Congress and the Scope of Government

VI. Summary (pp. 386-387)

LEARNING OBJECTIVES

After studying Chapter 12, you should be able to:

1. Describe the characteristics of our senators and representatives, and the nature of their jobs.

2. Explain what factors have the greatest influence in congressional elections.

3. Explain the structure of power and leadership in the United States Congress, and the role of committees.

4. Identify what members of Congress do and discuss the congressional process and the many influences on legislative decision making.

5. Evaluate Congress in terms of American democracy and the scope of government.

The following exercises will help you meet these objectives:

Objective 1: Describe the characteristics of our senators and representatives, and the nature of their jobs.

1.   List seven perks members of Congress receive.

      1.

      2.

      3.

      4.

      5.

      6.

      7.

2.   Describe a "typical" member of Congress in terms of the following categories.

Sex:

Race:

Age:

Religion:

Prior Occupation:

Wealth:

3.   What is the difference between descriptive and substantive representation?

Descriptive:

Substantive:

Objective 2: Explain what factors have the greatest influence in congressional elections.

1. List and explain five advantages incumbents have over their opponents in congressional elections.

   1.

   2.

   3.

   4.

   5.

2. What is the difference between casework and pork barrel?

   Casework:

   Pork barrel:

3. What are the main criticisms of Political Action Committees?

4. List and explain three ways that an incumbent might be defeated.

   1.

   2.

   3.

5.   List three criticisms of term limitations.

        1.

        2.

        3.

Objective 3: Explain the structure of power and leadership in the United States Congress, and the role of committees.

    1.   What are the main functions of the House Rules Committee?

    2.   List four formal powers of the Speaker of the House.

        1.

        2.

        3.

        4.

    3.   List the four types of congressional committees.

        1.

        2.

        3.

        4.

4.   What is meant by legislative oversight?

5.   How does the seniority system work?

6.   What is the difference between the personal staff and the committee staff?

7.   List three congressional staff agencies.

      1.

      2.

      3.

Objective 4: Identify what members of Congress do and discuss the congressional process and the many influences on legislative decision making.

1.   Draw a diagram of how a bill becomes a law.

2.   List the ten times a president must usually win in order to hope for final passage of his or her proposed legislation.

      1.

      2.

      3.

4.

5.

6.

7.

8.

9.

10.

3.   What is the difference between trustees, instructed delegates, and politicos?

Trustees:

Instructed Delegates:

Politicos:

4.   List three ways Congress can frustrate the activities of lobbyists.

1.

2.

3.

Objective 5: Evaluate Congress in terms of American democracy and the scope of government.

1.   Present the arguments of supporters and critics on the effectiveness of Congress.

Supporters:

Critics:

2. How does the organization of Congress contribute to the expanding scope of government?

KEY TERMS

Identify and describe:

incumbents

casework

pork barrel

bicameral legislature

House Rules Committee

filibuster

Speaker of the House

majority leader

whips

minority leader

standing committees

joint committees

conference committees

select committees

legislative oversight

committee chairs

seniority system

caucus

bill

Compare and contrast:

casework and pork barrel

majority leader, minority leader, and whips

standing committees and select committees

joint committees and conference committees

committee chairs and seniority system

Name that term:

1.   They usually win congressional elections.

    _____

2.   Two houses.

    _____

3.   Unlimited debate in the U.S. Senate.

    _____

4.   Reviews most of the bills coming from a House committee before they go to the full House.

    _____

5. He or she exercises substantial control over which bills get assigned to which committees in the House.

_____

6. This monitoring process is handled mainly through congressional hearings.

_____

7. A grouping of members of Congress sharing some interest.

_____

8. A proposed law, drafted in precise, legal language.

_____

USING YOUR UNDERSTANDING

1. Investigate one or more of the members of Congress from your state or congressional district. Find out about their membership on congressional committees and their leadership positions. Also find out whether or not one of your members might be considered a policy entrepreneur and why. See how well your representatives are doing in the media, and whether or not they have achieved a reputation for servicing their constituency and representing it adequately in Washington. Do your representatives tend to act as trustees, delegates, or politicos on particular issues? Profile your representatives or senators in terms of how well they seem to be performing their many duties.

2. Study the legislative history of a particular law in a particular policy area. Trace the law from its original sources to its enactment. Try to find out when and where the bill originated, where its support came from (the president, interest groups, etc.), how it was altered by congressional committees, who voted for it, and whether or not the president actually signed it into law. Assess how long the process took from beginning to end and how much the law changed during the process. How did the final product compare with the original intent? Evaluate the legislative process in terms of this particular law and your perspective on how the system works.

REVIEW QUESTIONS

Check ☑ the correct answer:

1. In recent years, congressional tasks have become more and more difficult.
   ☐ True
   ☐ False

2. The foremost attraction to a congressperson's job is
   ☐ a. power.
   ☐ b. money.
   ☐ c. easy work.
   ☐ d. leisure time.

3. Members of Congress use their virtually unlimited franking privileges to
   ☐ a. pay staff salaries.
   ☐ b. travel to their home state.
   ☐ c. communicate with constituents.
   ☐ d. get research services from the Library of Congress.

4. Who of the following would NOT be allowed to take a seat in the Senate?
   ☐ a. someone who was a citizen for ten years
   ☐ b. someone who had been a resident of their state for only one year
   ☐ c. a 28 year old
   ☐ d. none of the above

5. Which of the following statements concerning members of Congress is FALSE?
   ☐ a. The dominant occupation of members of Congress is law.
   ☐ b. There are no Hispanics in the Senate.
   ☐ c. Proportionately, women are well represented in Congress today.
   ☐ d. Most members of Congress share the beliefs and attitudes of a large proportion of their constituents.

6. Most members of Congress are better at substantive representation than descriptive representation.
   ☐ True
   ☐ False

7. The single most important advantage when running for Congress is being
   ☐ a. photogenic.
   ☐ b. an incumbent.
   ☐ c. better funded than the opponent.
   ☐ d. a challenger.

8.   Which of the following is NOT a reason for greater competition for senatorial seats in Congress?
- [ ] a.   Senators have less personal contact with their constituents.
- [ ] b.   Senators have more visibility and media coverage.
- [ ] c.   An entire state is usually less diverse than a single congressional district.
- [ ] d.   Senators tend to draw more visible challengers.

9.   Most congressional incumbents have a strong feeling of vulnerability.
- [ ] True
- [ ] False

10.   Incumbents do well in congressional elections because of
- [ ] a.   voter awareness of how members of Congress vote on important policy decisions.
- [ ] b.   presidential coattails.
- [ ] c.   favorable economic conditions.
- [ ] d.   advertising, credit-claiming, and position-taking.

11.   For members of Congress, the principal goal of advertising is
- [ ] a.   raising money.
- [ ] b.   convincing other members to support their positions.
- [ ] c.   visibility.
- [ ] d.   avoiding constituents.

12.   Issues play a greater role in House elections than in Senate elections.
- [ ] True
- [ ] False

13.   Which of the following is NOT an incumbency advantage?
- [ ] a.   credit-claiming
- [ ] b.   position-taking on issues important to the constituency
- [ ] c.   weak opponents
- [ ] d.   scandal or a charge of corruption

14.   Which of the following statements about Political Action Committees (PACs) is FALSE?
- [ ] a.   PACs contribute about a one-fourth of the funds raised by candidates for Congress.
- [ ] b.   PACs sometimes make contributions after the election.
- [ ] c.   Challengers receive more PAC money than incumbents.
- [ ] d.   PACs make contributions to candidates because they want access to policymakers.

15. PACs will often give money to the winning candidate even if they supported his or her opponent during the election.
☐ True
☐ False

16. Money in congressional campaigns is more important to
☐ a. incumbents.
☐ b. challengers.
☐ c. members of the House.
☐ d. members from safe seats.

17. When a state loses population, reapportionment is likely to favor the state's minority party.
☐ True
☐ False

18. Safe seats in Congress make it more difficult for citizens to "send a message to Washington."
☐ True
☐ False

19. A bicameral legislature is one that
☐ a. uses committees.
☐ b. has two houses.
☐ c. is elected.
☐ d. holds biannual sessions.

20. (bonus) The only state that does not have a bicameral legislature is
☐ a. California.
☐ b. Texas.
☐ c. Rhode Island.
☐ d. Nebraska.

21. The House of Representatives
☐ a. is more centralized than the Senate.
☐ b. is less hierarchical than the Senate.
☐ c. is more likely to have party-line voting.
☐ d. has fewer leaders than the Senate.

22. The House Rules Committee
☐ a. reviews most bills coming from a House committee.
☐ b. schedules bills on the calendar.
☐ c. allots time for debating bills.
☐ d. all of the above

23. Setting the legislative agenda in the Senate is the responsibility of
☐ a. the Rules Committee.
☐ b. the president of the Senate.
☐ c. party leaders.
☐ d. the minority leader.

24. Which of the following statements about filibusters is FALSE?
☐ a. They are used in both houses.
☐ b. They can tie up the legislative agenda.
☐ c. They are used to talk a bill to death.
☐ d. Rules adopted over the years make it easier to close off debate.

25. Which of the following is NOT one of the roles of the Speaker of the House?
☐ a. presiding over the House when it is in session
☐ b. making committee assignments and appointing leaders
☐ c. serving as vice president of the United States
☐ d. influencing the assignment of bills to committees

26. Which of the following is NOT among the roles of the House majority leader?
☐ a. being the Speaker's principal party ally
☐ b. scheduling bills in the House
☐ c. rounding up votes along with the party whips
☐ d. presiding over the House when it is in session

27. Vice presidents usually ignore their senatorial chores, leaving power in the Senate up to party leaders.
☐ True
☐ False

28. (bonus) Who referred to himself as the "Majority Pleader"?
☐ a. President Ronald Reagan
☐ b. Vice President Dan Quayle
☐ c. Senator Robert Dole
☐ d. House Speaker Tip O'Neil

29. Members from both the House and Senate belong to
☐ a. standing committees.
☐ b. joint committees.
☐ c. conference committees.
☐ d. both b. and c.

30. The Senate committee that looked into Watergate was a
☐ a. standing committee.
☐ b. joint committee.
☐ c. conference committee.
☐ d. select committee.

31. Which of the following statements about committees is FALSE?
☐ a. A committee's work is done when the marked-up bill is submitted to the full House or Senate.
☐ b. Committee members often serve as floor managers.
☐ c. Some standing committee members later become members of conference committees.
☐ d. Legislative oversight keeps committee members busy monitoring bureaucratic agencies.

32. The process of monitoring the bureaucracy and its administration of policy is called
☐ a. filibustering.
☐ b. oversight.
☐ c. caucus.
☐ d. legislating.

33. Oversight does not give Congress any real power to pressure agencies to comply with their wishes.
☐ True
☐ False

34. Incentives for increasing oversight activities include
☐ a. the increasing size and complexity of government.
☐ b. tight budgets.
☐ c. charges that the executive branch had become too powerful.
☐ d. all of the above

35. Members seek committees that will help them achieve all of the following goals EXCEPT
☐ a. re-election.
☐ b. influence in Congress.
☐ c. more PAC money.
☐ d. the opportunity to make policy in areas they think are important.

36. Committee chairs play a dominant role in
☐ a. scheduling hearings.
☐ b. hiring staff.
☐ c. appointing subcommittees.
☐ d. all of the above

37. The seniority system is
☐ a. based on party loyalty.
☐ b. based on competence.
☐ c. still the general rule for selecting committee chairs.
☐ d. both a. and b.

38. The caucus is
☐ a. the basis of the committee structure in Congress.
☐ b. an informal group of members of Congress.
☐ c. a formal group of members of Congress based strictly on party affiliation.
☐ d. an interest group outside of Congress.

39. Personal staff help members of Congress with
☐ a. constituent problems.
☐ b. drafting legislation.
☐ c. negotiating agreements.
☐ d. all of the above

40. Bills can be formally submitted for consideration by
☐ a. the president.
☐ b. members of Congress.
☐ c. interest groups.
☐ d. all of the above

41. Which of the following statements about presidents is FALSE?
☐ a. They lobby through their congressional liaison office.
☐ b. They have many resources to use in influencing Congress.
☐ c. They are designated as the chief legislator by the Constitution.
☐ d. They are both partners and antagonists with Congress.

42. George Edwards points out that presidential leadership of Congress is
☐ a. at the margins.
☐ b. insignificant.
☐ c. at an all-time high.
☐ d. totally dominant.

43. Differences between the parties are sharpest on questions of social welfare and economic policy.
☐ True
☐ False

44. Edmund Burke favored the concept of a legislator as
☐ a. instructed delegate.
☐ b. constituent.
☐ c. trustee.
☐ d. politico.

45. The greatest way for constituents to influence members of Congress is to
☐ a. answer public opinion polls.
☐ b. write to them.
☐ c. vote for candidates who match their positions.
☐ d. join a single-issue group.

46. Which of the following statements is FALSE?
☐ a. It is difficult even for well-intentioned legislators to know what people want.
☐ b. Legislators whose votes are out-of-step with the views of their constituents are rarely re-elected.
☐ c. On obscure issues, legislators can safely ignore constituency opinion.
☐ d. On a typical issue, the prime determinant of a congressional member's vote is personal ideology.

47. Which of the following statements about lobbying is FALSE?
☐ a. Lobbyists have a dismal image.
☐ b. Lobbyists can provide members of Congress with information and campaign contributions.
☐ c. Congress has not attempted to regulate lobbyists.
☐ d. Members of Congress can ignore lobbyists.

48. John Kingdon found that no single influence was important enough to determine a congressperson's votes.
☐ True
☐ False

49. Which of the following statements about Congress is FALSE?
☐ a. Some aspects of Congress are very unrepresentative.
☐ b. Citizens have a direct role in determining leadership in Congress.
☐ c. Congress does not callously disregard people's opinions.
☐ d. Legislators find it hard to know what constituents want.

50.   Critics have charged that Congress is responsive to too many interests so that policy is uncoordinated, fragmented, and decentralized.
☐ True
☐ False

51.   Constituency service may provide members of Congress the incentive to tolerate, and even expand, big government.
☐ True
☐ False

ESSAY QUESTIONS

1.   What is the congressperson's job like? What are the characteristics of members of Congress?

2.   What is the effect of incumbency in congressional elections? What other factors are associated with congressional electoral success?

3.   What is the role of money in congressional campaigns? Assess the influence of interest groups and Political Action Committees (PACs) on members of Congress.

4.   How do the House of Representatives and the Senate differ? How does the structure of leadership differ between the two?

5.   Describe the committee system in Congress. What are the different roles of committees in the legislative process?

6.   How does a bill become a law? What factors influence the legislative process and how does their influence differ?

7.   Is Congress representative in its membership and its policymaking role? Explain.

CHAPTER 13

THE PRESIDENCY

CHAPTER OUTLINE

I. The Presidents (pp. 392-397)
    A. Great Expectations
    B. Who They Are
    C. How They Got There
        1. Elections: The Normal Road to the White House
            a. The **Twenty-second Amendment** limits presidents to two terms.
            b. Only 13 presidents have served two or more terms.
        2. Succession and Impeachment
            a. **Impeachment** is the political equivalent of an indictment in criminal law.
            b. The House Judiciary Committee voted to recommend Richard Nixon's impeachment as a result of the **Watergate** scandal.
            c. The **Twenty-fifth Amendment** permits the vice president to become acting president if the president is disabled.

II. Presidential Powers (pp. 397-400)
    A. Constitutional Powers
    B. The Expansion of Power
    C. Perspectives on Presidential Power

III. Running the Government: The Chief Executive (pp. 400-407)
    A. The Vice President
    B. The **Cabinet** consists of the heads of the executive departments.
    C. The Executive Office
        1. The **National Security Council (NSC)** links the president's key foreign and military policy advisors.
        2. The **Council of Economic Advisors (CEA)** advises the president on economic policy.
        3. The **Office of Management and Budget (OMB)** prepares the president's budget.
    D. The White House Staff
    E. The First Lady

IV. Presidential Leadership of Congress: The Politics of Shared Powers (pp. 408-415)
    A. Chief Legislator
        1. The Constitution gives the president power to **veto** congressional

legislation.
2. A **pocket veto** occurs if Congress adjourns within ten days after submitting a bill and the president fails to sign it.
B. Party Leadership
1. The Bonds of Party
2. Slippage in Party Support
3. Leading the Party
a. **Presidential coattails** refer to voters casting their ballots for congressional candidates of the president's party because those candidates support the president.
b. The president's party typically loses seats in midterm elections.
C. Public Support
1. Public Approval
2. Mandates
D. Legislative Skills

V. The President and National Security Policy (pp. 415-421)
A. Chief Diplomat
1. The president alone extends diplomatic recognition to foreign governments.
2. The president has sole power to negotiate treaties.
3. Presidents can negotiate *executive agreements* with heads of foreign governments.
B. Commander in Chief
C. War Powers
1. The **War Powers Resolution** mandated the withdrawal of forces after 60 days unless Congress declared war or granted an extension.
2. The use of the War Powers Resolution may constitute a **legislative veto** violating the doctrine of separation of powers.
D. Crisis Manager
1. A **crisis** is a sudden, unpredictable, and potentially dangerous event.
2. Presidents can instantly monitor events almost anywhere and act quickly.
E. Working with Congress

VI. Power from the People: The Public Presidency (pp. 421-427)
A. Going Public
B. Presidential Approval
C. Policy Support
D. Mobilizing the Public

VII. The President and the Press (pp. 427-430)
A. Presidents and the press tend to be in conflict.
B. The president's *press secretary* serves as a conduit of information from the White House to the press.

C. The best known direct interaction between the president and the press is the presidential press conference.

D. Most of the news coverage of the White House focuses on the president's personal and official activities.

E. News coverage of the presidency often tends to emphasize the negative.

VIII. Understanding the American Presidency (pp. 430-431)
   A. The Presidency and Democracy
   B. The Presidency and the Scope of Government

IX. Summary (pp. 431-432)

LEARNING OBJECTIVES

After studying Chapter 13, you should be able to:

1. Describe the American presidents—who they are, how they got there, and what they do.

2. List the constitutional powers of the president and explain how these powers have expanded.

3. Explain how the office of the presidency is organized to make policy.

4. Discuss the relationship between the president and Congress and the ways in which the president is able to lead Congress.

5. Explain the role of the president in developing national security policy.

6. Discuss the importance of public opinion to the president and his ability to obtain the support of the public.

7. Examine the relationship between the president and the media.

8. Understand the place of the presidency in American democracy and the effect the presidency has had on the scope of government.

The following exercises will help you meet these objectives:

Objective 1: Describe the American presidents—who they are, how they got there, and what they do.

1.   What are the two contradictory expectations that Americans have about the presidency?

      1.

      2.

2.   Make a list of whom you believe are the ten "best" presidents in history and briefly explain why.

      1.

      2.

      3.

      4.

      5.

      6.

      7.

      8.

      9.

      10.

3.   Outline the procedure for removing a president from office.

Objective 2: List the constitutional powers of the president and explain how these powers have expanded.

    1.   Look at Table 13.3 on page 399 and choose one constitutional power of the president from each category that you believe is the most important.

         1.

         2.

         3.

         4.

    2.   Describe two ways in which the power of the president has expanded from its constitutional base.

         1.

         2.

Objective 3: Explain how the office of the presidency is organized to make policy.

    1.   What is the cabinet and what does it do?

    2.   List and explain the function of three major policymaking bodies of the Executive Office.

         1.

2.

3.

3.   What is the difference between a hierarchical organization and a wheel-and-spokes system of White House management?

     Hierarchical:

     Wheel-and-Spokes:

4.   Make a list of four First Ladies and how they have influenced the presidency.

     1.

     2.

     3.

     4.

Objective 4: Discuss the relationship between the president and Congress and the ways in which the president is able to lead Congress.

     1.   List the three options the president has once Congress passes a bill.

          1.

          2.

          3.

2.   What is the difference between a veto, a pocket veto, and a line-item veto?

Veto:

Pocket Veto:

Line-Item Veto:

3.   Explain what is meant by the term "presidential coattails."

4.   What are the two indicators of public support for the president?

1.

2.

5.   What is meant by the president's "honeymoon" period?

Objective 5: Explain the role of the president in developing national security policy.

1.   What is an executive agreement and how does it differ from a treaty?

2.   What are the main provisions of the War Powers Resolution?

3.   Why is the president more equipped to handle a crisis than Congress?

4.   What are the "two presidencies"?

1.

2.

Objective 6: Discuss the importance of public opinion to the president and his or her ability to obtain the support of the public.

1.   What is the difference between the president as head of state and head of government?

Head of State:

Head of Government:

2.   Rank the past ten presidents in terms of their ability to garner public support.

1.

2.

3.

4.

5.

6.

7.

8.

9.

10.

Objective 7: Examine the relationship between the president and the media.

    1.   What is the role of the president's press secretary?

    2.   In what way(s) are the press biased in their coverage of the president?

Objective 8: Understand the place of the presidency in American democracy and the effect the presidency has had on the scope of government.

    1.   In what way(s) is the institution of the presidency undemocratic?

    2.   How does the presidency increase and decrease the scope of government?

KEY TERMS

Identify and describe:

Twenty-second Amendment

impeachment

Watergate

Twenty-fifth Amendment

cabinet

National Security Council (NSC)

Council of Economic Advisors (CEA)

Office of Management and Budget (OMB)

veto

pocket veto

presidential coattails

War Powers Resolution

legislative veto

crisis

Compare and contrast:

impeachment and Watergate

Twenty-second Amendment and Twenty-fifth Amendment

National Security Council, Council of Economic Advisors, and Office of Management and Budget

veto, pocket veto, and legislative veto

War Powers Resolution and legislative veto

Name that term:

1. It limits the president to two terms of office.

   _____

2. Because of this scandal, the House Judiciary Committee voted to recommend the impeachment of President Nixon.

   _____

3. Although not in the Constitution, every president has had one.

   _____

4. It links the president's key foreign and military advisors.

   _____

5.   A two-thirds vote in each house of Congress can override it.

_____

6.   Few congressional races are actually determined by this factor today.

_____

7.   A sudden, unpredictable, and potentially dangerous event.

_____

USING YOUR UNDERSTANDING

1.   Compare and contrast the Clinton presidency with the Bush presidency in terms of the principal roles the president plays. Identify particular policies in which the president is involved as head of state, commander in chief, chief legislator, and so on. You may want to collect newspaper or news magazine items that illustrate contemporary policy problems that both presidents faced. Pay special attention to presidential roles with respect to specific policy areas and national security.

2.   All presidents seem to want to hold a prominent place in history. People are sometimes asked to identify the "top presidents" in our nation's history. Make a list of those presidents that you believe played prominent roles, for better or worse. You may even wish to rank them. Justify your choices by making a statement or two about each president's success or notoriety in one of the presidential roles, in policymaking achievements in domestic or foreign policy, in relations with Congress, and/or in terms of his image of power. Compare your choices with those of your colleagues. On the basis of your assessment, briefly describe what you believe to be the factors that help ensure that a president will have a prominent place in history.

REVIEW QUESTIONS

Check ☑ the correct answer:

1.   Powerful, strong, leader of the free world, and commander in chief describe
☐ a.   the intentions of the Founders for the chief executive.
☐ b.   common popular images of the American president.
☐ c.   how the presidency has evolved in the twentieth century.
☐ d.   the constitutional powers of the president.

2. Richard Neustadt has emphasized that presidential power is the power to
    ☐ a.   command.
    ☐ b.   lead.
    ☐ c.   control.
    ☐ d.   persuade.

3. Which of the following statements about the presidents is FALSE?
    ☐ a.   All have been white males.
    ☐ b.   All have been Protestant.
    ☐ c.   They must be natural-born citizens and at least 35 years old.
    ☐ d.   There has been much variety in their backgrounds.

4. Americans expect
    ☐ a.   very little out of their presidents.
    ☐ b.   presidents will be corrupt.
    ☐ c.   presidents to ensure peace, prosperity, and security.
    ☐ d.   Congress to be more powerful than the president.

5. The Twenty-second Amendment
    ☐ a.   limits presidents to two terms.
    ☐ b.   sets out procedures for presidential impeachment.
    ☐ c.   provides for succession to the presidency.
    ☐ d.   none of the above

6. (bonus) The most "accidental" president was
    ☐ a.   Calvin Coolidge.
    ☐ b.   Harry Truman.
    ☐ c.   Lyndon Johnson.
    ☐ d.   Gerald Ford.

7. Impeachment of a president requires a
    ☐ a.   two-thirds vote in the Senate.
    ☐ b.   majority vote in the House of Representatives.
    ☐ c.   Supreme Court ruling.
    ☐ d.   popular election.

8. In 1974, the House of Representatives, as a result of the Watergate scandal,
    impeached President Nixon.
    ☐ True
    ☐ False

9. According to the Twenty-fifth Amendment, the vice president can become acting president if both he or she and the president's cabinet determine that the president is disabled.
☐ True
☐ False

10. After the vice president, the next person in the order of presidential succession is the
☐ a. Speaker of the House.
☐ b. president pro tempore of the Senate.
☐ c. Secretary of State.
☐ d. majority leader of the Senate.

11. The contemporary presidency closely resembles the one designed by the framers in 1787.
☐ True
☐ False

12. The Founders preserved the balance of power without jeopardizing the independence of the separate branches by checking those powers that they believed to be most dangerous.
☐ True
☐ False

13. The expansion of presidential power can be attributed to
☐ a. the increased prominence of the United States in the world.
☐ b. technological advances.
☐ c. presidential initiatives.
☐ d. all of the above

14. Which of the following is NOT a constitutional power of the president?
☐ a. commander in chief of the armed forces
☐ b. declare war
☐ c. veto legislation
☐ d. grant reprieves and pardons

15. The presidential role that receives the LEAST amount of publicity is
☐ a. presiding over the administration of government.
☐ b. appealing to the public for support for policy initiatives.
☐ c. dealing with Congress.
☐ d. negotiating with foreign powers.

16. Today, new presidents have only a very few high-level positions available for appointment.
☐ True
☐ False

17. (bonus) Which vice president commented that the vice presidency was "not worth a warm bucket of spit"?
☐ a. Richard Nixon
☐ b. John Nance Garner
☐ c. Dan Quayle
☐ d. Spiro Agnew

18. The president's cabinet
☐ a. was provided for by the Constitution.
☐ b. serves as the president's board of directors.
☐ c. has increased over the years with newly established executive departments approved by Congress.
☐ d. can veto the president on matters of executive policy.

19. Members of the president's cabinet do not need congressional approval.
☐ True
☐ False

20. Which of the following is NOT one of the main policymaking bodies in the Executive Office of the President?
☐ a. the National Security Council
☐ b. the Council of Economic Advisors
☐ c. the Office of Management and Budget
☐ d. the Attorney General

21. The Council of Economic Advisors
☐ a. prepares the president's budget.
☐ b. advises the president on economic policy.
☐ c. reviews legislative proposals from the cabinet.
☐ d. all of the above

22. The president's clearinghouse for agency ideas is the
☐ a. cabinet.
☐ b. Office of Management and Budget.
☐ c. vice president.
☐ d. press secretary.

23. The organization of most White House staffs has been
    ☐ a. hierarchical.
    ☐ b. pluralistic.
    ☐ c. representative.
    ☐ d. disorganized.

24. In the wheel-and-spokes system of White House management,
    ☐ a. aides have very little power.
    ☐ b. aides are organized hierarchically.
    ☐ c. aides have equal status and are balanced against one another.
    ☐ d. power and responsibility are widely delegated.

25. President Reagan dispersed and delegated power widely among his advisors.
    ☐ True
    ☐ False

26. The president usually operates independently of Congress.
    ☐ True
    ☐ False

27. Which of the following is NOT mentioned in the Constitution?
    ☐ a. the requirement that the president give a State of the Union address to Congress
    ☐ b. the designation of the president as chief legislator
    ☐ c. the requirement that the president bring important matters to Congress's attention from time to time
    ☐ d. the power of the president to veto congressional legislation

28. A pocket veto
    ☐ a. allows a president to kill a bill without either signing or vetoing it.
    ☐ b. is a law sent back to Congress with the president's reasons for rejecting it.
    ☐ c. is a bill that automatically becomes law.
    ☐ d. can be overridden by a two-thirds vote in each house of Congress.

29. Which of the following statements about the president's party leadership in Congress is FALSE?
    ☐ a. Presidents can rely on their fellow party members to always vote on their programs.
    ☐ b. Party leadership in Congress provides the nucleus of coalitions supporting presidential proposals.
    ☐ c. Party leadership in Congress is a principal task of every president.
    ☐ d. Presidents are highly dependent on their party to move their programs.

30. When the president's party is in the majority in Congress, all he has to do is make sure his party members show up to vote.
☐ True
☐ False

31. When constituency opinion and the president's proposals conflict, members of Congress are more likely to vote with their constituents.
☐ True
☐ False

32. The influence of presidential coattails
☐ a. is highest in midterm elections.
☐ b. has diminished in significance.
☐ c. is especially important in Senate races.
☐ d. creates dramatic swings in the composition of Congress.

33. Since 1953, most Republican presidents have lacked a majority in one or both houses of Congress during most of their terms.
☐ True
☐ False

34. Public approval of the president
☐ a. strengthens opposition to the president's policies.
☐ b. allows the president to control Congress.
☐ c. gives the president leverage at the margins of coalition building.
☐ d. does not affect opportunities for policy change.

35. Public approval gives the president leverage, not control.
☐ True
☐ False

36. Which of the following is NOT true of electoral mandates?
☐ a. They are powerful symbols in American politics.
☐ b. They give legitimacy and credibility to new presidents.
☐ c. They change the premises of decisions.
☐ d. They are guaranteed by large electoral majorities.

37. Which of the following is NOT among the legislative strategies of the president?
☐ a. making personal appeals
☐ b. avoiding bargains to build majorities
☐ c. exploiting the honeymoon period
☐ d. establishing priorities among legislative proposals

38. The president does not have to bargain with every member of Congress to receive support.
☐ True
☐ False

39. Which of the following statements is TRUE?
☐ a. After accounting for party and public support, presidents differ greatly in terms of legislative success.
☐ b. The president's legislative skills are at the core of presidential leadership of Congress.
☐ c. Successful presidents exploit favorable configurations of political forces.
☐ d. Most presidents have been able to change the political landscape and create opportunities for change.

40. The president must receive Senate approval prior to extending diplomatic recognition to foreign governments.
☐ True
☐ False

41. When the Constitution was written,
☐ a. the president was not considered commander in chief.
☐ b. no one expected the United States to have a permanent army.
☐ c. the United States was involved in several military alliances.
☐ d. the United States had a large standing army.

42. The power to declare war belongs to
☐ a. the president.
☐ b. Congress.
☐ c. the Secretary of Defense.
☐ d. the National Security Council.

43. The War Powers Resolution
☐ a. strengthens presidential power during times of war.
☐ b. limits congressional power during time of war.
☐ c. is part of the Constitution.
☐ d. provides for a legislative veto to end American involvement in overseas hostilities.

44. Since its passage in 1973, most presidents have regarded the War Powers Resolution as an unconstitutional infringement on presidential power.
☐ True
☐ False

45. Because of its access to information, Congress has become most prominent in handling crises.
☐ True
☐ False

46. When it comes to national security,
☐ a. Congress has no constitutional role.
☐ b. presidential leadership in policymaking is central.
☐ c. members of Congress usually initiate policies.
☐ d. presidents always get their way.

47. In matters of national security, the role of Congress has typically been oversight of the executive rather than initiation of policy.
☐ True
☐ False

48. Perhaps the greatest source of influence a president has is
☐ a. public support.
☐ b. party leadership.
☐ c. ability to parcel out favors.
☐ d. constitutional powers.

49. Which of the following statements is FALSE?
☐ a. Presidents sometimes rely on persuasion.
☐ b. Presidents are passive followers of public opinion.
☐ c. The White House is a virtual whirlwind of public relations activity.
☐ d. Most presidents make frequent public appearances.

50. Ceremonial responsibilities are not considered important by presidents and are usually given to the vice president.
☐ True
☐ False

51. Which of the following is NOT a key explanation of the public's support for a president?
☐ a. a predisposition
☐ b. party affiliation
☐ c. the honeymoon period
☐ d. first-hand experiences

52. Rally events have an enduring impact on presidential approval scores.
☐ True
☐ False

53. All presidents since Truman have had media advice from experts on lighting, makeup, stage settings, camera angles, clothing, pacing of delivery, and other facets of making speeches.
☐ True
☐ False

54. Which of the following presidents was NOT considered an effective speaker?
☐ a.   Franklin D. Roosevelt
☐ b.   John Kennedy
☐ c.   Richard Nixon
☐ d.   Ronald Reagan

55. Which of the following statements is FALSE?
☐ a.   Modern presidents monitor the media closely.
☐ b.   As long as their goals differ, the president and the media are likely adversaries.
☐ c.   Most of what people know about the president comes through the mass media.
☐ d.   White House staff members generally ignore the media.

56. The person who most often deals directly with the press is the president's press secretary.
☐ True
☐ False

57. The term "body watch" refers to the media's
☐ a.   preoccupation with the president's physical health.
☐ b.   analysis of the body of issues on the executive agenda.
☐ c.   step-by-step account of the president's personal and official activities.
☐ d.   presence at presidential press conferences.

58. Studies have shown that the media are systematically biased against the president.
☐ True
☐ False

59. Major policy change is virtually impossible under a divided government.
☐ True
☐ False

60. Most recently, the institution that has championed constraints on government and limits on spending has been
   ☐ a. Congress.
   ☐ b. the presidency.
   ☐ c. interest groups.
   ☐ d. the bureaucracy.

ESSAY QUESTIONS

1. What are the characteristics of American presidents? How do presidents and vice presidents get into office?

2. What are the formal constitutional powers of the presidency and how have these powers expanded over the years?

3. How is the presidency organized? On whom does the president depend for advice about governmental and policy matters?

4. Explain the factors that affect presidential leadership of Congress. Why are some presidents more effective leaders than others?

5. What roles does the president play as leader of national security policy? How do these roles conflict with the role of Congress in the area of national security?

6. What factors affect presidential popularity and approval? How is popularity related to power and to policymaking?

7. Why is the press so important to the president? Give examples of the relationship between the press and the presidency.

8. How does the contemporary presidency differ from that envisioned by the Founders? Take a position on whether or not the president has become too powerful, and how this might affect democracy and the scope of government.

CHAPTER 14

THE CONGRESS, THE PRESIDENT, AND THE BUDGET:
THE POLITICS OF TAXING AND SPENDING

CHAPTER OUTLINE

I.   Introduction (pp. 434-436)
    A.   Central to public policy are the questions of who bears the burdens of paying for government and who receives the benefits.
    B.   A **budget** is a policy document allocating burdens (taxes) and benefits (expenditures).
    C.   A budget **deficit** occurs when **expenditures** exceed **revenues** in a fiscal year.

II.   Sources of Federal Revenue (pp. 436-445)
    A.   Income Tax
        1.   Individuals are required to pay the government a portion of the money they earn, called an **income tax.**
        2.   The **Sixteenth Amendment** permitted Congress to levy an income tax.
    B.   Social Insurance Taxes
    C.   Borrowing
        1.   The **federal debt** is all of the money borrowed over the years that is still outstanding.
        2.   Government borrowing may crowd out private borrowers from the loan marketplace.
        3.   The federal government does not have a capital budget.
    D.   Taxes and Public Policy
        1.   Tax loopholes consist of a tax break or tax benefit.
        2.   **Tax expenditures** are revenue losses attributable to provisions of the federal tax laws.
        3.   Tax reduction has frequently been called for.
        4.   Tax reform has simplified taxes and made them more equitable.

III. Federal Expenditures (pp. 445-452)
    A.   Big Governments, Big Budgets
    B.   The Rise and Decline of the National Security State
    C.   The Rise of the Social Service State
        1.   The **Social Security Act** intended to provide a minimal level of sustenance to older Americans.
        2.   **Medicare** provides both hospital and physician coverage to the elderly.

D. Incrementalism
   1. **Incrementalism** means that the best predictor of this year's budget is last year's budget plus a little bit more.
   2. The budgetary process is affected by groups with interests in taxes and expenditures.
E. "Uncontrollable" Expenditures
   1. **Uncontrollable expenditures** result from policies that make some group automatically eligible for some benefit.
   2. **Entitlements** are policies in which Congress has obligated itself to pay X level of benefits to Y number of recipients each year.

IV. The Budgetary Process (pp. 452-459)
   A. Budgetary Politics
      1. Stakes and Strategies
      2. The Players
         a. The interest groups
         b. The agencies
         c. The Office of Management and Budget (OMB)
         d. The president
         e. The Tax Committees in Congress
            (1) **House Ways and Means Committee**
            (2) **Senate Finance Committee**
         f. The Budget Committees and the Congressional Budget Office
         g. The subject-matter committees
         h. The Appropriations Committees and their subcommittees
         i. The Congress as a whole
         j. The Government Accountability Office (GAO)
   B. The President's Budget
   C. Congress and the Budget
      1. Reforming the Process
         a. The **Congressional Budget and Impoundment Act of 1974**
            (1) A fixed budget calendar.
            (2) A budget committee in each house.
            (3) The **Congressional Budget Office (CBO)**.
         b. A **budget resolution** is supposed to set limits on expenditures based on revenue projections.
         c. Budget **reconciliation** revises program authorizations to achieve required savings.
         d. An **authorization bill** is an act of Congress that establishes a discretionary government program or an entitlement.
         e. An **appropriations bill** must be passed to actually fund programs established by authorization bills.

2. The Success of the 1974 Reforms
   a. **Continuing resolutions** are laws that allow agencies to spend at the previous year's level.
   b. The 1974 reforms have helped Congress view the entire budget early in the process.
3. More Reforms
   a. The Gramm-Rudman-Hollings Act mandated maximum allowable deficit levels for each year until the budget was to be balanced in 1993.
   b. In 1990 Congress switched from a focus on controlling the size of the deficit to controlling increases in spending.
   c. Republican efforts to balance the budget.

V. Understanding Budgeting (pp. 460-463)
   A. Democracy and Budgeting
   B. The Budget and the Scope of Government

VI. Summary (p. 463)

LEARNING OBJECTIVES

After studying Chapter 14, you should be able to:

1. Describe the major sources of federal revenues.

2. Understand the nature of the tax system in America.

3. Explain the nature of federal expenditures and why so much of the budget is uncontrollable.

4. Discuss how the budgetary process works, who is involved, and the politics of budgetary reform.

5. Understand how budgeting affects democracy and the scope of government in America.

The following exercises will help you meet these objectives:

Objective 1: Describe the major sources of federal revenues.

1. List four sources of federal revenues.

   1.

254

2.

3.

4.

2.   How does the federal government borrow money?

3.   What is meant by a capital budget?

Objective 2: Understand the nature of the tax system in America.

1.   Define tax expenditures and give three examples.

Definition:

Examples:
      1.

      2.

      3.

2.   What were the three major reforms of the Tax Reform Act of 1986?

1.

2.

3.

Objective 3: Explain the nature of federal expenditures and why so much of the budget is uncontrollable.

1.   Name the two conditions associated with government growth in America.

      1.

      2.

2.   What is meant by the phrase "military industrial complex"?

3.   Explain how Social Security is a kind of intergenerational contract.

4.   List four features of incremental budgeting.

      1.

      2.

      3.

      4.

5.   Explain how entitlements are "uncontrollable expenditures."

Objective 4: Discuss how the budgetary process works, who is involved, and the politics of budgetary reform.

1.   How might each of the following political actors have a stake in the federal budget?

Mayors:

Defense contractors:

Scientists:

Bureaucratic agencies:

Members of Congress:

Presidents:

Farmers:

2.   List the ten main actors in the budgetary process.

1.

2.

3.

4.

5.

6.

7.

8.

9.

10.

3.   Explain the three main provisions of the Congressional Budget and Impoundment Control Act of 1974.

     1.

     2.

     3.

4.   What is meant by a budget resolution?

5.   Explain the two ways in which laws are changed to meet the budget resolution.

     1.

     2.

6.   What was the Gramm-Rudman-Hollings Act and why did it fail?

Objective 5: Understand how budgeting affects democracy and the scope of government in America.

     1.   List three possible explanations as to why democracies have seen a substantial growth in government in the twentieth century.

          1.

          2.

          3.

2. How could the budgetary process limit government?

KEY TERMS

Identify and describe:

budget

deficit

expenditures

revenues

income tax

Sixteenth Amendment

federal debt

tax expenditures

Social Security Act

Medicare

incrementalism

uncontrollable expenditures

entitlements

House Ways and Means Committee

Senate Finance Committee

Congressional Budget and Impoundment Control Act of 1974

Congressional Budget Office (CBO)

budget resolution

reconciliation

authorization bill

appropriations bill

continuing resolutions

Compare and contrast:

budget and deficit

expenditures and revenues

income tax and Sixteenth Amendment

income tax and tax expenditures

Social Security Act and Medicare

uncontrollable expenditures and entitlements

House Ways and Means Committee and Senate Finance Committee

reconciliation and authorization bill

Name that term:

1. A policy document allocating burdens and benefits.

    _____

2. All of the money borrowed over the years and still outstanding.

    _____

3. This was intended to provide a minimal level of sustenance to older Americans.

    _____

4. Revenue losses attributable to provisions of the federal tax laws that allow a special exemption, exclusion, or deduction.

    _____

5. The best predictor of this year's budget is last year's budget, plus a little bit more.

    _____

6. These result from policies that make some group automatically eligible for some benefit.

    _____

7. This agency advises Congress on the probable consequences of its budget decisions.

    _____

8. This occurs in Congress every April.

    _____

9. An act of Congress that actually funds programs within limits established by authorization bills.

    _____

10. These allow agencies to spend at the previous year's level.

    _____

USING YOUR UNDERSTANDING

1. Take a look at a recent edition of the *United States Budget in Brief.* Identify expenditure categories that relate to specific policy arenas, such as equality, the economy, social welfare, technology, and national security. Create your own policy arenas using broad or specific categories. Briefly describe what you found in terms of the policy priorities represented by the budget. Evaluate the budget according to where you believe your tax dollars should be spent.

2. This chapter has emphasized the budget of the United States government. Locate a budget document for your state or community. These should be available in the Government Documents section of your school library, through state and local government offices, or on the Internet. Assess the sources of revenues on which this unit of government depends and the types of expenditures it makes in various policy areas. Take note of whether or not the budget represents a deficit (expenditures exceeding revenues) or a surplus (revenues exceeding expenditures), and the magnitude of the amount. Compare the major features of this budget to those of the budget of the United States. Investigate the politics of the budgetary process at the state or local level and compare what you find to the national level. Alternatively you could examine a budget of another Western democracy and compare it to that of the United States using these same guidelines.

REVIEW QUESTIONS

Check ☑ the correct answer:

1. The budget deficit or surplus is equal to
   - ☐ a. expenditures divided by revenues.
   - ☐ b. revenues plus expenditures.
   - ☐ c. revenues divided by expenditures.
   - ☐ d. expenditures times revenues.

2. (bonus) Who said, "Taxes are what we pay for civilization"?
   - ☐ a. Aaron Wildavsky
   - ☐ b. Oliver Wendell Holmes, Jr.
   - ☐ c. Jean-Baptiste Colbert
   - ☐ d. Bill Clinton

3. Congress was given permission to levy an income tax by the
   - ☐ a. Supreme Court case of *Pollock* v. *Farmer's Loan and Trust Co.*
   - ☐ b. Sixteenth Amendment.
   - ☐ c. Thirteenth Amendment.
   - ☐ d. Internal Revenue Service.

4. The largest percentage of the government's income comes from
   - ☐ a. excise taxes.
   - ☐ b. income taxes.
   - ☐ c. social insurance taxes.
   - ☐ d. borrowing.

5. Corporate taxes yield more revenues than individual income taxes do.
   - ☐ True
   - ☐ False

6. Social Security taxes
   - ☐ a. come from both employers and employees.
   - ☐ b. do not go into the government's general fund.
   - ☐ c. are earmarked for a specific purpose.
   - ☐ d. all of the above

7. The federal debt
   - ☐ a. is the amount by which expenditures exceed revenues in a given year.
   - ☐ b. has the impact of crowding out private borrowing.
   - ☐ c. finances mainly capital projects.
   - ☐ d. was never greater than under Ronald Reagan.

8. The federal government's budget acts like a capital budget.
   - ☐ True
   - ☐ False

9. A tax loophole is also a
   - ☐ a. tax benefit.
   - ☐ b. tax expenditure.
   - ☐ c. tax break.
   - ☐ d. all of the above

10. Tax loopholes are forbidden by the IRS Code.
    - ☐ True
    - ☐ False

11. Which of the following is an example of a tax expenditure?
    ☐ a.   direct government support of a charity
    ☐ b.   a tax reform
    ☐ c.   mortgage interest deduction
    ☐ d.   the Social Security system

12. Tax expenditures are most beneficial to poorer people.
    ☐ True
    ☐ False

13. Ronald Reagan's 1981 tax reforms
    ☐ a.   reduced individual and corporate taxes.
    ☐ b.   provided tax incentives for personal savings and corporate investment.
    ☐ c.   indexed taxes to the cost of living.
    ☐ d.   all of the above

14. Ronald Reagan's 1981 tax reforms
    ☐ a.   increased social service expenditures.
    ☐ b.   did not help people at the lower end of the income ladder.
    ☐ c.   resulted in a balanced budget.
    ☐ d.   raised taxes for the rich.

15. The Tax Reform Act of 1986
    ☐ a.   eliminated or reduced the value of many tax deductions.
    ☐ b.   increased the number of possible tax expenditures.
    ☐ c.   greatly reduced the number of tax brackets.
    ☐ d.   both a. and c.

16. The policies and programs the government spends money on change over time.
    ☐ True
    ☐ False

17. (bonus) Which of the following countries has the highest tax revenues as percentage of GDP?
    ☐ a.   United Kingdom
    ☐ b.   Sweden
    ☐ c.   United States
    ☐ d.   Germany

18. Total military expenditures have declined as a percentage of our GNP since the end of World War II.
    ☐ True
    ☐ False

19. The Reagan budgets brought defense back as the biggest slice of the budget pie.
☐ True
☐ False

20. Which of the following statements is TRUE?
☐ a.   From the mid-1960s to the early 1980s, military expenditures more than doubled.
☐ b.   Ronald Reagan substantially increased the defense budget during his second term.
☐ c.   Procurement is used to draft military personnel.
☐ d.   The cost of military weapons is more expensive than their predecessors.

21. Social Security checks go only to retired persons.
☐ True
☐ False

22. Which of the following statements is TRUE?
☐ a.   Medicare is mainly for poor persons.
☐ b.   Social Security was originally designed as a disability program.
☐ c.   As the 1980s began, the Social Security program was going broke.
☐ d.   Conservatives favor expansion of Social Security.

23. The Social Security system combines all social policies of the federal government.
☐ True
☐ False

24. Which of the following is NOT among the features of incremental budgeting?
☐ a.   little attention to the budget base
☐ b.   rapid growth in the federal budget
☐ c.   heated debate over the proposed increment
☐ d.   growth in agency budgets by only a little bit every year

25. Incrementalism
☐ a.   fully describes American budgetary politics.
☐ b.   facilitates budgetary reform.
☐ c.   does not describe the budget process for every agency.
☐ d.   makes it easy to pare the budget.

26. Uncontrollable expenditures result from
☐ a.   failure to focus attention on the budgetary base.
☐ b.   the increased costs of military procurement.
☐ c.   incremental budgeting.
☐ d.   policies that make some group automatically eligible for some benefit.

27. About two-thirds of the federal budget is uncontrollable.
☐ True
☐ False

28. Policies that obligate Congress to pay X level of benefits to Y number of recipients are called
☐ a. entitlements.
☐ b. increments.
☐ c. allowances.
☐ d. tax expenditures.

29. The biggest uncontrollable item in the federal budget is
☐ a. Social Security.
☐ b. welfare.
☐ c. grants-in-aid.
☐ d. defense.

30. The process of creating the national budget is confined to a few politicians in Washington, D.C.
☐ True
☐ False

31. Lobbying for a group's needs takes place
☐ a. in the agencies.
☐ b. with the president.
☐ c. before congressional committees.
☐ d. all of the above

32. Which of the following is NOT among the congressional players in the budgetary process?
☐ a. Office of Management and Budget
☐ b. tax committees
☐ c. subject-matter committees
☐ d. Congressional Budget Office

33. The body that audits, monitors, and evaluates what agencies do with their budgets is the
☐ a. House Ways and Means Committee.
☐ b. Congressional Budget Office.
☐ c. Government Accountability Office.
☐ d. Senate Finance Committee.

34. The Budget and Accounting Act of 1921
   ☐ a. created the Congressional Budget Office.
   ☐ b. mandated the reconciliation reduction.
   ☐ c. required the president to propose an executive budget to Congress.
   ☐ d. gave Congress impoundment power.

35. The Office of Management and Budget (OMB)
   ☐ a. receives budget requests from Congress.
   ☐ b. audits, monitors, and evaluates what agencies are doing with their budgets.
   ☐ c. supervises preparation of the budget and advises the president on budgetary matters.
   ☐ d. adjudicates disputes over the budget.

36. Preparation of the federal budget takes almost one year.
   ☐ True
   ☐ False

37. According to the Constitution, federal appropriations must be authorized by
   ☐ a. the Office of Management and Budget.
   ☐ b. the president.
   ☐ c. three-fifths of the states.
   ☐ d. Congress.

38. Which of the following was NOT established by the Congressional Budget and Impoundment Control Act of 1974?
   ☐ a. a fixed budget calendar
   ☐ b. the elimination of tax expenditures
   ☐ c. a committee on the budget in each house
   ☐ d. the Congressional Budget Office

39. The budget resolution requires that
   ☐ a. the president and Congress agree on the budget.
   ☐ b. Congress and the bureaucracy set limits on program spending.
   ☐ c. both houses of Congress initially agree on a total expenditure level.
   ☐ d. this year's budget roughly equals last year's budget.

40. The purpose of budget reconciliation is to
   ☐ a. critique and analyze the president's proposed budget.
   ☐ b. establish a discretionary government program or entitlement.
   ☐ c. adjudicate disputes over the budget.
   ☐ d. revise program authorizations to achieve required savings.

41. Which of the following does an authorization bill NOT provide for?
    - ☐ a. a discretionary program or an entitlement
    - ☐ b. program goals
    - ☐ c. program funds
    - ☐ d. eligibility requirements for entitlement programs

42. An appropriations bill actually funds programs, within limits established by authorizations, for the lifetime of the specific program.
    - ☐ True
    - ☐ False

43. When Congress is unable to reach agreement and pass appropriations bills, it may allow agencies to spend at the previous year's level by passing a
    - ☐ a. continuing resolution.
    - ☐ b. budget resolution.
    - ☐ c. budget reconciliation.
    - ☐ d. authorization bill.

44. The purpose of the Gramm-Rudman-Hollings Act was to
    - ☐ a. decrease the spiraling defense budget.
    - ☐ b. stabilize deficit spending at a manageable level.
    - ☐ c. introduce a constitutional amendment to balance the budget.
    - ☐ d. mandate maximum allowable deficit levels until the budget was balanced in 1993.

45. The Gramm-Rudman-Hollings Act resulted in significantly reducing the deficit.
    - ☐ True
    - ☐ False

46. The 1990 budget law
    - ☐ a. facilitated the ability of Congress to shift budget priorities across categories.
    - ☐ b. shifted the focus to controlling increases in spending.
    - ☐ c. increased the functions of the congressional budget committees.
    - ☐ d. reduced the power of the Office of Management and Budget.

47. One reason all democracies have experienced substantial growth in government is because policymakers spend public money on things voters will like.
    - ☐ True
    - ☐ False

48. Allen Meltzer and Scott Richard argue that government grows in a democracy because of
☐ a.   corrupt politicians.
☐ b.   the equality of suffrage.
☐ c.   the need for strong defense.
☐ d.   an apathetic public.

49. Which of the following statements is FALSE?
☐ a.   Many politicians willingly cooperate with the desire of working class voters to expand their benefits.
☐ b.   Corporate elites are especially opposed to big government.
☐ c.   Low-income and wealthy voters alike have voted for parties and politicians who promised them benefits.
☐ d.   Government grows by responding to groups and their demands.

50. Ronald Reagan won election to the presidency twice by promising to
☐ a.   raise taxes.
☐ b.   spend less money.
☐ c.   provide more services.
☐ d.   increase the scope of government.

51. Americans have chosen to tax less and spend less on public services than almost all other democracies with developed economies.
☐ True
☐ False

52. Since 1980, policymaking in the American government could be characterized as the politics of scarcity.
☐ True
☐ False

53. The budget
☐ a.   is the scope of government.
☐ b.   can be used to rein in the government.
☐ c.   can be used to expand the role of government.
☐ d.   all of the above

ESSAY QUESTIONS

1. Why is government so big? What are the political implications of big government, and who benefits from it?

2. What are the principal sources of revenue for the federal government? What public policy problems or issues do taxation and government borrowing raise?

3. What are the principal categories of government expenditures? What are the reasons for the increasing expenditures for Social Security?

4. What is incrementalism? How do uncontrollable expenditures contribute to incremental budget-making?

5. Who are the players in budgetary politics? What stake do they have in the budget process, and what roles do they play?

6. Compare the role of the president and the role of Congress in the budgetary process. Where does their authority in the process come from?

7. Explain how the budgetary process has been reformed. How successful have the reforms been? Why is it so difficult to reform the budgetary process?

8. How does the budgetary process affect democracy and the scope of government? How have budgetary reforms affected the scope of government and the democratic process?

CHAPTER 15

THE FEDERAL BUREAUCRACY

CHAPTER OUTLINE

I.   Introduction (pp. 466-468)
   A.   Bureaucracies are central to our lives.
   B.   Max Weber's conception of **bureaucracy**
      1.   Bureaucracies have a hierarchical authority structure.
      2.   Bureaucracies use task specialization.
      3.   Bureaucracies develop extensive rules.
      4.   Bureaucracies operate on the merit principle.
      5.   Bureaucracies behave with impersonality.

II.   The Bureaucrats (pp. 468-475)
   A.   Some Bureaucratic Myths and Realities
      1.   Americans dislike bureaucrats.
      2.   Bureaucracies are growing bigger each year.
      3.   Most federal bureaucrats work in Washington, DC.
      4.   Bureaucracies are ineffective, inefficient, and always mired in red tape.
   B.   Who They Are and How They Got There
      1.   Civil Service: From Patronage to Protection
         a.   **Patronage** is a hiring and promotion system based on knowing the right people.
         b.   The **Pendleton Civil Service Act** created the federal civil service.
         c.   All **civil service** systems are based on merit and the desire to create a nonpartisan government service.
         d.   The **merit principle** uses entrance exams and promotion ratings to reward qualified individuals.
         e.   The **Hatch Act** prohibits civil service employees from active participation in partisan politics while on duty.
         f.   The **Office of Personnel Management (OPM)** is in charge of hiring for most federal agencies.
         g.   Each civil service job is assigned a **GS (General Schedule) rating**.
         h.   The very top of the civil service system is the **Senior Executive Service.**
      2.   The Other Route to Federal Jobs: Recruiting from the Plum Book
         a.   The plum book lists top federal jobs available for direct presidential appointment.

b. The most important trait of presidential appointees is their transience.

III. How Bureaucracies Are Organized (pp. 475-480)
    A. The Cabinet Departments
    B. The Regulatory Agencies
        1. Each **independent regulatory agency** has responsibility for some sector of the economy.
        2. Interest groups are closely involved with independent regulatory agencies.
    C. The **government corporations** provide a service that could be provided by the private sector and charge for their service.
    D. The **independent executive agencies** are essentially all the rest of the government.

IV. Bureaucracies as Implementors (pp. 480-489)
    A. What Implementation Means
        1. **Policy implementation** is the stage of policymaking between the establishment of a policy and its consequences.
        2. Implementation is the continuation of policymaking by other means.
    B. Why the Best-Laid Plans Sometimes Flunk the Implementation Test
        1. Program Design
        2. Lack of Clarity
        3. Lack of Resources
        4. Administrative Routine
            a. **Standard operating procedures** (SOPs) help bureaucrats make everyday decisions.
            b. SOPs may become "red tape" and obstacles to action.
        5. Administrators' Dispositions
            a. **Administrative discretion** is the authority of administrative actors to select among various responses to a given problem.
            b. **Street-level bureaucrats** are those bureaucrats who are in constant contact with the public and have considerable discretion.
        6. Fragmentation
    C. A Case Study: The Voting Rights Act of 1965

V. Bureaucracies As Regulators (pp. 489-493)
    A. Regulation in the Economy and in Everyday Life
        1. Government **regulation** is the use of governmental authority to control or change some practice in the private sector.
        2. A Full Day of Regulation
    B. Regulation: How It Grew, How It Works
        1. In the **command-and-control policy**, the government tells business how to reach certain goals, checks that these commands are followed, and punishes offenders.
        2. An **incentive system** uses taxes and rewards to promote certain behavior.

C.   Toward **Deregulation**

VI.   Understanding Bureaucracies (pp. 493-499)
      A.   Bureaucracy and Democracy
            1.   Presidents Try to Control the Bureaucracy
                  a.   They appoint the right people to head the agency.
                  b.   They issue **executive orders**.
                  c.   They alter an agency's budget
                  d.   They reorganize an agency.
            2.   Congress Tries to Control the Bureaucracy
                  a.   They influence the appointment of agency heads.
                  b.   They alter an agency's budget.
                  c.   They hold hearings.
                  d.   They rewrite the legislation or make it more detailed.
            3.   Iron Triangles and Issue Networks
                  a.   When agencies, groups, and committees all depend on one another and are in close, frequent contact, they form what are sometimes called **iron triangles**, or subgovernments.
                  b.   The system of subgovernments is now overlaid with an amorphous system of *issue networks*.
      B.   Bureaucracy and the Scope of Government

VII.   Summary (p. 499)

LEARNING OBJECTIVES

After studying Chapter 15, you should be able to:

1.   Describe the bureaucrats—who they are, how they got there, and what they do.

2.   Discuss how the federal bureaucracy is organized.

3.   Explain how bureaucracies function as implementors of public policy.

4.   Explain how bureaucracies function as regulators.

5.   Evaluate the problem of controlling bureaucracies in a democratic government and how bureaucracies affect the scope of government.

The following exercises will help you meet these objectives:
Objective 1: Describe the bureaucrats—who they are, how they got there, and what they do.

1.   List five elements of the Weberian model of bureaucracy.

    1.

    2.

    3.

    4.

    5.

2.   List four prevalent myths about bureaucracy.

    1.

    2.

    3.

    4.

3.   What is the difference between patronage and the merit principle?

    Patronage:

    Merit Principle:

4.   What is the purpose of the Hatch Act?

5.   What are some of the common characteristics of plum book appointees?

Objective 2: Discuss how the federal bureaucracy is organized.

    1.   What are the four basic types of agencies in the federal executive branch?

           1.
           2.

           3.

           4.

    2.   Explain the relationship between interest groups and independent regulatory agencies.

    3.   In what two ways are government corporations like private corporations and different from other parts of the government?

           1.

           2.

4.   What are the three biggest independent executive agencies?

           1.

           2.

           3.

Objective 3: Explain how bureaucracies function as implementors of public policy.

    1.   What are the three minimum elements of implementation?

           1.

           2.

           3.

2.   List six reasons why policy implementation might fail.

   1.
   2.

   3.

   4.

   5.

   6.

3.   What are three advantages of using standard operating procedures?

   1.

   2.

   3.

4.   What is meant by administrative discretion? Give an example.

Objective 4: Explain how bureaucracies function as regulators.

   1.   What was the significance of *Munn* v. *Illinois* (1877)?

   2.   List three elements common to all regulation.

      1.

      2.

      3.

3.   What is the difference between command-and-control policy and incentive system?

       Command-and-Control:

       Incentive:

4.   List three criticisms of regulation.

       1.

       2.

       3.

Objective 5: Evaluate the problem of controlling bureaucracies in a democratic government and how bureaucracies affect the scope of government.

       1.   List four methods in which the president can control the bureaucracy.

              1.

              2.

              3.

              4.

       2.   List four methods in which Congress can control the bureaucracy.

              1.

              2.

              3.

4.

3.   Explain the difference between an iron triangle and an issue network.

       Iron Triangle:

       Issue Network:

4.   What effect does bureaucracy have on the scope of government?

KEY TERMS

Identify and describe:

bureaucracy

patronage

Pendleton Civil Service Act

civil service

merit principle

Hatch Act

Office of Personnel Management (OPM)

GS (General Schedule) rating

Senior Executive Service

independent regulatory agency

government corporations

independent executive agencies

policy implementation

standard operating procedures

administrative discretion

street-level bureaucrats

regulation

deregulation

command-and-control policy

incentive system

executive orders

iron triangles

Compare and contrast:

patronage and merit principle

Pendleton Civil Service Act and civil service

civil service and merit principle

GS (General Schedule) rating and Senior Executive Service

independent regulatory agencies, government corporations, and independent executive agencies

standard operating procedures and administrative discretion

administrative discretion and street-level bureaucrats

regulation and deregulation

command-and-control policy and incentive system

Name that term:

1. This law created the federal civil service.

   _____

2. This law limits the political activity of government employees.

   _____

3. This agency is in charge of hiring for most federal agencies.

   _____

4. The Federal Trade Commission is an example.

   _____

5. The U.S. Postal Service is an example.

   _____

6. This is needed because most policies are not self-executing.

   _____

7. Examples might include a police officer or a welfare worker.

   _____

8. Presidents sometime use these to control the bureaucracy.

   _____

9. Also known as subgovernments.

   _____

USING YOUR UNDERSTANDING

1.   The organization of the federal government is very complex; policy responsibilities are delegated among many different agencies and offices. Take a look at the simplified organization chart of the bureaucracy. (See for example, Figure 15.3, p. 476.) Based on what you know about the particular responsibilities of these many offices, try to categorize them according to different policy arenas such as the economy, social welfare, equality issues, environment, technology, or national security. Keep in mind that these policy arenas encompass many different types of policies. Take note of any agencies that fall within one or more of the policy groups. Briefly describe what you found in terms of the relative organizational emphasis on each of the policy arenas.

2.   Regulations affect many different aspects of our everyday lives. (See the section, "A Full Day of Regulation," p. 490.) Keep a record of your regulated day from the time you wake up to the time you go to bed, recording which aspects of your life are regulated and what federal agency is doing the regulation. After your record is complete, make an overall assessment as to the degree to which federal regulation affects you. Based on your assessment, consider whether or not the costs of regulation exceed the benefits it provides you. Also consider whether or not any of the regulations you recorded are not necessary or could be handled to your satisfaction by some other method or by a private means as compared to governmental means.

REVIEW QUESTIONS

Check ☑ the correct answer:

1.   The Constitution outlines in detail the form and rules for establishing the federal bureaucracy.
☐ True
☐ False

2.   Which of the following elements is NOT part of Max Weber's model of bureaucracy?
☐ a.   the personal touch
☐ b.   a hierarchical authority structure
☐ c.   task specialization
☐ d.   the merit principle and extensive rules

3. Which of the following statements about bureaucracies is FALSE?
   - ☐ a. Americans tend to dislike bureaucrats.
   - ☐ b. Most federal bureaucrats work in the states.
   - ☐ c. As a percentage of America's work force, federal employment has been shrinking.
   - ☐ d. Federal bureaucrats are no more inefficient than private bureaucrats.

4. Which of the following myths about bureaucracies is partly TRUE?
   - ☐ a. Americans dislike bureaucrats.
   - ☐ b. Most federal bureaucrats work in Washington, D.C.
   - ☐ c. Bureaucracies are growing bigger and bigger each year.
   - ☐ d. Government bureaucracies are less efficient than private bureaucracies.

5. The vast majority of tasks carried out by governments at all levels are noncontroversial.
   - ☐ True
   - ☐ False

6. Which of the following agencies employ the most civilian workers?
   - ☐ a. the Department of Defense
   - ☐ b. the Department of Health and Human Services
   - ☐ c. the Department of Veterans Affairs
   - ☐ d. the U.S. Postal Service

7. The permanent bureaucracy is less representative of the American people than legislators, judges, and presidential appointees to the executive branch.
   - ☐ True
   - ☐ False

8. Patronage is a hiring and promotion system based on
   - ☐ a. the merit principle.
   - ☐ b. knowing the right people.
   - ☐ c. the Pendleton Act.
   - ☐ d. talent and skill.

9. (bonus) Who was Charles Guiteau?
   - ☐ a. Chester A. Arthur's vice president
   - ☐ b. the first man hired under the civil service system
   - ☐ c. the man who shot President James A. Garfield
   - ☐ d. the man who coined the term "spoils system"

10. Most federal bureaucrats get their jobs through
☐ a. a political contact.
☐ b. presidential appointment.
☐ c. the civil service system.
☐ d. elections.

11. The Hatch Act prevents public employees from
☐ a. being fired for partisan reasons.
☐ b. being promoted for political reasons.
☐ c. voting in federal elections.
☐ d. active participation in partisan politics while on duty.

12. The GS (General Schedule) rating is used to
☐ a. select three eligible job applicants.
☐ b. assign salaries to federal employees.
☐ c. nominate members of the Senior Executive Service.
☐ d. evaluate federal employees prior to dismissal.

13. The plum book
☐ a. lists all civil service jobs.
☐ b. is published by the Office of Personnel Management.
☐ c. lists top federal jobs available with presidential appointment, often with Senate confirmation.
☐ d. provides rules for hiring minorities and women.

14. (bonus) Who referred to the top administrative policymakers as "government of strangers"?
☐ a. President Chester A. Arthur
☐ b. Charles Guiteau
☐ c. President Franklin D. Roosevelt
☐ d. Hugh Heclo

15. Of the 15 cabinet departments, all are headed by a secretary except the
☐ a. Department of Justice.
☐ b. Department of Labor.
☐ c. Department of Veterans Affairs.
☐ d. Department of State.

16. From the 1970s until 1995, the largest government agency in dollars spent was the
☐ a. Department of Defense.
☐ b. Department of Health and Human Services.
☐ c. Treasury Department.
☐ d. Department of Commerce.

17. The agency that was created to regulate business practices and control monopolistic behavior is the
☐ a. Securities and Exchange Commission.
☐ b. Federal Trade Commission.
☐ c. Federal Communications Commission.
☐ d. National Labor Relations Board.

18. The president cannot easily fire regulatory commission members.
☐ True
☐ False

19. The idea of "capture" refers to
☐ a. regulatory reforms pushed by groups.
☐ b. regulation of economic monopolies.
☐ c. control of regulators by regulatees.
☐ d. presidential influence on regulation.

20. Government corporations
☐ a. provide a service that the private sector could provide.
☐ b. typically charge for the services they provide.
☐ c. are different from other parts of the government.
☐ d. all of the above

21. Which of the following agencies is NOT a government corporation?
☐ a. Tennessee Valley Authority
☐ b. U.S. Postal Service
☐ c. Amtrak
☐ d. Department of Veterans Affairs

22. The General Services Administration, the National Science Foundation, and the National Aeronautics and Space Administration are
☐ a. cabinet departments.
☐ b. independent executive agencies.
☐ c. regulatory commissions.
☐ d. government corporations.

23. Most public policies are self-executing.
☐ True
☐ False

24. The policy implementation process includes all of the following activities EXCEPT
☐ a. creation of a new agency or assignment of responsibility to an old one.
☐ b. translation of policy goals into operation.
☐ c. coordination of agency resources.
☐ d. passage of a law.

25. Successful policy implementation is more likely with
☐ a. good program design.
☐ b. lack of clarity.
☐ c. very broad policies.
☐ d. limited budgets.

26. The case of assuring equal opportunity in college athletics demonstrates that bureaucracies usually resolve policy problems that Congress fails to resolve.
☐ True
☐ False

27. Bureaucratic agencies frequently lack the staff, training, funding, supplies, and equipment to carry out the tasks it has been assigned.
☐ True
☐ False

28. Administrative routine
☐ a. is made possible by standard operating procedures.
☐ b. is not essential to bureaucracy.
☐ c. makes it impossible to exchange personnel.
☐ d. prevents policies from being applied uniformly.

29. Standard operating procedures
☐ a. save time.
☐ b. bring uniformity to complex organizations.
☐ c. make personnel interchangeable.
☐ d. all of the above

30. A paradox of bureaucracy is the coexistence of
☐ a. routines and discretion.
☐ b. equity and efficiency.
☐ c. rules and regulations.
☐ d. red tape and detail.

31. Administrative discretion is greatest when rules do not fit.
☐ True
☐ False

32. An example of a street-level bureaucrat is a
☐ a. Supreme Court justice.
☐ b. member of Congress.
☐ c. welfare worker.
☐ d. presidential appointee.

33. It is not easy to control the exercise of administrative discretion because
☐ a. it is not easy to fire bureaucrats in the civil service.
☐ b. removing appointed officials may be politically embarrassing to the president.
☐ c. special bonuses are rare in the public sector.
☐ d. all of the above

34. Policies within the areas of human services and homeland security are
☐ a. well-coordinated.
☐ b. highly fragmented.
☐ c. handled by a single agency.
☐ d. uniform.

35. Government reorganization to reduce fragmentation is difficult because
☐ a. congressional committees would gain jurisdiction over too many agencies.
☐ b. too many agencies want to remain within a broader bureaucratic unit.
☐ c. interest groups do not want to give up the close relationships they have with their agencies.
☐ d. all of the above

36. The Voting Rights Act of 1965 was a successful case of implementation for each of the following reasons EXCEPT
☐ a. it was popular with everyone.
☐ b. its goal was clear.
☐ c. its implementation was straightforward.
☐ d. the authority of the implementers was clear.

37. Which of the following statements about regulation is FALSE?
☐ a. Regulation pervades the everyday lives of Americans.
☐ b. Regulation is the least controversial bureaucratic role.
☐ c. The idea of a total free enterprise economy is out of date.
☐ d. Almost all bureaucratic agencies are regulators.

38. In the case of *Munn* v. *Illinois* (1877), the Supreme Court
☐ a. upheld the right of government to regulate business.
☐ b. struck down the authority of the states to regulate.
☐ c. held that government regulation was unconstitutional.
☐ d. upheld the creation of the Interstate Commerce Commission.

39. Government agencies are not permitted to go to court to enforce their rules and guidelines.
☐ True
☐ False

40. Which of the following is NOT among the key elements of all government regulation?
☐ a. a grant of power and set of directions from Congress
☐ b. a set of rules and guidelines by the regulatory agency
☐ c. permits and licenses for regulated industries
☐ d. some means of enforcing compliance with congressional goals and agency regulations

41. Proponents of deregulation argue that regulation
☐ a. keeps prices low.
☐ b. enhances competition abroad.
☐ c. is reasonably effective.
☐ d. distorts market forces.

42. Critics of regulation claim that it
☐ a. raises prices.
☐ b. hurts America's competitive position abroad.
☐ c. doesn't work.
☐ d. all of the above

43. Advocates of deregulation include conservatives and liberals.
☐ True
☐ False

44. Bureaucracies are America's only unelected policymaking institution.
☐ True
☐ False

45. Which of the following is NOT among the key methods used by presidents to control the bureaucracy?
☐ a. pay raises
☐ b. appointments
☐ c. budgets
☐ d. executive orders

46. Congress finds a big bureaucracy congenial because it can provide services to constituents.
☐ True
☐ False

47. Congress can oversee the bureaucracy by
☐ a. influencing the appointment of agency heads.
☐ b. holding hearings.
☐ c. rewriting the legislation.
☐ d. all of the above

48. Which of the following would NOT be part of an iron triangle?
☐ a. a congressional committee
☐ b. a government agency
☐ c. a political party
☐ d. an interest group

49. Subgovernments or iron triangles can foster
☐ a. democracy.
☐ b. centralization.
☐ c. fragmentation.
☐ d. policy cooperation.

50. Issue networks have
☐ a. created new iron triangles.
☐ b. challenged formerly closed subgovernments.
☐ c. replaced the system of subgovernments.
☐ d. decreased participation in bureaucratic policymaking.

51. Which of the following statements regarding the scope of the bureaucracy is FALSE?
☐ a. The federal bureaucracy has not grown over the past two generations.
☐ b. Originally the bureaucracy had a modest role in promoting the economy.
☐ c. The bureaucracy has been able to prevent much of the deregulation attempted by Congress and the president.
☐ d. Today, the bureaucracy is expected to play an active role in dealing with social and economic problems.

ESSAY QUESTIONS

1. How does one become a bureaucrat? What myths surround the bureaucracy in the United States?

2. Compare and contrast the different theories of bureaucracy. Which one do you believe best reflects reality?

3. How is the United States bureaucracy organized? What policymaking roles do the different federal executive agencies play?

4. What is policy implementation and what are its main features? What factors facilitate and what factors hinder successful implementation of a public policy? Use specific examples of implementation to illustrate your points.

5.   What is needed for an agency to perform its regulatory role? What are the pros and cons of deregulation?

6.   How does politics permeate bureaucracies? What factors make it difficult to control bureaucracies? What methods are available to the president and Congress to control bureaucracies?

7.   What is the role of bureaucracies in the federal system? Is the federal bureaucracy too big? What are the pros and cons of a large bureaucracy?

CHAPTER 16

THE FEDERAL COURTS

CHAPTER OUTLINE

I. The Nature of the Judicial System (pp. 504-506)
- A. Introduction
    1. In criminal law cases, an individual is charged by the government with violating a specific law.
    2. Civil law involves no charge of criminality, but concerns a dispute between two parties.
- B. Participants in the Judicial System
    1. Litigants
        - a. Every case is a dispute between a plaintiff and a defendant.
        - b. **Standing to sue** means that litigants must have serious interest in a case.
        - c. **Class action suits** permit a small number of people to sue on behalf of all other people similarly situated.
        - d. **Justiciable disputes** are issues that are capable of being settled by legal methods.
    2. Groups sometimes try to influence courts by using particular cases and litigants and *amicus curiae* **briefs.**
    3. Attorneys

II. The Structure of the Federal Judicial System (pp. 507-511)
- A. Introduction
    1. Congress has created *constitutional courts* and *legislative courts.*
    2. Courts with **original jurisdiction** are those in which a case is heard first, usually in a trial.
    3. Courts with **appellate jurisdiction** hear cases brought to them on appeal from a lower court.
- B. District Courts
    1. The entry point for most litigation in the federal courts is one of the 91 **district courts.**
    2. Most of the cases handled in the district courts are routine.
- C. Courts of Appeal
    1. The U.S. **courts of appeal** are appellate courts empowered to review all final decisions of district courts.
    2. The courts of appeal focus on correcting errors of procedure and law that occurred in the original proceedings of legal cases.

D. The Supreme Court
   1. The pinnacle of the American judicial system is the U.S. **Supreme Court.**
   2. Almost all of the business of the Court comes from the appellate process.

III. The Politics of Judicial Selection (pp. 511-516)
   A. The Lower Courts
      1. According to **senatorial courtesy**, nominations for lower court positions are not confirmed when opposed by a senator of the president's party from the state in which the nominee is to serve.
      2. The president usually has more influence in the selection of judges to the federal courts of appeal than to the federal district courts.
   B. The Supreme Court
      1. Nominations to the Court may be a president's most important legacy to the nation.
      2. The president operates under fewer constraints in nominating members to the Supreme Court.

IV. The Background of Judges and Justices (pp. 516-520)
   A. Judges serving on the federal district and circuit courts are all lawyers and overwhelmingly white males.
   B. Supreme Court justices are an elite group.

V. The Courts as Policymakers (pp. 520-527)
   A. Accepting Cases
      1. The most common way for the Court to put a case on its docket is by issuing to a lower federal or state court a *writ of certiorari,* a formal document that calls up a case.
      2. The **solicitor general** is in charge of the appellate court litigation of the federal government.
   B. Making Decisions
      1. *Amicus curiae* ("friend of the court") briefs are briefs from parties who are interested in the outcome of the case but are not formal litigants.
      2. An **opinion** is a statement of the legal reasoning behind the decision.
      3. The vast majority of cases reaching the courts are settled on the principle of *stare decisis*, meaning that an earlier decision should hold for the case being considered.
      4. All courts rely heavily upon **precedent**, the way similar cases were handled in the past, as a guide to current decisions.
      5. **Original intent** holds that judges and justices should determine the intent of the framers of the Constitution regarding a particular matter and decide cases in line with that intent.
   C. Implementing Court Decisions
      1. **Judicial implementation** refers to how and whether court decisions are translated into actual policy, affecting the behavior of others.

2.   Implementation of court decisions involves an interpreting, implementing, and consumer population.

VI.   The Courts and the Policy Agenda (pp. 527-532)
    A.   A Historical Review
        1.   John Marshall and the Growth of Judicial Review
            a.   In *Marbury* **v.** *Madison* (1803), Chief Justice Marshall established the power of **judicial review**, the power of the courts to hold acts of Congress, and by implication the executive, in violation of the Constitution.
        2.   The "Nine Old Men"
        3.   The Warren Court
        4.   The Burger Court
            a.   The Burger Court was more conservative than the liberal Warren Court.
            b.   In *United States* **v.** *Nixon* (1974), the Burger Court ordered President Nixon to turn over White House tapes to the courts.
        5.   The Rehnquist Court

VII.   Understanding the Courts (pp. 532-536)
    A.   The Courts and Democracy
    B.   What Courts Should Do: The Scope of Judicial Power
        1.   **Judicial restraint** is when judges adhere closely to precedent and play minimal policymaking roles.
        2.   **Judicial activism** is when judges make bolder policy decisions, even charting new constitutional ground.
        3.   The doctrine of **political questions** is a means to avoid deciding some cases, principally those regarding conflicts between the president and Congress.
        4.   If an issue is one of **statutory construction,** in which a court interprets an act of Congress, the legislature routinely passes legislation that clarifies existing laws.

VIII.   Summary (pp. 536-537)

LEARNING OBJECTIVES

After studying Chapter 16, you should be able to:

1.   Understand the nature of the judicial system.

2.   Explain how courts in the United States are organized and the nature of their jurisdiction.

3.   Describe the role of judges in the judicial process, including their backgrounds and how they were selected.

4.   Discuss Supreme Court policymaking and judicial implementation.

5.   Explain the role of the courts in shaping the policy agenda in America.

6.   Evaluate how the courts operate in a democratic system and how their activities affect the scope of government.

The following exercises will help you meet these objectives:

Objective 1: Understand the nature of the judicial system.

1.   Explain the difference between criminal law and civil law.

      Criminal Law:

      Civil Law:

2.   List three regular participants in the judicial system other than judges.

      1.

      2.

      3.

3.   What is meant by "justiciable disputes"?

Objective 2: Explain how courts in the United States are organized and the nature of their jurisdiction.

1.   What are the differences between constitutional courts and legislative courts?

Constitutional Courts:

Legislative Courts:

2.   Complete the following table on the structure of the federal judicial system.

Court	Number of Courts	Number of Judges	Jurisdiction	Policy Implications
District Court				
Court of Appeal				
Supreme Court				

3.   What is the role of a U.S. attorney?

Objective 3: Describe the role of judges in the judicial process, including their backgrounds and how they were selected.

1.   Explain the practice of "senatorial courtesy."

2.   Name three conditions in which nominations to the Supreme Court are more likely to run into trouble.

1.

2.

3.

3.   Present a demographic profile of the "typical" federal judge.

4.   List six criteria that have been important in choosing Supreme Court justices over the years.

      1.

      2.

      3.

      4.

      5.

      6.

Objective 4: Discuss Supreme Court policymaking and judicial implementation.

1.   What are the four key functions of the solicitor general?

      1.

      2.

      3.

      4.

2.   What are the functions of *amicus curiae* briefs?

3.   What is the difference between a majority opinion, a dissenting opinion, and a concurring opinion?

Majority Opinion:

Dissenting Opinion:

Concurring Opinion:

4. What is the difference between *stare decisis* and precedent?

    Stare Decisis:

    Precedent:

5. List and explain the three elements of judicial implementation according to Charles Johnson and Bradley Canon.

    1.

    2.

    3.

Objective 5: Explain the role of the courts in shaping the policy agenda in America.

    1. Explain the principle of judicial review.

2.   Complete the following table on public policy and the Supreme Court.

Court	Basic Ideology	Judicial Restraint or Judicial Activism	Key Cases
Warren Court			
Burger Court			
Rehnquist Court			

Objective 6: Evaluate how the courts operate in a democratic system and how their activities affect the scope of government.

1.   In what ways might it be said that courts are not a very democratic institution?

2.   Explain the difference between judicial activism and judicial restraint.

Judicial Activism:

Judicial Restraint:

3. Define the terms "political question" and "statutory construction" as they apply to the Supreme Court and give an example of each.

Term	Definition	Example
Political Question		
Statutory Construction		

KEY TERMS

Identify and describe:

standing to sue

class action suits

justiciable disputes

amicus curiae briefs

original jurisdiction

appellate jurisdiction

district courts

courts of appeal

Supreme Court

senatorial courtesy

solicitor general

opinion

stare decisis

precedent

original intent

judicial implementation

Marbury v. *Madison*

judicial review

United States v. *Nixon*

judicial restraint

judicial activism

political questions

statutory construction

Compare and contrast:
standing to sue and class action suits

original jurisdiction and appellate jurisdiction

district courts, courts of appeal, and Supreme Court

stare decisis and precedent

Marbury v. *Madison* and judicial review

judicial restraint and judicial activism

political questions and statutory construction

Name that term:

1. Capable of being settled by legal methods.

    _____

2. The way of disposing of state-level federal judicial nominations.

    _____

3. This office represents the government before the Supreme Court.

    _____

4. Interested parties who are not litigants submit these.

    _____

5. A statement of the legal reasoning behind a Supreme Court decision.

    _____

6. How and whether court decisions are translated into policy.

    _____

7. This is sometimes referred to as strict constructionism.

    _____

8. This Supreme Court case hastened the resignation of a president.

    _____

9. The doctrine used to avoid deciding some cases.

    _____

USING YOUR UNDERSTANDING

1.   Investigate the composition of the current Supreme Court in terms of the different types of individuals that are found there. Find out who appointed them, their political party affiliation, their age, their ethnicity, their religion, their home state, their previous occupation, and other such defining characteristics. Then see if you can find out how the different justices voted on some recent court cases having to do with public policy issues. Try to develop a profile of the Supreme Court in which you relate the characteristics of its members to their voting behavior. Briefly discuss the implications of a justice's background for the way he or she behaves on the bench.

2.   Conduct a study of judicial selection by comparing the two Supreme Court nominations from the Clinton administration (Ruth Bader Ginsburg and Stephen G. Breyer) with the two nominations from the George W. Bush administration (Samuel A. Alito and John G. Roberts). How do Bush's choices differ from Clinton's choices? How did the nominations differ? What were the most important factors influencing the presidents' choices? Who else was considered as a potential nominee by each president, and why were the successful candidates chosen instead of any of the others? How did the public react to the nominations? How did the Senate react to the nominations? Compare the confirmation hearings of the nominees. How did they differ and how were they similar? Evaluate the judicial selection process for Supreme Court justices in light of these cases. Is the process fair? How might the process be improved?

REVIEW QUESTIONS

Check ☑ the correct answer:

1.   The Supreme Court makes the majority of American judicial policy.
      ☐ True
      ☐ False

2.   Federal judges
      ☐ a.   actively initiate cases.
      ☐ b.   issue advisory opinions on hypothetical cases.
      ☐ c.   cannot resolve justiciable disputes.
      ☐ d.   are impartial arbiters between two contending views.

3.   Which of the following is NOT associated with civil law?
      ☐ a.   a plaintiff and a defendant
      ☐ b.   a charge that a law has been violated
      ☐ c.   statutes and common law
      ☐ d.   a dispute between two parties

4.   Most civil and criminal cases begin and end in the state courts.
      ☐ True
      ☐ False

5.   Every judicial case involves
      ☐ a.   a plaintiff and defendant.
      ☐ b.   a jury.
      ☐ c.   a federal judge.
      ☐ d.   criminal law.

6.   Litigants must have
      ☐ a.   a jury trial.
      ☐ b.   standing to sue.
      ☐ c.   original jurisdiction.
      ☐ d.   a civil dispute.

7.   The concept of standing to sue has been broadened by the use of
      ☐ a.   class action suits.
      ☐ b.   appellate jurisdiction.
      ☐ c.   common law.
      ☐ d.   justiciable disputes.

8.   Which of the following is NOT a justiciable dispute?
      ☐ a.   a divorce proceeding
      ☐ b.   a dispute over an insurance claim
      ☐ c.   a suit calling for the abolishment of a federal program
      ☐ d.   a murder trial

9.   Interest groups ignore the judicial process because of its limited impact on public policy.
      ☐ True
      ☐ False

10.   The federal government provides legal assistance to the poor through the
      ☐ a.   National Association for the Advancement of Colored People.
      ☐ b.   American Civil Liberties Union.
      ☐ c.   Legal Services Corporation.
      ☐ d.   all of the above

11.   The Constitution specifically created the
        ☐ a.   Supreme Court.
        ☐ b.   federal district courts.
        ☐ c.   federal courts of appeal.
        ☐ d.   all of the above

12.   Courts with appellate jurisdiction
        ☐ a.   review the factual record of cases.
        ☐ b.   hear the majority of court cases in the United States.
        ☐ c.   review the legal issues involved in cases.
        ☐ d.   are all federal courts.

13.   The Court of Military Appeals and the Tax Court are
        ☐ a.   constitutional courts.
        ☐ b.   legislative courts.
        ☐ c.   state courts.
        ☐ d.   local courts.

14.   Each state has at least one federal district court.
        ☐ True
        ☐ False

15.   Cases in the federal district courts
        ☐ a.   are usually presided over by one judge.
        ☐ b.   cannot involve litigants from different states.
        ☐ c.   are heard on appeal from state courts.
        ☐ d.   involving civil law are rarely settled.

16.   Duties of the federal magistrates include all of the following EXCEPT
        ☐ a.   issuing warrants for arrest.
        ☐ b.   hearing motions subject to review by the district judge.
        ☐ c.   representing the U.S. government in civil cases.
        ☐ d.   presiding over some trials.

17.   Most of the cases handled in the district courts
        ☐ a.   are settled by a jury.
        ☐ b.   are routine.
        ☐ c.   result in policy innovations.
        ☐ d.   are published by the U.S. government.

18.   Cases in the federal courts of appeal
        ☐ a.   involve trials and testimony.
        ☐ b.   focus on the correction of errors in procedure and law.
        ☐ c.   rarely come from the federal district courts.
        ☐ d.   must be decided by a unanimous vote.

19. Which of the following is NOT among the functions of the Supreme Court?
- [ ] a. maintaining national supremacy in the law
- [ ] b. ensuring uniformity in interpretations of national laws
- [ ] c. enforcing the orders of state regulatory agencies
- [ ] d. resolving conflicts among the states

20. Few cases arise under the Supreme Court's original jurisdiction.
- [ ] True
- [ ] False

21. Cases appealed to the Supreme Court from state courts must involve
- [ ] a. a crime.
- [ ] b. at least $50,000 in a civil case.
- [ ] c. a substantial federal question.
- [ ] d. all of the above

22. Federal judges and justices
- [ ] a. serve for life.
- [ ] b. cannot be impeached.
- [ ] c. can be removed for political reasons.
- [ ] d. are elected to office.

23. (bonus) The only Supreme Court justice who was tried but not convicted by the Senate was
- [ ] a. Robert Bork.
- [ ] b. Samuel Chase.
- [ ] c. John Marshall.
- [ ] d. William Rehnquist.

24. Senatorial courtesy allows any senator to prevent the confirmation of a federal judiciary nominee.
- [ ] True
- [ ] False

25. Nominees for the federal judiciary are evaluated by
- [ ] a. the Department of Justice.
- [ ] b. the Federal Bureau of Investigation.
- [ ] c. sitting judges.
- [ ] d. all of the above

26. The president's appointments to the Supreme Court may be his or her most important legacy.
- [ ] True
- [ ] False

27.   Which of the following does the president rely on most to identify and screen candidates for the Supreme Court?
☐ a.   the Senate Judiciary Committee
☐ b.   the attorney general and the Department of Justice
☐ c.   sitting justices
☐ d.   the American Bar Association

28.   Candidates for the Supreme Court usually aggressively pursue the position, especially by politicking the Senate Judiciary Committee.
☐ True
☐ False

29.   Which of the following works to the advantage of a Supreme Court nominee?
☐ a.   a reputation for judicial activism
☐ b.   nomination by a president at the end of his term
☐ c.   nomination by a president whose party is in the minority in the Senate
☐ d.   ethics, competence, and a low profile

30.   Which of the following statements is TRUE?
☐ a.   Federal judges are highly representative of the American people.
☐ b.   The Constitution does not require federal judges to be lawyers.
☐ c.   Most federal judges have never been involved in politics.
☐ d.   The Reagan administration ignored ideology in making judicial appointments.

31.   The race and gender of nominees for Supreme Court justice have become less salient in recent years.
☐ True
☐ False

32.   Many Supreme Court justices, including some of the most distinguished ones, have not had previous judicial experience.
☐ True
☐ False

33.   An important influence on the selection of judges and justices is
☐ a.   partisanship.
☐ b.   ideology.
☐ c.   politics.
☐ d.   all of the above

34. Which of the following statements is FALSE?
- ☐ a. Partisan politics affects judicial appointments.
- ☐ b. Presidents usually nominate judges and justices who share their ideological beliefs.
- ☐ c. Members of the federal bench may time their retirement so that the president can choose compatible successors.
- ☐ d. Presidents can always rely on their judicial appointees to vote the way the president wants them to vote.

35. Which of the following statements is FALSE?
- ☐ a. Republican judges are somewhat more conservative than Democratic judges.
- ☐ b. Judges who are former prosecutors are somewhat less sympathetic toward defendant rights.
- ☐ c. Judges' ethnicity and gender strongly influences their judicial behavior.
- ☐ d. The influence of background on judicial decision making is generally limited.

36. A *writ of certiorari* is a formal document that
- ☐ a. calls up a case for review by the Supreme Court.
- ☐ b. is used to sentence convicted criminals.
- ☐ c. initiates a civil law suit.
- ☐ d. requires a witness to testify in federal court.

37. The solicitor general of the United States
- ☐ a. represents the United States before the Supreme Court.
- ☐ b. is a presidential appointee.
- ☐ c. typically has the confidence of the Supreme Court.
- ☐ d. all of the above

38. A Supreme Court decision without explanation is known as
- ☐ a. a *writ of certiorari*.
- ☐ b. a *writ of mandamus*.
- ☐ c. a *per curiam* decision.
- ☐ d. an *amicus curiae* brief.

39. Which of the following is NOT a characteristic of *amicus curiae* briefs?
- ☐ a. Parties who are formal litigants file them.
- ☐ b. They are intended to influence court decisions.
- ☐ c. Some are filed by the solicitor general on behalf of the government.
- ☐ d. They raise additional points of view and information.

40. The written opinion in a Supreme Court case
☐ a. is irrelevant compared to the decision itself.
☐ b. is a statement of the legal reasoning behind a decision.
☐ c. is always prepared by the chief justice.
☐ d. always represents the views of all nine justices.

41. Opinions written not only to support a majority decision but also to stress a different constitutional or legal basis are called
☐ a. majority opinions.
☐ b. dissenting opinions.
☐ c. opposing opinions.
☐ d. concurring opinions.

42. The vast majority of cases reaching the courts are settled on the principle of *stare decisis*.
☐ True
☐ False

43. When judicial precedents are clear, the Supreme Court tends to be divided in ideological terms.
☐ True
☐ False

44. The idea of original intent refers to
☐ a. original jurisdiction.
☐ b. the intent of the Constitution's framers.
☐ c. the ideological positions of justices.
☐ d. the views of a popular majority.

45. How and whether court decisions are translated into actual policy is called
☐ a. judicial activism.
☐ b. judicial precedents.
☐ c. judicial implementation.
☐ d. judicial policymaking.

46. Which of the following is NOT among the key elements of judicial implementation according to Charles Johnson and Bradley Canon?
☐ a. interpreting population
☐ b. implementing population
☐ c. consumer population
☐ d. general population

47. From 1938 to the present, the Supreme Court has enlarged the scope of personal freedom and civil rights.
☐ True
☐ False

48. The case of *Marbury* v. *Madison* (1803) established the Supreme Court's
☐ a. power of judicial review.
☐ b. use of writs of *certiorari*.
☐ c. application of the principle of *stare decisis*.
☐ d. power to expand its original jurisdiction.

49. During the New Deal era, President Roosevelt sought to create a more sympathetic Supreme Court by
☐ a. getting Congress to expand the court's size.
☐ b. changing the chief justice.
☐ c. removing unsympathetic justices.
☐ d. directly influencing court decisions.

50. In the shift from the Warren Court to the Burger Court, the Supreme Court became more
☐ a. conservative.
☐ b. liberal.
☐ c. activist.
☐ d. none of the above

51. (bonus) Who said "It seems to me that there's nothing more antithetical to the idea of what a good judge should be than to think it has something to do with representative democracy"?
☐ a. Justice Potter Stewart
☐ b. Chief Justice William Rehnquist
☐ c. Justice Thurgood Marshall
☐ d. Alexander Hamilton

52. It may be said that the courts are not a very democratic institution because
☐ a. federal judges are not elected.
☐ b. it is almost impossible to remove judges.
☐ c. the courts are dominated by elites.
☐ d. all of the above

53. The Supreme Court is insulated from the normal forms of politics.
☐ True
☐ False

54.   Which of the following statements is FALSE?
- [ ] a.   In some ways, courts are very undemocratic.
- [ ] b.   Supreme Court decisions are often in line with public opinion.
- [ ] c.   Few major policy decisions actually end up in court.
- [ ] d.   Agencies and businesses commonly find themselves ordered by different courts to do opposite things.

55.   Which of the following is NOT a general characteristic of judicial restraint?
- [ ] a.   deference to Congress
- [ ] b.   deference to state legislatures
- [ ] c.   a minimum policymaking role
- [ ] d.   achieving political ends through judicial means

56.   The policy in which judges make bold policy decisions, even charting new constitutional ground, is called
- [ ] a.   judicial restraint.
- [ ] b.   judicial activism.
- [ ] c.   judicial liberalism.
- [ ] d.   judicial conservatism.

57.   Liberal members of the Supreme Court tend toward judicial activism whereas conservatives tend toward judicial restraint.
- [ ] True
- [ ] False

58.   The federal courts use the doctrine of "political questions"
- [ ] a.   to settle disputes regarding the political parties.
- [ ] b.   to make bold policy decisions.
- [ ] c.   when the federal government is one of the litigants.
- [ ] d.   as a means to avoid deciding some cases.

59.   Congress can influence the Supreme Court and its decisions by
- [ ] a.   beginning the process of amending the Constitution.
- [ ] b.   altering the structure of the courts.
- [ ] c.   passing legislation that clarifies existing laws and, in effect, overturns the courts.
- [ ] d.   all of the above

ESSAY QUESTIONS

1.   How do the courts work? Who are the key participants in the American judicial system and what do they do?

2.   Explain the structure of the American judicial system. What are the differences between the federal district courts, courts of appeal, and the Supreme Court?

3.   What is the process by which members of the Supreme Court are chosen? How does the appointment process for other federal courts differ?

4.   What are the typical characteristics of American judges and justices? How do their backgrounds and personal characteristics affect their judicial behavior?

5.   How do courts shape public policy in their decisions and in the opinions by judges used to justify decisions? What effect have the courts had on the policy agenda? Use historical examples in your answer.

6.   How do court decisions become public policy? What is involved in judicial implementation? Use examples to illustrate the potential problems of implementing court decisions.

7.   What is the role of courts in a democracy? What are the major criticisms of the court system in the United States today? In what ways might the courts be considered too strong or weak?

CHAPTER 17

ECONOMIC POLICYMAKING

CHAPTER OUTLINE

I.   Government, Politics, and the Economy (pp. 542-549)
    A.   Introduction
        1.   **Capitalism** is an economic system in which individuals and corporations own the principal means of production.
        2.   A **mixed economy** is a system in which the government, while not commanding the economy, is still deeply involved in economic decisions.
        3.   **Multinational corporations**, businesses with vast holdings in many countries, dominate the world's economy.
    B.   Economic Policy at Work: An Illustration
        1.   Government Regulation and Business Practices
            a.   The main government regulatory agency responsible for the regulation of business practices is the **Securities and Exchange Commission (SEC)**.
            b.   **Minimum wage** is the legal minimum hourly wage for large employers.
            c.   A **labor union** is a workers' organization for bargaining with an employer.
            d.   **Collective bargaining** consists of negotiations between representatives of labor unions and management to determine pay and acceptable working conditions.
        2.   Wal-Mart and the World Economy
    C.   "It's the Economy, Stupid": Voters, Politicians, and Economic Policy
        1.   Economic conditions are the best single predictors of voters' evaluation of the president.
        2.   Democrats stress the importance of employment; Republicans stress the importance of inflation.
    D.   Two Major Worries: Unemployment and Inflation
        1.   The **unemployment rate** has a direct affect on government and politics.
        2.   The **Consumer Price Index (CPI)** measures **inflation** (the rise in prices for consumer goods).

II.   Policies for Controlling the Economy (pp. 549-552)
    A.   **Laissez-faire** is the principle that government should not meddle with the economy.
    B.   Monetary Policy and "The Fed"

1.   **Monetary policy** is the manipulation of the supply of money and credit in private hands.
2.   **Monetarism** holds that the supply of money is the key to the nation's economic health.
3.   The main agency for making monetary policy is the Board of Governors of the **Federal Reserve System.**

  C. Fiscal Policy of Presidents and Parties
1.   **Fiscal policy** describes the impact of the federal budget on the economy.
2.   **Keynesian economic theory** holds that government spending can help the economy weather its normal ups and downs.
3.   **Supply-side economics** argues that the key task for government economic policy is to stimulate the supply of goods, not their demand.

III. Why it is Hard to Control the Economy (pp. 552-553)
  A. Instruments for controlling the economy are difficult to use.
  B. Economic policies take a long time to implement.
  C. Most of the budget expenditures are uncontrollable.
  D. The private sector dominates the economy.

IV. Politics, Policy, and the International Economy (pp. 553-556)
  A. Most emerging economies want to follow an economic policy of **protectionism**.
  B. The **World Trade Organization (WTO)** is an international organization that regulates international trade.
  C. The loss of American jobs overseas has become an important political issue.

V. Arenas of Economic Policymaking (pp. 556-559)
  A. Business and Public Policy
1.   Corporate Corruption and Concentration
    a. **Antitrust policy** ensures competition and prevents monopoly.
2.   Regulating and Benefiting Business
  B. Consumer Policy: The Rise of the Consumer Lobby
1.   The **Food and Drug Administration (FDA)** has broad regulatory powers over the manufacturing, contents, marketing, and labeling of food and drugs.
2.   The Federal Trade Commission (FTC) has become a defender of consumer interests in truth in advertising.
  C. Labor and Government
1.   The **National Labor Relations Act** guarantees workers the right of collective bargaining.
2.   The Taft-Hartley Act continued to guarantee collective bargaining, but prohibited unfair practices by unions as well.
3.   Section 14B of Taft-Hartley permitted right-to-work laws that forbid labor contracts from requiring workers to join unions to hold their jobs.

LEARNING OBJECTIVES

After studying Chapter 17, you should be able to:

1. Understand the relationship between politics and the economy.

2. Describe the policies and programs that policymakers use to affect the state of the economy.

3. Explain why it is hard to control both the domestic and international economy.

4. Discuss the major issues and policy directions that have been pursued in the areas of business, consumer, and labor policy.

5. Understand the relationship between democracy, the scope of government, and economic policymaking in the United States.

The following exercises will help you meet these objectives:

Objective 1: Understand the relationship between politics and the economy.

1. Briefly explain how Wal-Mart can be used to illustrate the following concepts:

Inflation:

Securities and Exchange Commission:

Labor union:

Collective bargaining:

Occupational Health and Safety Administration:

316

Globalization:

2.	Explain the basic difference between the Republican Party and the Democratic Party in terms of their approach to economic policies.

Republicans:

Democrats:

3.	Briefly explain how the unemployment rate is measured.

4.	What is meant by the Consumer Price Index (CPI) and why is it important?

Objective 2: Describe the instruments and programs that policymakers use to affect the state of the economy.

1.	Explain how the Fed works to affect the supply of money and credit.

2.	What is meant by fiscal policy?

3.	Explain the basic differences between Keynesian economic theory and supply-side economics.

Keynesian Theory:

Supply-Side Economics:

Objective 3: Explain why it is hard to control both the domestic and international economy.

1.   What is meant by the "political business cycle"?

2.   Explain how the American capitalist system imposes restraints on controlling the economy.

3.   What are the major arguments for and against the World Trade Organization?

Objective 4: Discuss the major issues and policy directions that have been pursued in the areas of business, consumer, and labor policy.

1.   Complete the following table listing one major congressional act and one major governmental policy for each of the arenas of economic policymaking discussed in the text.

Arena	Major Congressional Act	Major Government Policy
Business		
Consumers		
Labor		

2.   List four ways in which the government benefits business.

   1.

   2.

   3.

   4.

3.   How does the Food and Drug Administration (FDA) and the Federal Trade Commission (FTC) benefit consumers?

   FDA:

   FTC:

4.   What were the main provisions of the National Labor Relations Act and the Taft-Hartley Act?

   National Labor Relations Act:

   Taft-Hartley Act:

Objective 5: Understand the relationship between democracy, the scope of government, and economic policymaking in the United States.

1.   What does the conflict about jobs in the 2004 election tell us about democracy and economic policymaking?

2.   What is the main difference between the liberal and conservative view of the scope of government in economic policymaking?

      Liberals:

      Conservatives:

KEY TERMS

Identify and describe:

capitalism

mixed economy

multinational corporation

Securities and Exchange Commission

minimum wage

labor unions

collective bargaining

unemployment rate

inflation

Consumer Price Index (CPI)

laissez-faire

monetary policy

monetarism

Federal Reserve System

fiscal policy

Keynesian economic theory
supply-side economics

protectionism

World Trade Organization (WTO)

antitrust policy

Food and Drug Administration (FDA)

National Labor Relations Act

Compare and contrast:

capitalism and mixed economy

labor union and collective bargaining

inflation and Consumer Price Index (CPI)

laissez-faire, monetarism, and Keynesian economic theory

monetary policy and fiscal policy

Keynesian economic theory and supply-side economics

protectionism and World Trade Organization (WTO)

National Labor Relations Act and collective bargaining

Name that term:

1. Some of these have annual budgets exceeding those of foreign countries.

   _____

2. This agency was created during the New Deal to regulate stock fraud.

   _____

3. Today this amounts to $5.15 per hour.

   _____

4. The percentage of Americans actively seeking employment but unable to find work.

   _____

5. It regulates the lending practices of banks.

   _____

6. An economic theory popularized by President Reagan.

   _____

7. This is used to ensure competition and prevent monopoly.

   _____

8.   This agency is responsible for ascertaining the safety and effectiveness of new
      drugs before approving them for marketing in the United States.

_____

USING YOUR UNDERSTANDING

1.   Find copies of the government's objective indicators of economic conditions—the
      unemployment and inflation rates—for some recent years. Government Internet
      sources would be a good place to start. Try your hand at plotting these indicators
      on a graph. Then try to locate an indicator of the importance of these issues on
      the public agenda, as measured by public opinion about the seriousness of these
      economic problems. Plot this indicator along with the objective indicators you
      found. If a national election occurred during the time frame you are considering,
      draw a line representing when the election occurred. Briefly describe what you
      found in terms of the relationship between the government's measurement of
      economic problems and their place on the public's agenda. If applicable, describe
      the apparent impact of the election on the indicators you plotted.

2.   Using newspapers, newsmagazines and/or the Internet, collect some current
      examples of economic policymaking in the United States. Try to find items that
      illustrate the different tools that policymakers use to try to control the economy
      and the different sectors of the economy that they seek to control. Consider the
      impact of the political party in power on current economic policymaking and
      whether or not it is consistent with what would be expected. Describe what you
      found in terms of the direction and impact of contemporary policies in the
      economic arena.

REVIEW QUESTIONS

Check ☑ the correct answer:

1.   The "father of the American economy" is
      ☐ a.   George Washington.
      ☐ b.   James Madison.
      ☐ c.   Alexander Hamilton.
      ☐ d.   Thomas Jefferson.

2.   A system in which the government, while not commanding the economy, is
      deeply involved in economic decisions is called
      ☐ a.   capitalism.
      ☐ b.   a mixed economy.
      ☐ c.   socialism.
      ☐ d.   communism.

3. Some multinational corporations have budgets greater than many foreign governments.
   ☐ True
   ☐ False

4. Wal-Mart
   ☐ a. generated as much revenue as the state of California collected in taxes.
   ☐ b. is partly responsible for the low rate of inflation in the United States.
   ☐ c. has been responsible for 12 percent of all productivity growth in the United States.
   ☐ d. all of the above

5. The main regulatory agency responsible for regulation of business practices is the
   ☐ a. Federal Reserve Board.
   ☐ b. Securities and Exchange Commission.
   ☐ c. Department of Commerce.
   ☐ d. Justice Department.

6. Economic conditions are the best single predictor of voters' evaluations of how the president is doing his job.
   ☐ True
   ☐ False

7. People who feel that unemployment is a serious national problem tend to
   ☐ a. lean toward the Democratic party.
   ☐ b. lean toward the Republican party.
   ☐ c. be unaffected by party politics.
   ☐ d. not vote.

8. Which of the following statements is FALSE?
   ☐ a. Republicans appeal primarily to working-class voters.
   ☐ b. Voters concerned with unemployment are more likely to vote Democratic.
   ☐ c. The parties pay close attention to economic conditions when selecting their policies.
   ☐ d. Republicans worry more about inflation.

9. The coalition behind the Republican Party is most likely to be concerned with
   ☐ a. inflation.
   ☐ b. inflation and unemployment.
   ☐ c. unemployment.
   ☐ d. expanding government's role.

10. The Bureau of Labor Statistics measures the unemployment rate as the total number of adults without jobs.
☐ True
☐ False

11. Our key measure of inflation is called the
☐ a. Consumer Price Index (CPI).
☐ b. Gross National Product (GNP).
☐ c. Laffer Curve.
☐ d. National Inflation Index (NII).

12. Laissez-faire was an economic philosophy embraced by
☐ a. Herbert Hoover.
☐ b. Franklin D. Roosevelt.
☐ c. Lyndon Johnson.
☐ d. Jimmy Carter.

13. Monetarists seek to keep the money supply in line with the
☐ a. Consumer Price Index.
☐ b. gross domestic product.
☐ c. unemployment rate.
☐ d. amount of available credit.

14. According to monetarists, too much money and credit leads to
☐ a. recession.
☐ b. unemployment.
☐ c. inflation.
☐ d. a budget surplus.

15. The Board of Governors of the Federal Reserve System
☐ a. consists of 12 members.
☐ b. belong to the president's party.
☐ c. regulates the lending practices of banks.
☐ d. is formally controlled by Congress and the president.

16. The Fed attempts to affect the money supply by each of the following means EXCEPT
☐ a. determining tax rates.
☐ b. buying and selling government bonds.
☐ c. setting the federal funds rate.
☐ d. determining whether banks have more or less money to lend.

17. The financial dealings of the Federal Reserve Board directly or indirectly affect
    ☐ a. interest rates.
    ☐ b. inflation.
    ☐ c. availability of jobs.
    ☐ d. all of the above

18. The president has ultimate influence over the policies of the Federal Reserve System.
    ☐ True
    ☐ False

19. The impact of the federal budget—taxes, spending, and borrowing—on the economy describes
    ☐ a. laissez-faire policy.
    ☐ b. monetary policy.
    ☐ c. fiscal policy.
    ☐ d. economic policy.

20. Fiscal policy is almost entirely determined by
    ☐ a. Congress and the president.
    ☐ b. the Federal Reserve System.
    ☐ c. the Internal Revenue Service.
    ☐ d. the Office of Management and Budget.

21. The dominant economic philosophy most associated with the Roosevelt administration was
    ☐ a. laissez-faire.
    ☐ b. monetarism.
    ☐ c. Keynesianism.
    ☐ d. supply-side economics.

22. Which of the following statements is TRUE?
    ☐ a. Fiscal policy uses the Federal Reserve System.
    ☐ b. Supply-side economics holds that tax cuts will stimulate the economy.
    ☐ c. Conservative politicians have long favored Keynesian economic theory.
    ☐ d. The Laffer Curve shows the relationship between inflation and unemployment.

23. (bonus) Who, according to legend, wrote his economic theory on the back of a cocktail napkin?
    ☐ a. Karl Marx
    ☐ b. John Maynard Keynes
    ☐ c. Arthur Laffer
    ☐ d. Adam Smith

24.   Economists have shown that decisions to artificially influence the economy at
        election time have been made on a regular basis.
        ☐ True
        ☐ False

25.   Our capitalist system presents a restraint on controlling the economy because
        ☐ a.   the private sector dominates the economy.
        ☐ b.   big business dominates economic policymaking.
        ☐ c.   no one can predict American consumer behavior.
        ☐ d.   none of the above

26.   Emerging economies tend to favor an economic policy of
        ☐ a.   Keynesianism.
        ☐ b.   protectionism.
        ☐ c.   globalization.
        ☐ d.   laissez-faire capitalism.

27.   Which of the following statements regarding free trade is FALSE?
        ☐ a.   Both Republican and Democratic presidents have supported free trade.
        ☐ b.   The World Trade Organization was established to promote free trade.
        ☐ c.   Free trade became increasingly popular after World War II.
        ☐ d.   Trade unions tend to be the strongest supporters of free trade.

28.   (bonus) Who said, "the business of America is business"?
        ☐ a.   John Maynard Keynes
        ☐ b.   Calvin Coolidge
        ☐ c.   Herbert Hoover
        ☐ d.   Ronald Reagan

29.   At the center of the American economy has long stood the
        ☐ a.   corporation.
        ☐ b.   family farm.
        ☐ c.   consumer.
        ☐ d.   labor union.

30.   The beginning of the twenty-first century showed
        ☐ a.   a new respect for American corporations.
        ☐ b.   a sharp rise in the stock market.
        ☐ c.   an increase in corporate corruption.
        ☐ d.   a decrease in corporate concentration.

31. Since the 1980s, corporate capitalism was characterized by
    ☐ a. hard times.
    ☐ b. increased regulation.
    ☐ c. an increased number of mergers.
    ☐ d. nationalism.

32. Antitrust policy is implemented by the
    ☐ a. Justice Department.
    ☐ b. General Service Administration.
    ☐ c. Small Business Administration.
    ☐ d. Patent Office.

33. The Clinton administration filed a major antitrust suit against
    ☐ a. International Business Machines (IBM).
    ☐ b. General Motors.
    ☐ c. Microsoft.
    ☐ d. Exxon.

34. The government aids American business by
    ☐ a. collecting data on products and markets.
    ☐ b. issuing and protecting patents.
    ☐ c. providing research and development funds.
    ☐ d. all of the above

35. The first major consumer protection policy was the
    ☐ a. Food and Drug Act.
    ☐ b. Consumer Product Safety Act.
    ☐ c. Consumer Credit Protection Act.
    ☐ d. Wagner Act.

36. The agency that became a zealous defender of consumer interests in truth in advertising in the 1960s and 1970s was the
    ☐ a. Small Business Administration.
    ☐ b. Food and Drug Administration.
    ☐ c. Consumer Product Safety Commission.
    ☐ d. Federal Trade Commission.

37. Perhaps the biggest change in economic policymaking over the past century has been the virtual 180-degree turn in public policy toward
    ☐ a. consumers.
    ☐ b. business.
    ☐ c. labor unions.
    ☐ d. farmers.

38. The National Labor Relations Act
   ☐ a.   provided for a right-to-work law.
   ☐ b.   enforced "yellow dog contracts."
   ☐ c.   exempted unions from antitrust laws.
   ☐ d.   guaranteed the right of collective bargaining.

39. The Taft-Hartley Act
   ☐ a.   continued to guarantee unions the right of collective bargaining.
   ☐ b.   gave the president a means to halt major strikes.
   ☐ c.   permitted states to adopt right-to-work laws.
   ☐ d.   all of the above

40. Right-to-work laws forbid labor contracts from requiring workers to join unions to hold their jobs.
   ☐ True
   ☐ False

41. Voters rarely expect politicians to do much about the economy.
   ☐ True
   ☐ False

42. For the last two generations, U.S. policymakers have followed the near-universal advice of economists by supporting
   ☐ a.   protectionism.
   ☐ b.   free trade.
   ☐ c.   supply-side economics.
   ☐ d.   regulation.

43. Democracy regularly facilitates an economic policy that looks after general interests for long-term gain and ignores specific interests of particular groups.
   ☐ True
   ☐ False

44. In general, liberals would favor letting business and the free market create new jobs and prepare people for them.
   ☐ True
   ☐ False

45. Liberals tend to focus on the imperfections of
   ☐ a.   government.
   ☐ b.   the market.
   ☐ c.   regulatory agencies.
   ☐ d.   states.

ESSAY QUESTIONS

1. How are politics and economics related? Why do politicians and policymakers try to control the economy?

2. What are the principle instruments available to policymakers for controlling the economy? Compare monetarism, Keynesian economic theory, and supply-side economics.

3. What obstacles does the government face in attempting to control the domestic and international economy?

4. What policies has government used to try to control American business? Has the government been successful?

5. When and why did the consumer movement emerge? What are some of the major developments in consumer policy?

6. How has government policy toward labor changed in the last century? What public policies have emerged to protect workers?

7. How closely does economic policymaking in the United States conform to democratic theory?

CHAPTER 18

SOCIAL WELFARE POLICYMAKING

CHAPTER OUTLINE

I. What is Social Policy and Why is it so Controversial? (pp. 566-568)
   A. **Social welfare policies** refer to the programs through which government provides support and assistance to specific groups of people.
   B. **Entitlement programs** consist of government benefits that certain qualified individuals are entitled to by law, regardless of need.
   C. **Means-tested programs** are benefits provided only to people with specific needs.

II. Income, Poverty, and Public Policy (pp. 568-574)
   A. Who's Getting What?
      1. **Income distribution** describes the share of national income earned by various groups in the United States.
      2. **Income** is the amount of money collected between any two points in time.
      3. **Wealth** is the value of one's assets.
   B. Who's Poor in America?
      1. The **poverty line** takes into account what a family would need to spend to maintain an "austere" standard of living.
      2. Poverty may be more extensive than the poverty line suggests.
      3. Because of the high incidence of poverty among unmarried mothers and their children, experts on poverty often describe the problem today as the **feminization of poverty**.
   C. What Part Does Government Play?
      1. Taxation
         a. A **progressive tax** takes a bigger bite from the incomes of the rich than the poor.
         b. A **proportional tax** takes the same percentage from everyone.
         c. A **regressive tax** takes a higher percentage from the lower income levels than from the rich.
         d. Through the **Earned Income Tax Credit (EITC)**, the poorest of the poor receive a check from Washington instead of sending one.
      2. Government Expenditures
         a. **Transfer payments** transfer money from the general treasury to those in specific need.
         b. Social Security and Medicare are the most costly social welfare programs.

III. Helping the Poor? Social Policy and Poverty (pp. 574-578)
    A.   "Welfare" as We Knew It
          1.   The **Social Security Act of 1935** brought together scattered, uneven state programs under a single federal umbrella.
          2.   President Johnson's Great Society expanded welfare programs.
          3.   President Reagan limited social welfare spending.
    B.   Ending Welfare as We Knew It: The Welfare Reforms of 1996
          1.   The **Personal Responsibility and Work Opportunity Reconciliation Act (PRWORA)** gave each state a fixed amount of money, required welfare recipients to work, and placed a time limit on welfare.
          2.   **Temporary Assistance to Needy Families (TANF)** replaced AFDC as the means-tested aid to the poor.

IV. Living on Borrowed Time: Social Security (pp. 578-582)
    A.   The New Deal, the Elderly, and the Growth of Social Security
          1.   Social Security is the most expensive public policy in the United States.
          2.   Both employee and employer contributions are paid into the **Social Security Trust Fund**.
          3.   Currently, the Trust Fund receives more money than it pays out, but this will soon change.
    B.   How George W. Bush Tried and Failed to Reform Social Security
          1.   Bush proposed diverting a small portion of Social Security contributions to private retirement funds.
          2.   Democrats argued privatization would hasten the bankruptcy of Social Security.
          3.   Bush lost control of domestic policy due to Iraq, immigration politics, and weak showing in the polls.
    C.   Social Welfare Policy Elsewhere (pp. 582-584)
          1.   Most industrial nations are more generous with social policy benefits than the United States.
          2.   European nations tend to support greater governmental responsibility for poverty.
          3.   Europeans pay high taxes for social welfare policies.

VI. Understanding Social Welfare Policy (pp. 584-585)
    A.   Social Welfare Policy and the Scope of Government
    B.   Democracy and Social Welfare

VII. Summary (p. 585)

LEARNING OBJECTIVES

After studying Chapter 18, you should be able to:

1. Understand the debate over social welfare policy in the United States and why it is so controversial.

2. Discuss the nature of wealth and poverty and how public policy affects income in the United States.

3. Explain the evolution of social welfare programs in the United States.

4. Understand the debate concerning the future of social welfare policy.

5. Explain how social welfare policy in other countries differs from the United States.

6. Understand the place for social welfare policies in a democracy and how they contribute to the scope of government.

The following exercises will help you meet these objectives:

Objective 1: Understand the debate over social welfare policy in the United States.

1. Define "social welfare policies."

2. What is the difference between entitlement programs and means-tested programs?

Entitlement Programs:

Means-Tested Programs:

Objective 2: Discuss the nature of wealth and poverty and how public policy affects income in the United States.

1. What is the difference between income and wealth?

Income:

Wealth:

2.   How does the U.S. Bureau of the Census define poverty?

3.   What are the three types of taxes and how can each affect citizens' incomes?

      1.

      2.

      3.

4.   What is meant by a transfer payment? Give an example.

5.   Make a list of three entitlement programs and three means-tested programs.

Entitlement Programs	Means-Tested Programs

Objective 3:   Explain the evolution of social welfare programs in the United States.

    1.   Complete the following table by briefly summarizing the major emphasis of social welfare and listing a major social welfare act during the New Deal (Roosevelt), Great Society (Johnson), Reagan and Clinton eras.

Era	Social Welfare Emphasis	Social Welfare Act/Program
New Deal		
Great Society		
Reagan Years		
Clinton Years		

2.   List the three major provisions of the Personal Responsibility and Work Opportunity Reconciliation Act (PRWORA).

        1.

        2.

        3.

Objective 4: Understand the debate concerning the future of social welfare policy.

    1.   Briefly explain the major problem facing the Social Security program today.

    2.   What are the major arguments for and against the privatization of Social Security?

Objective 5: Explain how social welfare policy in other countries differs from the United States.

1. List three ways in which social welfare in the United States differs from most western European countries.

    1.

    2.

    3.

Objective 6: Understand the place for social welfare policies in a democracy and how they contribute to the scope of government.

1. In what ways has social welfare policy increased the scope of government?

2. What is the difference between the poor and the elderly in terms of their ability to influence social welfare policy?

    Poor:

    Elderly:

KEY TERMS

Identify and describe:

social welfare policies

entitlement programs

means-tested programs

income distribution

income

wealth

poverty line

feminization of poverty

progressive tax

proportional tax

regressive tax

Earned Income Tax Credit

transfer payments

Social Security Act of 1935

Personal Responsibility and Work Opportunity Reconciliation Act

Temporary Assistance to Needy Families

Social Security Trust Fund

Compare and contrast:

social welfare policies and transfer payments

entitlement programs and means-tested programs

income and wealth

progressive tax, proportional tax, and regressive tax

Personal Responsibility and Work Opportunity Reconciliation Act and Temporary Assistance for Needy Families

Name that term:

1. The share of national income earned by various groups in the United States.

    _____

2. A measure that takes into account what a family would need to spend to maintain an "austere" standard of living.

    _____

3. The increasing concentration of poverty among women.

    _____

4. An example is when the rich pay five percent of their income in taxes while the poor pay 50 percent of theirs.

    _____

5. A negative income tax.

    _____

6. Benefits that are paid either in cash or in kind.

    _____

7. This act created an entitlement program for the aged and a national program to assist the poor.

    _____

8. The new name for public assistance to needy families.

    _____

9. Both employee and employer contributions are paid into this.

    _____

USING YOUR UNDERSTANDING

1.   Look for various ways in which income is distributed in the United States. For example, you may want to find out how income differs among various regions, states, cities, age groups, races, and genders. Illustrate differences between groups using bar or pie charts. You may also want to examine how income has changed over time in the categories you use. Try to explain why incomes are higher for one group and not another. Identify public policies, such as taxes, that affect the incomes of the different groups.

2.   Develop a comparison of a social welfare policy in the United States with that of another western democracy. For example, Medicare and Medicaid could be compared with the National Health Service in Great Britain. Briefly describe the history of each policy. Examine the issues or controversies associated with the policy today. Find out how much the policy costs and what benefits are bestowed, in their entirety and on a per capita basis. Find out how the policy is paid for through taxes. Who are the primary recipients of the benefits? Consider whether one system has any advantages over the other.

REVIEW QUESTIONS

Check ☑ the correct answer:

1.   Benefits provided by law regardless of need are called
   ☐ a.   public assistance programs.
   ☐ b.   entitlements.
   ☐ c.   poverty programs.
   ☐ d.   means-tested programs.

2.   Government programs available only to persons below a poverty line are called
   ☐ a.   social welfare policies.
   ☐ b.   entitlement programs.
   ☐ c.   means-tested programs.
   ☐ d.   income distribution policies.

3.   Americans have the highest per capita income in the world.
   ☐ True
   ☐ False

4.   (bonus) Who responded to the remark that "The rich are different from you and me" with "Yes, they have more money"?
   ☐ a.   Ernest Hemingway
   ☐ b.   F. Scott Fitzgerald
   ☐ c.   Thomas B. Edsall
   ☐ d.   Dan Quayle

5.   The idea that the "rich get richer and the poor get poorer" was particularly applicable during the
   ☐ a.   1950s.
   ☐ b.   1960s.
   ☐ c.   1970s.
   ☐ d.   1980s.

6.   Which of the following is NOT considered wealth?
   ☐ a.   stocks and bonds
   ☐ b.   cars and houses
   ☐ c.   bank deposits
   ☐ d.   the amount earned between two points in time

7.   The percentage of wealth possessed by the top one percent of wealth-holders in the United States is about
   ☐ a.   one percent.
   ☐ b.   one-third.
   ☐ c.   one-quarter.
   ☐ d.   one-half.

8.   A study of overall incomes of Americans during their lifetimes showed that
   ☐ a.   the poverty line is an accurate portrayal of poverty in America.
   ☐ b.   about 50% of all working Americans experienced at least a year of poverty during their lifetimes.
   ☐ c.   poverty is not as extensive as the poverty line suggests.
   ☐ d.   a culture of poverty exists in the United States.

9.   Poverty is particularly common among
   ☐ a.   African Americans.
   ☐ b.   Hispanics.
   ☐ c.   unmarried women.
   ☐ d.   all of the above

10.   Poverty is particularly a problem among
   ☐ a.   unmarried women and children.
   ☐ b.   the elderly.
   ☐ c.   single men.
   ☐ d.   urban dwellers.

11. Government can directly affect people's income through
    ☐ a.   taxation.
    ☐ b.   expenditure policies.
    ☐ c.   regulation.
    ☐ d.   both a. and b.

12. (bonus) Who said, "Nothing is certain in life but death and taxes"?
    ☐ a.   George Bush
    ☐ b.   Abraham Lincoln
    ☐ c.   Benjamin Franklin
    ☐ d.   the Supreme Court

13. Taxes that take a bigger share of a rich family's income than a poor family's income are known as
    ☐ a.   progressive taxes.
    ☐ b.   proportional taxes.
    ☐ c.   regressive taxes.
    ☐ d.   none of the above

14. Many taxes are purposively regressive.
    ☐ True
    ☐ False

15. State sales taxes tend to be
    ☐ a.   progressive.
    ☐ b.   proportional.
    ☐ c.   regressive.
    ☐ d.   neutral.

16. In general, federal taxes are
    ☐ a.   progressive.
    ☐ b.   proportional.
    ☐ c.   regressive.
    ☐ d.   none of the above

17. Earned Income Tax Credit benefits
    ☐ a.   the wealthiest individuals who overpay taxes.
    ☐ b.   the poorest of the poor.
    ☐ c.   college students.
    ☐ d.   the working poor.

18. Transfer payments can be either cash or in-kind payments.
    ☐ True
    ☐ False

19. An example of an in-kind transfer payment is
☐ a. a Social Security check.
☐ b. a federal pension.
☐ c. unemployment compensation.
☐ d. food stamps.

20. Social welfare programs were far more extensive during the early history of the United States than they were in Great Britain.
☐ True
☐ False

21. The act that brought together scattered, uneven state social welfare programs under a single federal umbrella is called the
☐ a. Medicare Act.
☐ b. Medicaid Act.
☐ c. Social Security Act.
☐ d. Omnibus Budget Reconciliation Act.

23. Lyndon Johnson's poverty programs were known as
☐ a. the New Deal.
☐ b. the War on Poverty.
☐ c. the New Frontier.
☐ d. a More Kind and Gentle America.

23. As one major way to cut government spending, Ronald Reagan chose to target
☐ a. entitlements.
☐ b. poverty programs.
☐ c. military spending.
☐ d. all of the above

24. President Reagan
☐ a. cut welfare benefits.
☐ b. lowered the number of Americans on welfare rolls.
☐ c. cut benefits for many beneficiaries.
☐ d. all of the above

25. A study by Martin Gilens showed that Americans tend to see welfare recipients as overwhelmingly
☐ a. elderly.
☐ b. female.
☐ c. African American.
☐ d. southern.

26. The 1996 Welfare Reform Bill
   ☐ a. gave each state a fixed amount of money to run its own welfare programs.
   ☐ b. required people on welfare to find work within two years or lose all their benefits.
   ☐ c. placed a lifetime maximum of five years on welfare.
   ☐ d. all of the above

27. The 1996 Welfare Reform Bill failed to reduce the number of people on welfare.
   ☐ True
   ☐ False

28. George W. Bush's emphasis on welfare reform has been to
   ☐ a. increase government expenditures.
   ☐ b. promote education and training among the poor.
   ☐ c. spend more on in-kind transfers.
   ☐ d. encourage people to marry.

29. Social Security is the most expensive public policy in the United States.
   ☐ True
   ☐ False

30. The Social Security Trust Fund is funded by
   ☐ a. employee contributions.
   ☐ b. employer contributions.
   ☐ c. state taxes.
   ☐ d. both a. and b.

31. At some point in the near future, Social Security payouts will exceed income.
   ☐ True
   ☐ False

32. George W. Bush and Republican solutions to the Social Security problem tend to emphasize
   ☐ a. higher taxes.
   ☐ b. privatization.
   ☐ c. abolishing Social Security.
   ☐ d. reorganization.

33. The scope of social benefits in the United States is far less than in most Western democracies.
   ☐ True
   ☐ False

34. France provides
☐ a. far more social welfare policies than the U.S.
☐ b. far fewer social welfare policies than the U.S.
☐ c. about the same social welfare policies as the U.S.
☐ d. no social welfare policy benefits.

35. Compared to Americans, Europeans
☐ a. tend to support greater governmental responsibility for social welfare problems.
☐ b. have more positive attitudes toward government.
☐ c. pay higher taxes to support social welfare programs.
☐ d. all of the above

36. The growth of government has been driven by the growth of social welfare policies.
☐ True
☐ False

37. The elderly are poorly organized and lack political and economic capital to wield much influence in social welfare policies.
☐ True
☐ False

38. It is difficult for the poor to influence political decisions because they
☐ a. vote less frequently.
☐ b. lack strong, focused organizations.
☐ c. lack money.
☐ d. all of the above

ESSAY QUESTIONS

1. Explain the nature of the distribution of income and wealth in the United States. What are the characteristics of poverty and poor people in the United States?

2. How does public policy affect the distribution of income in the United States?

3. What are the different types of social welfare programs in the United States and how do they compare to social welfare programs in other countries?

4. How have social welfare programs evolved in the United States? In particular, compare the New Deal legislation and Great Society legislation with President Reagan's policies and welfare reforms of 1996.

5.   What are the major problems facing social welfare programs today? Speculate on the future of social welfare in the United States.

6.   Describe the debate concerning the causes of poverty and whether social welfare policies really work in our democracy. Take sides on the debate and defend your position.

CHAPTER 19

POLICYMAKING FOR HEALTH CARE AND THE ENVIRONMENT

CHAPTER OUTLINE

I.   Health Care Policy (pp. 590-600)
      A.   The Health of Americans
      B.   The Cost of Health Care
      C.   Uneven Coverage, Uneven Care
           1.   Health Insurance
           2.   Managed Care **Health Maintenance Organizations (HMO)** provide all or most of a person's health care for a yearly fee.
      D.   The Role of Government in Health Care
           1.   Much medical research is financed through the National Institutes of Health (NIH).
           2.   **National health insurance** is a proposal for a compulsory insurance program to finance all Americans' medical care.
           3.   **Medicare** is part of the Social Security system and covers more than 38 million people.
           4.   **Medicaid** is a program designed to provide health care for the poor.
      E.   Policymaking for Health Care
           1.   The Politics of Health Care
                a.   Many interests are involved in health care policies (elderly, workers, business, and insurance companies).
           2.   Two Presidents, Two Health Care Plans
           3.   The Health Policy Issues Ahead

II.   Environmental Policy (pp. 600-605)
      A.   Introduction
      B.   Environmental Policies in America
           1.   The **Environmental Protection Agency (EPA)** is the nation's largest federal regulatory agency.
           2.   Clean Air: The **Clean Air Act of 1970** charges the Department of Transportation with the responsibility of reducing automobile emissions.
           3.   Clean Water: The **Water Pollution Control Act of 1972** is designed to control pollution in the nation's lakes and rivers.
           4.   Wilderness Preservation.
           5.   Endangered Species: The **Endangered Species Act of 1973** created an endangered species protection program in the U.S. Fish and Wildlife Service.

6.   Toxic Wastes: The **Superfund** was created to clean up toxic wastes by taxing chemical products.

III.   Energy Policy (pp. 605-609)
        A.   Energy Sources and Energy Politics (coal, oil, nuclear)
        B.   The Global Warming Gridlock

IV.   Groups, Energy and Environment (pp. 609-610)

V.   Understanding Health Care and Environmental Policy (pp. 610-611)
        A.   Democracy, Health Care, and Environmental Policy
        B.   The Scope of Government and Health Care and Environmental Policy

VI.   Summary (pp. 611-612)

LEARNING OBJECTIVES

After studying Chapter 19, you should be able to:

1.   Explain the nature of health care and health care policy in the United States.

2.   Discuss the issues surrounding the environment and the programs and policies to deal with them.

3.   Understand the issues surrounding energy policy and global warming.

4.   Understand the relationship between health and environmental policy and democracy and the scope of government.

The following exercises will help you meet these objectives:

Objective 1: Explain the nature of health care and health care policy in the United States.

1.   How do life expectancy and infant mortality rates in the United States compare with other nations?

     Life Expectancy:

     Infant Mortality:

2.   What is meant by "defensive medicine"?

3.   In what ways is access to health insurance unequal in the United States?

4.   What are some of the advantages and disadvantages of managed care?

5.   What is the difference between Medicare and Medicaid?

Medicare:

Medicaid:

6.   List and explain the involvement of three interest groups in health care policy.

1.

2.

3.

7.   How did President George W. Bush's health care reform proposals differ from President Clintons?

8. Explain the major issues involved in the controversy over stem cell research.

Objective 2: Discuss the issues surrounding the environment and the programs and policies to deal with them.

1. What is the mission of the Environmental Protection Agency?

2. List the main provisions of the Clean Air Act of 1970, the Water Pollution Control Act of 1972, the Endangered Species Act of 1973, and the Superfund.

Clean Air Act:

Water Pollution Control Act:

Endangered Species Act:

Superfund:

Objective 3: Understand the issues surrounding energy policy and global warming.

1. What are the four most important sources of energy in the United States?

1.

2.

3.

4.

2.	What are the main problems for each of the following energy sources?

Coal:

Petroleum:

Nuclear:

3.	What are the main arguments against the 1997 treaty on global warming?

4.	What has been the primary argument of opponents of strict environmental laws?

Objective 4: Understand the relationship between health and environmental policy and democracy and the scope of government.

1.	Why are individual citizens rarely involved in policymaking for technological issues?

2.	How have technological issues affected the scope of government?

KEY TERMS

Identify and describe:

health maintenance organizations (HMOs)

national health insurance

Medicare

Medicaid

Environmental Protection Agency (EPA)

Clean Air Act of 1970

Water Pollution Control Act of 1972

Endangered Species Act of 1973

Superfund

Compare and contrast:

health maintenance organizations and National health insurance

national health insurance and Medicare

Medicare and Medicaid

Name that term:

1. A popular managed care system designed to keep health care costs down.

   _____

2. Our largest federal regulatory agency.

   _____

3. The law that requires the government to actively protect each of hundreds of species listed as endangered.

   _____

4. It is funded through taxes on chemical products.

   _____

USING YOUR UNDERSTANDING

1. Drawing from newspapers, newsmagazines, or the Internet, find some current examples of cases where public policy may be affected in the areas of health, energy, and/or the environment. High-tech medicine and medical research may evoke ethical, policy, or legal questions concerning life itself. The need for cheap and abundant energy may pose a threat to the environment. Make a list of the issues involved in each case and how it was resolved. Identify the tradeoffs involved and who would benefit and suffer from the different policy options available. Who are the individuals and groups, in and out of government, most involved in the issue and how much influence do they have on policy decisions? Consider how your examples reflect the current agenda in each policy area.

2. Every project utilizing federal funds is required to submit to the government an environmental impact statement. Analyze an environmental impact statement and report on its contents. It may be particularly useful to examine an EIS on an energy project, such as a power plant. Pay particular attention to the numerous types of environmental impacts predicted by the statement. Compare the amount of attention paid to physiographic, biological, social, and economic impacts, and

evaluate the sophistication of the analysis. Analyze the comment section of the statement and determine who commented on the proposal, what they said, and whether their views were incorporated into the body of the report. Identify the groups in favor of the project and those who opposed it. Find out whether the proposed project or policy was actually implemented.

REVIEW QUESTIONS

Check ☑ the correct answer:

1. Infant mortality rates in the United States are the lowest in the world.
   ☐ True
   ☐ False

2. What percentage of the gross national product goes to the health industry?
   ☐ a. one-seventh
   ☐ b. one-fifth
   ☐ c. one-third
   ☐ d. one-half

3. (bonus) Which of the following countries has the highest life expectancy rate?
   ☐ a. Canada
   ☐ b. United States
   ☐ c. Japan
   ☐ d. Britain

4. Health care costs are increasing rapidly in the United States because
   ☐ a. American medicine is high-tech medicine.
   ☐ b. health care providers are insulated from competing with each other to offer less expensive care.
   ☐ c. insurance companies pay for most health care expenses.
   ☐ d. all of the above

5. "Defensive medicine" refers to
   ☐ a. the increase in the use of prescription drugs.
   ☐ b. the emphasis on diet and environment to prevent disease.
   ☐ c. doctors ordering extra tests to ensure that they are not sued.
   ☐ d. public policies designed to alleviate crime and poverty.

6. Access to medical care in the United States is not universal.
   ☐ True
   ☐ False

7.   Which of the following groups is most likely to have good access to medical care in the United States?
   ☐ a.   African Americans
   ☐ b.   employed persons
   ☐ c.   Hispanics
   ☐ d.   uninsured persons

8.   People without health insurance face a 25 percent higher risk of dying than those with insurance.
   ☐ True
   ☐ False

9.   Health maintenance organizations
   ☐ a.   restrict physician lists for the provision of care.
   ☐ b.   negotiate with physician groups and hospitals on fees and costs.
   ☐ c.   try to monitor most aspects of care to control unnecessary use.
   ☐ d.   all of the above

10.   What percentage of America's total health bill is paid for by government sources?
   ☐ a.   16 percent
   ☐ b.   26 percent
   ☐ c.   46 percent
   ☐ d.   66 percent

11.   The National Institutes of Health
   ☐ a.   is a government-run hospital in Washington, D.C. for federal employees.
   ☐ b.   finances much of the medical research in the United States.
   ☐ c.   is the name of the federally funded national health insurance program.
   ☐ d.   none of the above

12.   National health insurance
   ☐ a.   is supported by the American Medical Association.
   ☐ b.   was first proposed in the 1980s.
   ☐ c.   would provide compulsory insurance for all Americans.
   ☐ d.   is a voluntary system of health care.

13.   Medicare is
   ☐ a.   the name of America's national health insurance.
   ☐ b.   entirely voluntary.
   ☐ c.   entirely compulsory.
   ☐ d.   part of the Social Security system.

14. Medicaid provides health care assistance for
    ☐ a. poor Americans.
    ☐ b. workers.
    ☐ c. elderly people.
    ☐ d. states.

15. One reason for uneven government and private health care policies involves the representation of interests.
    ☐ True
    ☐ False

16. Which of the following groups would be LEAST likely to support any kind of national health insurance?
    ☐ a. the elderly
    ☐ b. workers in low-paying service jobs
    ☐ c. business groups
    ☐ d. insurance companies

17. President Clinton's health care reform plan failed because
    ☐ a. it was considered too bureaucratic and complicated.
    ☐ b. it was the target of an aggressive advertising campaign mounted by opponents.
    ☐ c. it was characterized as expensive and experimental.
    ☐ d. all of the above

18. The centerpiece of the George W. Bush plan for American health care has been
    ☐ a. the privatization of Medicare.
    ☐ b. national health insurance.
    ☐ c. massive drug benefits to older Americans.
    ☐ d. federal support of stem cell research.

19. Indications are that medical care is likely to get cheaper in the decades ahead.
    ☐ True
    ☐ False

20. Debate over American health care policy tends to focus on
    ☐ a. cost containment.
    ☐ b. access to medical care.
    ☐ c. moral issues.
    ☐ d. all of the above.

21. Medical care in the United States is often rationed.
    ☐ True
    ☐ False

22. Americans tend to favor doing something about the environment but often oppose specific programs to protect the environment.
☐ True
☐ False

23. The Environmental Protection Agency is the largest federal regulatory agency.
☐ True
☐ False

24. Responsibility for implementing the Clean Air Act of 1970 rests with
☐ a.   the Environmental Protection Agency.
☐ b.   the Department of Transportation.
☐ c.   Congress.
☐ d.   the president.

25. The Clean Air Act Amendments of 1990
☐ a.   relaxed air pollution requirements.
☐ b.   established strict ozone controls to curb global warming.
☐ c.   established the nondegredation standard.
☐ d.   established the policy of emissions trading.

26. The Water pollution Control Act of 1972 resulted in all of the following EXCEPT
☐ a.   an increase in the number of waterfowl in U.S. waters.
☐ b.   safer waters for fishing.
☐ c.   control of runoff pollution.
☐ d.   point source regulation of water.

27. Ever since 1916, the United States has been a world leader in wilderness preservation.
☐ True
☐ False

28. What percent of the United States is designated as wilderness?
☐ a.   4 percent
☐ b.   14 percent
☐ c.   24 percent
☐ d.   40 percent

29. The Endangered Species Act
☐ a.   makes exceptions for economic effects on surrounding regions.
☐ b.   requires the government to protect hundreds of species.
☐ c.   is administered by the Environmental Protection Agency.
☐ d.   was strongly supported by President Reagan.

30. Which of the following statements about the Superfund law is FALSE?
   □ a.   A single party can be liable for cleaning up an entire site.
   □ b.   The Superfund includes retroactive liability.
   □ c.   The Superfund has virtually eliminated haphazard dumping of toxic waste.
   □ d.   The Superfund has successfully cleaned up most toxic waste sites.

31. Superfund was created to
   □ a.   clean up toxic waste sites.
   □ b.   fund the Environmental Protection Agency.
   □ c.   help agencies file environmental impact statements.
   □ d.   provide money for environmental research.

32. America's most abundant, but dirtiest, fuel is
   □ a.   coal.
   □ b.   oil.
   □ c.   natural gas.
   □ d.   hydroelectric power.

33. Nonrenewable resources are not replaced by nature once consumed.
   □ True
   □ False

34. The nuclear power industry was devastated because of
   □ a.   accidents.
   □ b.   cost overruns.
   □ c.   the environmental movement.
   □ d.   all of the above

35. The United States has not initiated any new nuclear power plants since 1978.
   □ True
   □ False

36. Opponents of the 1997 global warming treaty argue that
   □ a.   it is unfair that the developed nations should bear the burden of cutting greenhouse emissions.
   □ b.   cutting greenhouse emissions will cost too much.
   □ c.   it will increase energy costs.
   □ d.   all of the above

37. Environmental concerns often conflict with concerns about
   □ a.   foreign trade.
   □ b.   economic growth.
   □ c.   jobs.
   □ d.   all of the above

359

38. Environmental interest groups
☐ a. have been particularly effective during the George W. Bush administration.
☐ b. grew rapidly in the 1960s and 1970s.
☐ c. have virtually no opposition.
☐ d. all of the above

39. (bonus) "NIMBY" refers to
☐ a. National Industrial, Mining, and Business Year.
☐ b. National Innovative Movement for Better Byproducts.
☐ c. Not In My Back Yard.
☐ d. New International Management of Business Youth.

40. Policymaking for technological issues seems to rely heavily on
☐ a. individual citizens.
☐ b. political parties.
☐ c. group representation.
☐ d. presidential leadership.

41. Most Americans believe that high-technology issues should be a private matter and not involve government interference.
☐ True
☐ False

ESSAY QUESTIONS

1. Describe the nature of American health. How does the health of the American public compare with that of other nations?

2. How has the American government been involved in the public's health? What factors tend to influence policymaking for health care?

3. Describe and evaluate American environmental policy. What are the biggest obstacles to a clean environment?

4. Describe the American energy profile. What resources do we have? What resources do we use? What political and policy issues are involved with each energy resource?

5. How do democracies handle technological issues? What is the impact of technological issues on the scope of American government?

CHAPTER 20

NATIONAL SECURITY POLICYMAKING

CHAPTER OUTLINE

I.   American Foreign Policy: Instruments, Actors, and Policymakers (pp. 616-623)
- A. **Foreign policy** involves making choices about relations with the rest of the world.
- B. Instruments of Foreign Policy
  1. Military
  2. Economic
  3. Diplomacy
- C. Actors on the World Stage
  1. International organizations like the **United Nations (UN)** play an increasingly important role on the world stage.
  2. Regional organizations have proliferated in the post-World War II era.
     - a. The **North Atlantic Treaty Organization (NATO)** is a military alliance between the United States, Canada, and most of Western Europe.
     - b. The **European Union (EU)** is an economic alliance of the major western European nations.
  3. Multinational corporations are sometimes more powerful than the governments under which they operate.
  4. Nongovernmental organizations are important actors on the global stage.
  5. Individuals are also actors on the global stage.
- D. The Policymakers
  1. The President
  2. The Diplomats
     - a. The **secretary of state** has traditionally been the key advisor to the president on foreign policy matters.
     - b. Some recent presidents have established more personal systems for receiving foreign policy advice.
  3. The National Security Establishment
     - a. The **secretary of defense** is the president's main civilian advisor on national defense matters.
     - b. The commanding officers of each of the services, plus a chair, constitute the **Joint Chiefs of Staff.**
     - c. The National Security Council (NSC) was formed to coordinate foreign and military policies.
     - d. The **Central Intelligence Agency (CIA)** coordinates American information and data-gathering intelligence activities abroad.

4.   Congress

II.   American Foreign Policy: An Overview (pp. 624-630)
- A.   **Isolationism** was the foreign policy course followed throughout most of American history.
- B.   The Cold War
  1. Containment Abroad and Anticommunism at Home
     - a. The **containment doctrine** called for the United States to isolate the Soviet Union, contain its advances, and resist its encroachments.
     - b. At the height of the **Cold War**, the United States and the Soviet Union were often on the brink of war.
     - c. **McCarthyism** assumed that international communism was conspiratorial and infiltrating American institutions.
  2. The Swelling of the Pentagon
     - a. The military industrial complex refers to the interests shared by the armed services and defense contractors.
     - b. In the 1950s, the Soviet Union and the United States engaged in an **arms race.**
  3. The Vietnam War
- C.   The Era of Détente
  1. **Détente** represented a slow transformation from conflict thinking to cooperative thinking in foreign policy strategy.
  2. One major initiative emerging from détente was the Strategic Arms Limitation Talks (SALT).
- D.   The Reagan Rearmament
  1. President Reagan proposed the largest peacetime defense spending increase in American history.
  2. The **Strategic Defense Initiative (SDI)** was a plan for defense against missiles through a global umbrella in space.
- E.   The Final Thaw in the Cold War

III.   The War on Terrorism (pp. 631-633)
- A.   Introduction
- B.   Afghanistan and Iraq

IV.   The Politics of Defense Policy (pp. 633-638)
- A.   Defense Spending
- B.   Personnel
- C.   Weapons
- D.   Reforming Defense Policy

V.   The New Global Agenda (pp. 638-649)
- A.   The Changing Role of Military Power
  1. Humanitarian Interventions
  2. Economic Sanctions

B. Nuclear Proliferation
C. The International Economy
   3.   Today's international economy is characterized by **interdependency.**
   4.   International Trade
      a.   The **tariff** is a special tax added to the cost of imported goods.
      b.   The North American Free Trade Agreement would eliminate most tariffs among North American countries.
      c.   The General Agreement on Tariffs and Trade is the mechanism by which most of the world's nations negotiate trade agreements.
   5.   Balance of Trade
      a.   **Balance of trade** is the ratio of what a country pays for imports to what it earns from exports.
      b.   Year after year, the American balance of trade has been negative.
   6.   Energy **(Organization of Petroleum Exporting Countries, OPEC)**
   7.   Foreign Aid

VI. Understanding National Security Policymaking (pp. 649-651)
   A.   National Security Policymaking and Democracy
   B.   National Security Policymaking and the Scope of Government

VII. Summary (p. 651)

LEARNING OBJECTIVES

After studying Chapter 20, you should be able to:

1. Identify the many actors involved in making and shaping American foreign policy and discuss the roles they play.

2. Describe how American foreign policy has changed since the end of World War II.

3. Discuss the politics of defense policy.

4. Examine the new issues on the global agenda, particularly those concerning the world economy, energy, and environment.

5. Understand the role of foreign and defense policymaking in a democracy and how foreign and defense policy affects the scope of government.

The following exercises will help you meet these goals:

Objective 1: Identify the many actors involved in making and shaping American foreign policy and discuss the roles they play.

1.   What are the three types of tools that foreign policies ultimately depend on?

    1.

    2.

    3.

2.   List five types of actors on the world scene and give an example of each.

    1.

    2.

    3.

    4.

    5.

3.   List some of the primary foreign policy functions of the president.

4.   What is the purpose of the National Security Council?

5. Complete the following table on the major national security agencies. In the last column, comment on the agency's inclinations toward involvement in foreign ventures, giving an example when relevant.

Agency	Composition	Purpose	Comments
Joint Chiefs of Staff			
National Security Council			
Central Intelligence Agency			

Objective 2: Describe how American foreign policy has changed since the end of World War II.

1. Complete the following timeline on the Cold War by indicating the event or events that occurred during the year or years listed.

1946:

1947:

1948-1949:

1949:

1950-1953:

1954:

1964:

1972:

1973:
1975:

1979:

1983:

1989:

1992:

2.   What types of foreign policies were followed during the era of détente?

3.   What was the purpose of the Strategic Defense Initiative (SDI)?

4.   In what ways has American national security policy changed since the increasing threat posed by terrorist groups and hostile states supporting them?

5.   According to George W. Bush, which states belong to the "axis of evil?"

      1.

      2.

      3.

Objective 3: Discuss the politics of defense policy.

1.   What is meant by the "peace dividend"?

2.   What is the triad of nuclear weapons that the United States relies on for national defense?

      1.
      2.

3.

3. What were the main provisions of the Intermediate-range Nuclear Forces Treaty and the Strategic Arms Reduction Treaty?

Objective 4: Examine the new issues on the global agenda, particularly those concerning the world economy, energy, and environment.

1. Why isn't military power as important in foreign policy as it used to be?

2. Define "humanitarian interventions" and give three examples.

3. Define the term "interdependency" as it relates to the international economy.

4. What are the four major provisions of the General Agreement on Tariffs and Trade?

    1.

    2.

    3.

    4.

5.   List three consequences of a balance of trade deficit.

       1.

       2.

       3.

6.   What is the Organization of Petroleum Exporting Countries and why is it an important international actor?

7.   List four different types or forms of foreign aid.

       1.

       2.

       3.

       4.

Objective 5: Understand the role of foreign and defense policymaking in a democracy and how foreign and defense policy affects the scope of government.

1.   How might one argue that American foreign policymaking is a democratic process?

2.   How has foreign and defense policymaking contributed to the scope of government?

KEY TERMS

Identify and describe:

foreign policy

United Nations (UN)

North Atlantic Treaty Organization (NATO)

European Union (EU)

secretary of state

secretary of defense

Joint Chiefs of Staff

Central Intelligence Agency (CIA)

isolationism

containment doctrine

Cold War

McCarthyism

arms race

détente

Strategic Defense Initiative (SDI)

interdependency

tariff

balance of trade

Organization of Petroleum Exporting Countries (OPEC)

Compare and contrast:

foreign policy and isolationism

United Nations (UN), North Atlantic Treaty Organization (NATO), and European Union (EU)

secretary of state and secretary of defense

isolationism and interdependency

containment doctrine and McCarthyism

Cold War and détente

Organization of Petroleum Exporting Countries (OPEC) and interdependency

tariff and balance of trade

Name that term:

1. A regional organization involving the U.S. and most of Western Europe.

   _____

2. A major regional organization based on an economic alliance.

   _____

3. The commanding officers of each of the armed services.

   _____

4. They have often been involved in other nations' internal affairs.

   _____

5. This eventually resulted in a situation of mutual assured destruction.

   _____

6.   A change from conflict to cooperative thinking in foreign policy.

_____

7.   Also known as "Star Wars."

_____

USING YOUR UNDERSTANDING

1.   Organize your colleagues to try to simulate a military or foreign policy decision-making situation. The situation may be a political or economic crisis, such as a terrorist attack, an oil embargo, or some other crisis. Alternatively, it may be an ongoing policy problem, such as global inequalities in human rights, inequalities in the distribution of the world's wealth, or the continued over-consumption of the world commons and pollution of the global environment. Different students should represent each of the key international actors concerned with the situation and the policymaking actors responsible for addressing it. Representatives from nations other than the United States may also be present. Try to identify the major issues involved in the situation and the tradeoffs involved; keeping in mind that each of the actors on the stage has a different interest to protect. Collectively, try to come to agreement on a United States foreign policy that would contribute to a resolution of the situation.

2.   Given the end of the Cold War, international relations and the global agenda are changing dramatically. Find examples, using newspapers, newsmagazines, and/or the Internet that illustrate the changing global agenda. Include examples that stem from the decline of communism as well as the more traditional concerns about defense and military spending and the emerging agenda issues centering on terrorism, the economy, equality, energy, and environment. Identify those issues that seem to take a prominent position on the contemporary global agenda. At the same time, identify those issues that you see as important global concerns but that are not being given much attention. Assess the global agenda in terms of the relative importance of defense issues as compared to other policy issues and whether or not the agenda seems to be changing.

REVIEW QUESTIONS

Check ☑ the correct answer:

1.   The end of the Cold War has lessened the importance of national security policy.
    ☐ True
    ☐ False

2.   Foreign policy is like domestic policy because
    ☐ a.   the president is the dominant actor.
    ☐ b.   Congress sets the agenda.
    ☐ c.   public opinion has very little impact.
    ☐ d.   it involves choice-taking.

3.   The instruments of foreign policy are basically the same as those of domestic policy.
    ☐ True
    ☐ False

4.   The quietest of the principal foreign policy instruments is
    ☐ a.   the threat of war.
    ☐ b.   economic policy.
    ☐ c.   diplomacy.
    ☐ d.   war.

5.   The real seat of power in the United Nations is the
    ☐ a.   General Assembly.
    ☐ b.   Secretary General.
    ☐ c.   Security Council.
    ☐ d.   Secretariat.

6.   The North Atlantic Treaty Organization is
    ☐ a.   a regional military organization.
    ☐ b.   an economic federation.
    ☐ c.   a multinational corporation.
    ☐ d.   a branch of the United Nations.

7.   The European Union is
    ☐ a.   a regional military organization.
    ☐ b.   an economic federation.
    ☐ c.   a multinational corporation.
    ☐ d.   a foreign policymaking agency of the United States.

8. Which of the following statements about multinational corporations (MNCs) is FALSE?
   ☐ a. They account for more than one-tenth of the global economy.
   ☐ b. Most try not to become involved in internal politics.
   ☐ c. Some are wealthier than the governments under which they operate.
   ☐ d. Some have linked forces with the CIA to overturn governments.

9. The president's foreign policy duties include
   ☐ a. making treaties.
   ☐ b. acting as commander in chief of the armed forces.
   ☐ c. deploying troops abroad.
   ☐ d. all of the above

10. Which of the following presidents relied more on their special assistant for national security affairs than on their secretary of state?
    ☐ a. Richard Nixon
    ☐ b. Ronald Reagan
    ☐ c. George W. Bush
    ☐ d. Bill Clinton

11. The Secretary of Defense manages a budget larger than that of most nations.
    ☐ True
    ☐ False

12. The governmental body responsible for coordinating foreign and military policy is the
    ☐ a. National Security Council.
    ☐ b. Department of State.
    ☐ c. Joint Chiefs of Staff.
    ☐ d. Central Intelligence Agency.

13. The activities of the Central Intelligence Agency have included
    ☐ a. nurturing coups.
    ☐ b. training and supporting foreign armies.
    ☐ c. infiltrating American interest groups.
    ☐ d. all of the above

14. Which of the following is NOT among the foreign policy functions of the U.S. Congress?
    ☐ a. declaring war
    ☐ b. initiating treaties
    ☐ c. confirming ambassadorial appointments
    ☐ d. appropriating funds

15. Isolationism was reaffirmed by
    ☐ a. World War II.
    ☐ b. the Marshall Plan.
    ☐ c. the League of Nations.
    ☐ d. the Monroe Doctrine.

16. The containment doctrine proposed the containment of
    ☐ a. Germany during World War II.
    ☐ b. the Soviet Union after World War II.
    ☐ c. McCarthyism in the 1950s.
    ☐ d. nuclear arms in the 1980s.

17. The American policy of helping other nations oppose communism was enunciated in the
    ☐ a. Monroe Doctrine.
    ☐ b. Marshall Plan.
    ☐ c. Truman Doctrine.
    ☐ d. Isolationist Doctrine.

18. During the Cold War, the policy of "brinkmanship" meant that the United States
    ☐ a. was prepared to use nuclear weapons in order to influence the actions of the Soviet Union and China.
    ☐ b. would isolate the Soviet Union and contain its advances at all costs.
    ☐ c. would stay out of other nations' conflicts.
    ☐ d. was prepared to fight communist infiltration at home as well as abroad.

19. (bonus) The term "military-industrial complex" was coined by
    ☐ a. John F. Kennedy.
    ☐ b. Richard Nixon.
    ☐ c. Dwight Eisenhower.
    ☐ d. Joseph McCarthy.

20. The Vietnam War finally came to an end due to the superior firepower of the United States.
    ☐ True
    ☐ False

21. Which of the following does the Vietnam War NOT illustrate?
    ☐ a. a presidential campaign issue
    ☐ b. how war abroad can result in protest at home
    ☐ c. the ability of the government to lie to its citizens
    ☐ d. the superiority of United States military might

22. Détente refers to
☐ a. the irrevocable differences between the United States and the Soviet Union.
☐ b. the threat of nuclear war.
☐ c. a transformation from conflict thinking to cooperative thinking.
☐ d. Ronald Reagan's foreign policy.

23. The United States Senate approved the SALT II treaty in 1979.
☐ True
☐ False

24. The first president to extend formal diplomatic recognition to the People's Republic of China was
☐ a. Richard Nixon.
☐ b. Gerald Ford.
☐ c. Jimmy Carter.
☐ d. Ronald Reagan.

25. From the middle of the 1950s to 1981, the defense budget had generally been declining as a percentage of the total federal budget and gross national product.
☐ True
☐ False

26. The first president in recent history who committed more of the national budget to social services than to military services was
☐ a. Lyndon Johnson.
☐ b. Richard Nixon.
☐ c. Gerald Ford.
☐ d. Jimmy Carter.

27. Defense spending came to a standstill during the second term of Ronald Reagan's presidency.
☐ True
☐ False

28. The Strategic Defense Initiative (SDI) refers to
☐ a. Ronald Reagan's initiation of arms control talks.
☐ b. a defense system using high-tech devices to destroy invading missiles.
☐ c. an international organization bent on eliminating nuclear weapons.
☐ d. an arm of the Pentagon that prepares the country for defending against a nuclear attack.

29. The end of the cold war was characterized by the
   ☐ a.   fall of the Berlin Wall.
   ☐ b.   unification of East and West Germany.
   ☐ c.   split of the Soviet Union into 15 separate nations.
   ☐ d.   all of the above

30. China took a major step toward democratization as a result of the 1989 protests at Tiananmen Square.
   ☐ True
   ☐ False

31. According to George W. Bush, the "axis of evil" includes each of the following EXCEPT
   ☐ a.   Iraq.
   ☐ b.   Iran.
   ☐ c.   Afghanistan.
   ☐ d.   North Korea.

32. Critics of the war on terrorism argue
   ☐ a.   it is responding to a tactic when we should respond to the forces that generate it.
   ☐ b.   unilateral action has squandered America's moral authority.
   ☐ c.   the United States can not defend itself without the help of others.
   ☐ d.   all of the above

33. What fraction of the federal budget is devoted to defense?
   ☐ a.   about one-fifth
   ☐ b.   about one-fourth
   ☐ c.   about one-third
   ☐ d.   about one-half

34. Conservatives
   ☐ a.   believe the Pentagon wastes money.
   ☐ b.   insist that America needs to retain its readiness at a high level.
   ☐ c.   argue that a strong economy is the best defense.
   ☐ d.   believe the U.S. should invest in human capital.

35. Liberals credit the collapse of communism to
   ☐ a.   the American military build-up.
   ☐ b.   the ideological defects of communism.
   ☐ c.   defects at the core of the Soviet economy.
   ☐ d.   the Soviet Communist Party.

36. No other country in modern history has come close to the military predominance of the United States.
    ☐ True
    ☐ False

37. America's nuclear arsenal has relied primarily on
    ☐ a. ground-based intercontinental ballistic missiles.
    ☐ b. submarine-launched ballistic missiles.
    ☐ c. strategic bombers.
    ☐ d. all of the above

38. The first president to sign a treaty to reduce current levels of nuclear weapons was
    ☐ a. Richard Nixon.
    ☐ b. Gerald Ford.
    ☐ c. Jimmy Carter.
    ☐ d. Ronald Reagan.

39. The first accord mandating the elimination of strategic nuclear weaponry was
    ☐ a. SALT I.
    ☐ b. SALT II.
    ☐ c. the Intermediate-Range Nuclear Forces Pact.
    ☐ d. the Strategic Arms Reduction Treaty.

40. (bonus) How long did it take to win the Gulf War?
    ☐ a. one hour
    ☐ b. one day
    ☐ c. 100 hours
    ☐ d. 100 days

41. The United States is becoming increasingly dependent on other peoples to defeat terrorism, protect the environment, control weapons of mass destruction, regulate trade, and deal with other problems that cross national boundaries.
    ☐ True
    ☐ False

42. Military might has always been and remains America's primary instrument of foreign policy.
    ☐ True
    ☐ False

43. Economic sanctions
    ☐ a. are a recent tool of diplomacy.
    ☐ b. are often a first resort in times of crises.
    ☐ c. have never accomplished their goals.
    ☐ d. tend to receive wide support.

44. The primary means by which American policymakers have sought to halt the spread of nuclear weapons has been
☐ a. to encourage nations to agree that they would not acquire them.
☐ b. the use of economic sanctions.
☐ c. the threat of military force.
☐ d. through the United Nations.

45. The key word that describes today's international economy is
☐ a. isolationism.
☐ b. tariffs.
☐ c. interdependency.
☐ d. deficits.

46. Since the end of World War II,
☐ a. trade among nations has declined.
☐ b. a globalization of finances has taken place.
☐ c. tariffs have become the main instrument of international economic policy.
☐ d. interdependency has declined.

47. Nontariff barriers include
☐ a. quotas.
☐ b. subsidies.
☐ c. quality specifications.
☐ d. all of the above

48. The ratio of what we pay for imports to what we earn from exports is called
☐ a. interdependency.
☐ b. the balance of trade.
☐ c. a tariff.
☐ d. foreign aid.

49. Which of the following statements is FALSE?
☐ a. A decline in the dollar makes American products cheaper abroad.
☐ b. A poor balance of payments exacerbates unemployment.
☐ c. In recent years, America has had a balance of trade surplus.
☐ d. Trade deficits decrease the dollar's buying power.

50. The United States is more dependent on foreign sources of oil than any other country in the world.
☐ True
☐ False

51. American policy initiatives directed at the problem of world poverty include
☐ a. foreign-aid programs.
☐ b. Food for Peace programs.
☐ c. Peace Corps volunteers.
☐ d. all of the above

52. Foreign aid is very popular with Americans.
☐ True
☐ False

53. Which of the following statements is FALSE?
☐ a. Americans are usually more interested in domestic policy than foreign policy.
☐ b. When the American people hold strong opinions regarding international relations, they find policymakers responsive to them.
☐ c. The system of separation of powers plays a crucial role in foreign policy.
☐ d. Elitism is pervasive in the arena of international economic policy.

54. The decline of the United States as a world superpower has and will continue to reduce the scope of American government in foreign and defense policy.
☐ True
☐ False

ESSAY QUESTIONS

1. Who are the actors on the world's foreign policy stage? Who makes foreign policy in the United States?

2. What was the Cold War, and why did it emerge from isolationism? What were its consequences at home and abroad?

3. Compare the politics and policy of the Cold War to the politics and policy of détente. Be sure to include a discussion of the containment doctrine and the arms talks in your answer.

4. How did the Cold War end? What consequences does the end of the Cold War have on American foreign and defense policymaking?

5. Explain the nature of the war on terrorism. What are some of the major criticisms of the war on terrorism? Can the United States win the war on terrorism?

6. What are the politics of military spending? How do liberals and conservatives differ in regard to their view of defense spending?

7. Why does the United States often have troubles in its foreign policy initiatives?

8. What are the present characteristics of the international economy? How would you characterize the nature of international trade since the end of the Second World War?

9. Critique the statement "democracy has very little to do with the international relations of the United States." In what ways is American foreign and defense policymaking a democratic process, and in what ways is it not?

CHAPTER 21

The New Face of State and Local Government

CHAPTER OUTLINE

I.   Introduction (pp. 656-657)
    A.   **Sub-national governments** are state and local governments.
    B.   Revitalization
    C.   Diversity

II.   State Constitutions (pp. 657-659)
    A.   State constitutions provide far more detail than the federal constitution.
    B.   Amending State Constitutions

III.   State Elections (pp. 659-665)
    A.   Gubernatorial Elections
    B.   State Legislative Elections
        1.   Apportionment
        2.   Partisan Competition, Legislative Turnover, and Term Limits
        3.   Divided government
    C.   The Changing Face of State-Elected Officials

IV.   Governors and The Executive Branch (pp. 665-669)
    A.   The Job of Governor
        1.   Governors perform many roles.
        2.   The **line-item veto** allows governors to veto only certain parts of a bill while allowing the rest of it to pass into law.
    B.   Other Executive Officers
        1.   **Lieutenant governors** often preside over the state senate and are first in succession for governor.
        2.   Other state executives may include attorney general, treasurer, secretary of state, auditor, comptroller, and various commissioners.

V.   State Legislatures (pp. 670-672)
    A.   Legislative professionalism reforms have improved the effectiveness of state legislatures.
    B.   Some states have seen the beginning of a "de-professionalizing" trend.

VI.   State Court Systems (pp. 672-674)

A. State Court Organization
B. Selecting Judges
   1. In many states, voters elect judges for various courts.
   2. Many states follow a form of the **Merit Plan** that attempts to make appointments to the courts based upon merit.

VII. **Direct Democracy** (pp. 675-677)
   A. Under the legislative **initiative**, the people directly author and vote on legislation.
   B. Under the **referendum**, the people can approve or reject measures submitted to them by the legislature.
   C. Under the **recall**, voters can gather enough signatures to call an election to decide whether a representative should continue in office.

VIII. State and Local Government Relations (pp. 677-678)
   A. According to **Dillon's Rule**, local governments have only those powers that are explicitly given to them by the states.
   B. A **local charter** is the organizational statement and grant of authority from the state to a local government often used to give **home rule** to local governments.

IX. Local Governments (pp. 678-686)
   A. Types of Local Government
      1. Counties
      2. Townships
      3. Municipalities
         a. Originally, many local communities operated under a form of direct democracy called the **town meeting.**
         b. Mayor-council government.
         c. Council-manager government: An appointed **city manager** carries out policy with the city bureaucracy.
         d. Commission government.
      4. School Districts
      5. Special Districts
   B. Fragmentation, Cooperation, and Competition
      1. Each governing body in a fragmented metropolis tends to look at problems from its own narrow, partial perspective.
      2. A **council of governments** (COG) consists of officials from various localities who meet to discuss mutual problems and plan joint action.

X. State and Local Finance Policy (pp. 686-688)

XI. Understanding State and Local Governments (pp. 689-691)
   A. Democracy at the Subnational Level
   B. The Scope of Subnational Governments

XII. Summary (pp. 691-692)

LEARNING OBJECTIVES

After studying Chapter 21, you should be able to:

1. Describe the nature of state constitutions and how they differ from the U.S. Constitution.

2. Discuss the different types of state elections and how they differ from national elections.

3. Explain the function of state governors and the executive branch.

4. Understand the nature and function of state legislatures and how legislatures make policy.

5. Describe the structure of the state court systems.

6. Explain how direct democracy is used in the states.

7. Discuss the relationship between state and local governments.

8. Compare and contrast the different types of local government in the United States in terms of organization, functions, and policy roles.

9. Discuss the fiscal and budgetary policies of state and local governments.

10. Evaluate state and local government in the United States in terms of their contributions to democracy and the scope of government.

The following exercises will help you meet these objectives:

Objective 1: Describe the nature of state constitutions and how they differ from the U.S. Constitution.

1. Explain two important characteristics of subnational government.

    1.

    2.

2. What is the key difference between the federal and state constitutions?

3.   Explain three methods used by states to amend their constitutions.

    1.

    2.

    3.

Objective 2: Discuss the different types of state elections and how they differ from national elections.

    1.   Explain what is meant by the "presidentialization" of gubernatorial elections.

    2.   Explain what is meant by the "congressionalization" of state legislative elections.

    3.   What are the major consequences of divided government in the states?

    4.   List and explain three things that tend to increase legislative partisanship and polarize legislative deliberations in the states.

        1.

        2.

        3.

Objective 3: Explain the function of state governors and the executive branch.

    1.   Explain the two most important formal powers that governors have for controlling state government.

        1.

        2.

    2.   What is the role played by most lieutenant governors?

    3.   List four major executive positions elected in some states and explain their primary duties.

        1.

        2.

        3.

        4.

Objective 4: Understand the nature and function of state legislatures and how legislatures make policy.

    1.   List four functions performed by all state legislatures.

        1.

        2.

3.

4.

2. Explain the three legislative professionalism reforms.

   1.

   2.

   3.

3. Explain what is meant by the "de-professionalizing" trend in some state legislatures.

Objective 5: Describe the structure of the state court systems.

    1.   Complete the following table on the nature of state courts.

Court	Geographic Jurisdiction	Number of Presiding Judges	Types of Cases	Use of Jury
Trial Courts				
Intermediate Courts of Appeals				
Court of Last Resort				

    2.   What is the "Merit Plan"?

Objective 6: Explain how direct democracy is used in the states.

    1.   List and explain three procedures for direct democracy used in the states.

        1.

        2.

        3.

    2.   Give three examples of how initiatives have been used in the states.

        1.

2.

3.

Objective 7: Discuss the relationship between state and local governments.

    1.   Explain what is meant by Dillion's Rule.

    2.   What are three ways in which local governments can influence their own destiny?

        1.

        2.

        3.

Objective 8: Compare and contrast the different types of local government in the United States in terms of organization, functions, and policy roles.

    1.   What are the common functions of most counties?

2.   List the three modern forms of municipal government and complete the following table explaining where executive and legislative power lies and naming at least one city as an example.

Government Form	Executive	Legislature	Example

3.   Explain why regional cooperation at the local level is so difficult to achieve.

4.   What does a "council of government" mean and what purpose does it serve?

Objective 9: Discuss the fiscal and budgetary policies of state and local governments.

1.   List the three main sources of state revenues.

   1.

   2.

   3.

2.   List four main areas of state expenditures.

   1.

2.

3.

4.

3.   List the three main sources of local revenues.

1.

2.

3.

4.   List the three main areas of local expenditures.
1.

2.

3.

Objective 10: Evaluate state and local government in the United States in terms of their contributions to democracy and the scope of government.

1.   Give four reasons why state and local politics may fall short of the democratic ideal.

1.

2.

3.

4.

2. Explain two ways in which state and local governments have attempted to control spending, taxing, and employment growth.

1.

2.

KEY TERMS

Identify and describe:

subnational governments

line-item veto

lieutenant governor

Merit Plan

direct democracy

initiative

referendum

recall

Dillon's Rule

local charter

home rule

town meeting

city manager

council of governments

Compare and contrast:

direct democracy, initiative, referendum, and recall

Dillon's Rule and local charter

local charter and home rule

Name that term:

    1.   Also known as state and local governments.

        _____

2.	A governor's power to veto part of a bill while leaving the rest intact.

	_____

3.	The second-highest state executive officer.

	_____

4.	Under this system, state judges are appointed from a list of persons recommended by the state bar or a committee of officials.

	_____

5.	Under this system, all voting-age adults in a community gather once a year to make public policy.

	_____

6.	The local government administrator who implements and administers council-manager government.

	_____

7.	An organization of officials from various localities created to discuss mutual problems and plan cooperative action.

	_____

USING YOUR UNDERSTANDING

1.	Choose a state of interest to you, such as your home state or the state in which your college or university is situated. Compare the government of this state to the federal government on a number of dimensions including, but not necessarily limited to, constitutional arrangements, the structure and organization of government, the powers of the policymaking bodies, particularly the legislative and executive bodies, the judicial structure and the role of the courts, the budgetary process including how revenues are collected and spent, and the nature and extent of regulation, and bureaucratic involvement. You may wish to either write a comprehensive outline or use this exercise as the basis of a term paper.

2.	Explore the issue of federalism by choosing a federal policy that is implemented by the states. Examples include various environmental regulations or social welfare policies. How do states implement these policies? Which state bureaucracies are involved and how? Does the state legislature get involved in the act? Are any local governments involved and, if so, how? What individuals have the most impact on implementing the policy and how? What are the financial arrangements? Who controls how the money is spent? Evaluate the implementation of the policy on the basis of the policy's intention. This exercise may be a case study of one state or a comparison of different states.

REVIEW QUESTIONS

Check ☑ the correct answer:

1. Sub-national governments have gained importance in recent years.
    ☐ True
    ☐ False

2. Two important characteristics of sub-national governments today are
    ☐ a. conservatism and unity.
    ☐ b. revitalization and diversity.
    ☐ c. innovation and dominance.
    ☐ d. stagnation and indifference.

3. State constitutions are subordinate to
    ☐ a. the U.S. Constitution.
    ☐ b. laws of the United States.
    ☐ c. state laws.
    ☐ d. both a. and b.

4. Most state constitutions are shorter than the U.S. Constitution.
    ☐ True
    ☐ False

5. Typical of all state constitutions are provisions for
    ☐ a. separation of powers.
    ☐ b. taxation and finance.
    ☐ c. a bill of rights.
    ☐ d. all of the above

6. The most common method used by states to amend their constitution is the
    ☐ a. legislative proposal.
    ☐ b. constitutional convention.
    ☐ c. popular initiative.
    ☐ d. federal directive.

7.   Most governors are now elected during presidential years.
     ☐ True
     ☐ False

8.   In recent years, gubernatorial elections have become
     ☐ a.   less important.
     ☐ b.   linked to presidential elections.
     ☐ c.   more personalized.
     ☐ d.   less dependent on money.

9.   The result of the personalization of gubernatorial elections has been
     ☐ a.   less predictability in the outcomes.
     ☐ b.   more divided government in the states.
     ☐ c.   better-known candidates.
     ☐ d.   all of the above

10. Campaign costs for state legislative campaigns have skyrocketed.
     ☐ True
     ☐ False

11. Divided government in the states has facilitated coherent policy action.
     ☐ True
     ☐ False

12. In recent years, state legislatures have been characterized by
     ☐ a.   increased party competition.
     ☐ b.   divided government.
     ☐ c.   majority party switching.
     ☐ d.   all of the above

13. State governments have traditionally been characterized by less-than-representative percentages of women and ethnic minorities in elected officials.
     ☐ True
     ☐ False

14. Modernization in state governments has
     ☐ a.   resulted in enhanced powers for governors.
     ☐ b.   resolved the fragmentation of executive power.
     ☐ c.   spread power more evenly in state government.
     ☐ d.   resulted in more efficient and smaller government.

15. (bonus) Which of the following states has the strongest governor?
     ☐ a.   California
     ☐ b.   Rhode Island
     ☐ c.   Maryland
     ☐ d.   Vermont

16.   Most governors have the power of the line-item veto.
        ☐ True
        ☐ False

17.   The primary initiator of public policy in the states is/are
        ☐ a.   interest groups.
        ☐ b.   the speaker of the assembly.
        ☐ c.   legislative committee heads.
        ☐ d.   the governor.

18.   The individual who is next in line to succeed the governor is called the
        ☐ a.   vice governor.
        ☐ b.   lieutenant governor.
        ☐ c.   secretary of state.
        ☐ d.   state commissioner.

19.   State legislatures
        ☐ a.   make almost all of the basic laws of the state.
        ☐ b.   appropriate the money that is needed for state government to function.
        ☐ c.   oversee the activities of the executive branch.
        ☐ d.   all of the above

20.   Legislative professionalism reform has included
        ☐ a.   lengthening legislative sessions.
        ☐ b.   increasing legislators' salaries.
        ☐ c.   increasing the staff available to help legislators.
        ☐ d.   all of the above

21.   All state legislatures have become full-time professional bodies.
        ☐ True
        ☐ False

22.   The state courts that have taken on many of the functions of specialized courts are
        ☐ a.   courts of appeal.
        ☐ b.   state supreme courts.
        ☐ c.   trial courts.
        ☐ d.   circuit courts.

23.   The state courts that have the responsibility for administering and regulating the justice system in the state are the
        ☐ a.   trial courts.
        ☐ b.   courts of appeal.
        ☐ c.   state supreme courts.
        ☐ d.   circuit courts.

24. In the Merit Plan, judges are selected on the basis of
   ☐ a. competitive partisan election.
   ☐ b. recommendation by the state bar or other officials.
   ☐ c. competitive nonpartisan election.
   ☐ d. patronage.

25. The purest form of direct democracy would be the
   ☐ a. legislative proposal.
   ☐ b. constitutional convention.
   ☐ c. popular initiative.
   ☐ d. federal directive.

26. A form of direct democracy in which the legislature sends a bill to the voters instead of the governor for approval is called a
   ☐ a. legislative initiative.
   ☐ b. recall.
   ☐ c. referendum.
   ☐ d. popular initiative.

27. A form of direct democracy in which voters can decide whether a representative should continue in office is called a
   ☐ a. legislative initiative.
   ☐ b. recall.
   ☐ c. referendum.
   ☐ d. popular initiative.

28. The idea that local governments have only those powers that are explicitly given to them by the states is called
   ☐ a. Dillon's Rule.
   ☐ b. Merit Plan.
   ☐ c. Local Rule.
   ☐ d. State Rule.

29. The organizational statement and grant of authority from the state to a local government is called a
   ☐ a. constitution.
   ☐ b. local charter.
   ☐ c. council of government.
   ☐ d. intergovernmental agreement.

30.　(bonus) Which of the following states has the most number of local governments?
- a. New York
- b. California
- c. Illinois
- d. Texas

31.　Public policy is usually made in county governments by
- a. a county commission.
- b. row officers.
- c. a county administrator.
- d. the state.

32.　The type of local government that usually has the least amount of power is the
- a. county.
- b. municipality.
- c. township.
- d. special district.

33.　Most basic local programs and services are provided by
- a. municipalities.
- b. townships.
- c. school districts.
- d. special districts.

34.　At one time, most towns in the United States operated through direct democracy.
- True
- False

35.　Today, municipal governments take the form of
- a. mayor-council government.
- b. council-manager government.
- c. commission government.
- d. all of the above

36.　Traditionally, city council members
- a. represented the city at-large.
- b. were elected on a nonpartisan ballot.
- c. represented a district or ward.
- d. were appointed by the mayor.

37.　An unintended consequence of at-large representation in city councils is that
- a. the mayor's power has increased dramatically.
- b. the number of committees in the council has grown.
- c. minority group members have had difficulty gaining election.
- d. the role of the city council has diminished.

38. Most school systems in the United States are run as independent local governments.
☐ True
☐ False

39. Supreme Court decisions have put an end to legal discrimination in schools, but have not solved the financial problems of schools.
☐ True
☐ False

40. The fastest-growing form of local government is the
☐ a.   county.
☐ b.   municipality.
☐ c.   township.
☐ d.   special district.

41. Most metropolitan areas have created regional bodies to surmount the problems of metropolitan fragmentation and local parochialism.
☐ True
☐ False

42. Which of the following statements is TRUE?
☐ a.   There is no limit on the number of special districts.
☐ b.   Cities often compete with one another for desirable business facilities by offering incentives..
☐ c.   Local governments rarely need to compete with each other for economic development.
☐ d.   Regional coordination has become the norm in state government.

43. Councils of governments
☐ a.   are usually well-funded.
☐ b.   lack any real legislative power.
☐ c.   have large staffs.
☐ d.   are found in most metropolitan areas.

44. States receive the largest share of their revenue from
☐ a.   federal aid.
☐ b.   taxes.
☐ c.   state insurance programs.
☐ d.   charges for services.

45. The largest percentage of state money goes to
   ☐ a. aid local governments.
   ☐ b. administration.
   ☐ c. operate state programs.
   ☐ d. finance loans.

46. Local governments receive their revenues from
   ☐ a. taxes.
   ☐ b. user charges.
   ☐ c. intergovernmental aid.
   ☐ d. all of the above

47. The highest percentage of the local governments' monies is allocated to public education.
   ☐ True
   ☐ False

48. Democracy at the state and local levels may suffer because
   ☐ a. politics at the state level is poorly covered by the media.
   ☐ b. participation in state-wide elections is low.
   ☐ c. business interests have substantial leverage in state and city affairs.
   ☐ d. all of the above

49. For most of this century, growth in state and local government has
   ☐ a. been slowing down.
   ☐ b. been overshadowed by growth in the federal government.
   ☐ c. proceeded at a pace exceeding that of the federal government.
   ☐ d. remained unchanged.

50. Reforms and professionalization in sub-national governments have generally had the effect of reducing the scope of government.
   ☐ True
   ☐ False

51. Sunset legislation is used to
   ☐ a. increase democratic participation in state governments.
   ☐ b. appropriate money for state budgets.
   ☐ c. control the growth of state governments.
   ☐ d. create new programs and agencies in the states.

ESSAY QUESTIONS

1. Why are state and local governments important to the American political system and how has this importance increased in recent years?

2. What are the typical provisions found in state constitutions and how are these different from or similar to the provisions found in the U.S. Constitution?

3. What are the primary characteristics of state elections?

4. Compare the job of governor to the job of president of the United States. How are they different and how are they similar?

5. What is the role of state legislatures and how have they changed in recent years?

6. Write an outline of a state court system that includes how the courts are organized, their jurisdiction, and their role in policymaking.

7. Explain the relationship between state governments and their local governments.

8. List the different types of local governments in the United States, along with their organizational structure and responsibilities.

9. Where do state and local governments get their money and how do they spend it?

INTRODUCING GOVERNMENT IN TEXAS

CHAPTER OUTLINE

I.   Demographic trends in Texas (pp. 654–655)
    A. Texas is projected to grow rapidly.
    B. How that growth happens depends a lot on political decisions made today.

II.   Political Culture of Texas (pp. 656–658)
    A. What is Political Culture?
        1. **Political Culture** refers to a set of values, attitudes, and beliefs that are widely shared within society about government's role in society and in people's lives.
    B. Differences and similarities in political culture
        1. There are key shared principles that unite all Americans but there are considerable differences in emphasis from one region to another.
        2. Even within Texas, there are significant differences in political culture.
        3. Geography and history contribute to the political culture in Texas.
            a. Texas has been a nation of its own.
            b. Texas occupies a huge geographical area.
            c. Texas's large spaces have contributed to the belief that Texas is a land of opportunity where the individual can make it on his or her own.
    C. **Daniel Elazar** examined the political culture of the United States and identified three distinct political cultures.
        1. **Moralistic Subculture**
            a. Believes that government is needed to promote the public good and work for the benefit of all citizens
            b. Started with the Puritans in New England
            c. Strongest in the Northeast and Midwest of the U.S.
            d. Not very strong in Texas
        2. **Individualistic Subculture**
            a. Believes that government cannot correct the inequalities and injustices of society
            b. Believes that government should focus on maintaining the rules that protect people's right to pursue their interests
            c. Started with Germanic and English settlers in the mid-Atlantic regions

      d. With westward migration it spread to the upper south including parts of Texas

      e. Individualism in Texas strongest west of an imaginary line running from Texarkana to San Antonio

      f. Individualism is reflected in the social welfare policies of Texas and the belief that if someone is poor it is not government's responsibility to help them

3. **Traditionalistic Subculture**

      a. Believes that government's role should be preserving the existing social order

      b. Not terribly supportive of democracy and political participation by the masses

      c. Started with the plantation-based economy of the lower South and spread to eastern Texas

      d. There are some similarities between traditionalism and the political culture of Mexico which is dominated by large landowners; these two cultures have blended in some areas of southern and eastern Texas.

      e. Traditionalism is also bound up in the legacy of slavery and segregation in that it helped maintain elite control over minorities in the state.

D. Texas is settled by people who combine traditionalistic and individualistic political subcultures. They favor:

1. Limited government
2. Low taxation
3. Regressive taxation that favors the economic elites
4. Restrictive voting requirements designed to limit suffrage for minorities

III.   Population Growth and Changes (pp. 659–666)

A. Texas has been characterized by rapid population growth and this is likely to continue for the foreseeable future.

1. Texas' population has increased by more than 10% per decade since the 1850s.
2. In 1994, Texas became the second-most populated state in the U.S.
3. In the 1990s, Texas's population increased by more than population of 24 states.
4. Some projections indicate that the state population may more than double to 52 million by 2050.
5. Growth will continue to make Texas more ethnically and racially diverse.
6. Most of the growth will occur in the cities.

B. Anglos have been the majority of Texans since before statehood but this is rapidly changing.

1. Migration of Anglos to Texas starting in the 1820s rapidly made Hispanics a minority.

2. By 1860, they represented 60% of the population and by 1950 peaked at almost 75% of the population.
3. Within the last few years, the percentage of Anglos in the Texas population has declined to less than 50% of the population.

C. African Americans were the second-largest segment of the Texas population in the 1800s but were passed by Hispanics in the twentieth century.
   1. In the 1850s, African Americans accounted for 30% of the population and Hispanics represented only 5% of Texans.
   2. Currently African Americans account for 12% of the state's population and Hispanics account for 32% of Texans.

D. The largest group of "other" minorities is the rapidly-growing Asian population; from 1980 to 2000 they went from 1% of the population to 2.7%.

E. In 2004, Texas became a **minority-majority** state when Anglos dipped below 50% of the state population.

F. Hispanics represent most of the state growth in population and will become a majority in the state sometime between 2025 and 2035.

G. Demographic changes have already begun to affect Texas politics.
   1. The 2002 election saw the first major-party Hispanic nominee for Texas governor in Tony Sanchez.
   2. The Democrats nominated a diverse ticket with Sanchez running for governor, Ron Kirk, an African American for U.S. Senate, and John Sharp, an Anglo for Lt. Governor.
   3. Republican power in the state turned back all three candidates but the Republican hold on power could be threatened if they are unable to make inroads into minority, particularly Hispanic, communities in the future.

H. Texas has become increasingly urban in its demography.
   1. In the nineteenth century only 4% of the population was urban.
   2. By the early twenty-first century, about 83% of Texans lived in an urban environment,
   3. Three of the 10 largest cities in the U.S. are in Texas (Houston, San Antonio, and Dallas).
   4. The Dallas-Fort Worth area added 1.2 million in the 1990s which was more growth than 45 of the states registered.
   5. During the 1990s, almost all of the 98 Texas counties that lost population were rural.
   6. Despite the loss in population, rural areas maintain a disproportionate share of power in state government.

IV. Economic Development Trends (pp. 667–671)
    A. Politics and Economics Closely Related
       1. Taxes are related to business development.
       2. The economy impacts tax receipts and demands for services.
          a. When the economy is good, tax revenue is high and the use of government services is low.

        b.   When the economy, is bad tax revenue is low and the use of government services is high.

B. Major Economic Sectors in Texas
    1. Cotton and Cattle
        a. In the nineteenth century, these two products were the main elements of the Texas economy.
        b. Now less than 2% of the state population work on farms and ranches.
        c. Agriculture contributed approximately $36 billion to the state economy in 2004.

    2. Oil
        a. Oil was the primary driving force in the Texas economy for most of the twentieth century.
        b. The oil strike at Spindletop, near Beaumont, in 1901 resulted in a 20-fold increase in oil production in just three years.
        c. Oil riches have contributed to the individualistic political subculture by providing examples of people who got rich quickly through oil.
        d. Oil revenue contributes to higher education by funding the University of Texas and Texas A&M systems through the Permanent University Fund land grant which happened to be sitting on a large oil deposit.
        e. The state economy has been tied to the ups and downs of the oil and gas market, resulting in frequent boom and bust cycles as the price of oil has varied over time.

    3. High Tech
        a. The state's high tech industry stemmed in part from the oil bust of the 1980s which forced businesses to become more diversified.
        b. More high tech jobs were created in Texas during the 1990s than in any other state.
        c. When the tech bubble burst in 2000 it resulted in disproportionate job losses in this sector; 51% of all jobs lost in Texas from 2001 to 2003 were in this sector.
        d. High tech has diversified the economy; oil and gas now only account for 5% of economic activity in the state—down from 20% in 1982.

    4. The Effect of NAFTA
        a. The North American Free Trade Agreement (NAFTA) is an agreement between the United States, Mexico, and Canada to eliminate most tariffs and other trade barriers.
        b. The impact of NAFTA on the Texas economy remains unclear.
        c. Texas's exports to foreign countries has increased as a consequence of NAFTA.

          d. Some sectors have benefited more than others, with low-wage labor-intensive industries being most negatively affected by the new trade.

V.   Income and Education (pp. 672–679)
   A. Income Distribution
      1. In 2004 Texas was ranked 32nd out of 50 states in median household income.
      2. The national median income was $44,389 versus $41,326 in Texas.
      3. Historically, other than a brief period in the early 80s, Texans have enjoyed a lower per capita income than the national average.
   B. Geographic Distribution of Wealth
      1. Most economic growth takes place within the Texas Triangle which stretches from Houston to Dallas to San Antonio via Austin.
          a. Houston or Dallas/Fort Worth generally have the most economic growth.
          b. Austin has seen the greatest income growth in recent years.
          c. San Antonio tends to lag behind the other cities in growth.
          d. Dallas-Fort Worth is a major transportation hub.
          e. Austin relies on high tech, government, and higher education for most of its economic growth.
          f. Houston is the center of the oil business in the state.
          g. San Antonio is heavily reliant on its military bases and tourism as well as being a major transportation hub for south Texas.
          h. Since 1969, per capita income in the Triangle has usually been above the national average.
      2. Outside the Triangle, the rest of Texas sees its per capita income at about 70% of the national average.
          a. The poorest areas are along the Texas-Mexico border.
          b. Approximately 30% of the population in McAllen, Brownsville, and Laredo live below the poverty line; the national average is 12.7%.
          c. The statewide average of people living below the poverty line is 16.3%.
   C. Income Distribution
      1. The gap between rich and poor in Texas is greater than any other state save New York.
      2. The average income of the richest fifth is 8 times higher than that of the poorest fifth.
      3. In all measures of income distribution, Texas ranks among the bottom 10 states nationally.
   D. Race and Ethnicity
      1. The average income for Anglo households in Texas in 2000 was $47,162.

2. The average income for Hispanic households in Texas in 2000 was $29,873.
3. The average income for African-American households in Texas in 2000 was $29,305.
4. Minorities tend to be less educated and younger than Anglos in the state, which explains much of the income disparity.

E. Education level matters more in Texas than nationally
   1. People in Texas with a bachelor's degree earned an average of $59,781 versus $58,583 nationally.
   2. People in Texas with only a High School diploma earned an average of $27,603 versus $28,859 nationally.

F. Education
   1. For every dollar invested in education in Texas, it returns $5.50 to the state economy, according to the Texas State Comptroller.
   2. Educated people are more likely to be active and effective citizens because they are more knowledgeable about politics and policy and are therefore more likely to vote and be law-abiding.
   3. Educational Achievement
      a. Texas ranked last in the U.S. in terms of its high-school graduation rate at 78.3% compared to a national average of 85.2%.
      b. Texas ranks 35th with 24.5% of its population holding a college degree compared to the U.S. average of 27.7%.
      c. Anglos and African Americans do better than the national average in educational attainment rates, but Hispanics in Texas rank lower than the national average for Hispanics.
      d. Texas is at a competitive disadvantage because of the educational attainment of its workforce.
      e. Trends suggest that this disadvantage is likely to get worse and could seriously impact the growth of the Texas economy.
   4. Educational Goals for the Future
      a. Texas has made some gains in educational attainment with African Americans in particular showing the most growth.
      b. Educational goals set by the Texas Higher Education Coordinating Boards in 2000 are being exceeded by Anglos and African Americans, but Hispanics are falling well short of the goals.
      c. Some argue that, given the rapidly increasing population, goals are not being set high enough.
      d. Expenditures on public safety and correction increased 223% between 1985 and 2005 while education spending only increased 79% over the same period.
      e. Tuition increases at Texas universities have also increased the income gap between those who can afford to attend colleges and those who cannot.

VI.   Understanding Texas (pp. 680)
        A. Texas and Democracy
            1. Texas political culture tends to discourage active participation in the
                democratic process.
            2. Voter turnout in Texas has consistently been below the national average.
            3. Elites in Texas have set up systems that tend to encourage vast differences
                in income, education, and political opportunities.
            4. Changing demographics in the state may undermine the status quo in
                future years as we become a minority-majority and eventually a Hispanic
                majority state.
            5. Currently, minorities are underrepresented in the political process largely
                because of educational and age disadvantages but this is likely to change
                over time.
        B. Texas and the Scope of Government
            1. Political culture has also tended to limit the scope of government action in
                Texas.
            2. Texans do not like where Texas ranks in such measures as the poverty
                rate, children without health insurance, infant mortality, and educational
                attainment but do not see government as a solution to these problems.
            3. Aversion to taxes also means that the government is constrained from bold
                actions to address these concerns.
            4. The changing role of traditional minorities in the state may force Texas
                lawmakers to re-evaluate some of these kinds of positions in the future.

VII.   Summary (p. 681)

LEARNING OBJECTIVES:

After studying Chapter 21 you should be able to:

1. Discuss the changing demographics of Texas.
2. Identify the different political subcultures defined by Daniel Elazar and be able to apply
    them to studying the practices of Texas government.
3. Understand the key bases of the Texas economy.
4. Explain the roots of income differentials in Texas and why they tend to be larger than
    comparable figures from other states in the United States.
5. Explain the role of race in educational attainment and economic success both for
    individuals as well as the state as a whole.
6. Explain the impact of political culture on Texan's approaches to dealing with the
    problems facing Texas.

The following exercises will help you meet these objectives:

Objective 1: Discuss the changing demographics of Texas.

1. Look up U.S. Census information on Texas and compare it to other large U.S. states such as California, New York, and Pennsylvania.

2. How will the changing demographics of Texas impact politics and society in the state?

Objective 2: Identify the different political subcultures defined by Daniel Elazar and apply them to studying the practices of Texas government.

1. Investigate how Daniel Elazar's political cultures spread throughout the U.S.

2. Identify how these cultures affect politics differently in states where moralism is stronger than Texas such as New York or Washington state.

Objective 3: Understand the key bases of the Texas economy.

1. Look up census data on economic trends for Texas and compare them to the country as a whole. What are the similarities and differences?

2. Using historical data from the census and make a pie chart of the Texas economy as it existed in 1850, 1900, 1950, and 2000.

Objective 4: Explain the roots of income differentials in Texas and why they tend to be larger than comparable figures from other states in the United States.

1. Look up census data on the median income in Texas versus other states. Color in a map with relative median incomes for the states.

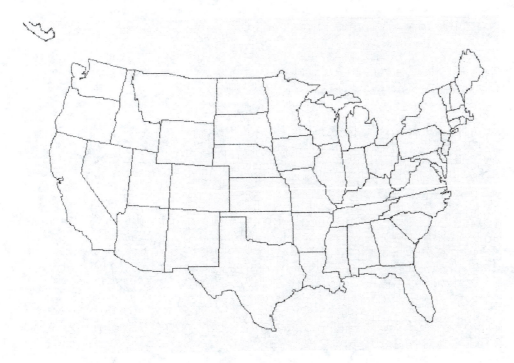

2. Compare that map with a map of Elazar's political cultures in the U.S. What conclusions can you reach from this comparison?

Objective 5: Explain the role of race in educational attainment and economic success both for individuals as well as the state as a whole.

1. Look up census data on educational attainment by race.

2. Look up census data on income level by race.

3. Compare the results of these two data sets. What conclusions can you reach?

411

Objective 6: Explain the impact of political culture on Texan's approaches to dealing with the problems facing Texas.

1. Look up data on voter turnout by state. Use the following U.S. map and color in the relative state-by-state totals.

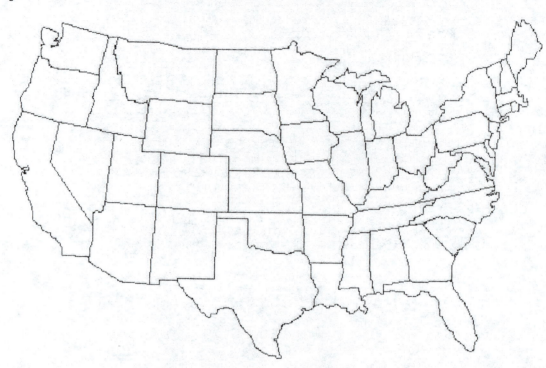

2. Compare this map to one made by Elazar about the relative strengths of political culture throughout the U.S. What conclusions do you reach?

KEY TERMS:

Identify and describe:

demography

political culture

Daniel Elazar

individualistic subculture

moralistic subculture

traditionalistic subculture

minority-majority

median household income

poverty rate

educational attainment

North American Free Trade Agreement

Name that term:

1. If no one racial group can claim a majority in the state then the state is considered to have a_____

2. Daniel Elazar proposed three: _____

3. If I believed in maintaining elite political control, I would probably come from the _____.

4. If I believed that government is an important actor in solving society's problems, I would probably come from the_____.

5. If I believed that government should stay out of individuals' lives as much as possible I would probably come from the _____.

6. In Texas, the _____ is higher than the national average.

7. In Texas, the level of _____ is lower than the national average.

8. Most economists believe that Texas has benefited from _____.

9. In Texas, the _____ is lower than the national average.

10. Predicting how many Texans there will be in the future is largely a function of _____.

USING YOUR UNDERSTANDING:

1) Pretend you are a state legislator:
   a. Make a list of 5 initiatives you would propose if your background were from the moralistic subculture.
   b. Make a list of 5 initiatives you would propose if your background were from the traditionalistic subculture.
   c. Make a list of 5 initiatives you would propose if your background were from the individualistic subculture.
   d. Come up with 3 initiatives that could be supported by legislators from both the traditionalistic and individualistic subcultures.

2) Research the Internet (a good place to start is with the research organizations of the House http://www.hro.house.state.tx.us/ and Senate http://www.senate.state.tx.us/SRC/Index.htm which present Bill Analyses of recent sessions) to find at least three major laws or proposed constitutional amendments that came out of the most recent Texas legislative session. See if you can match their principles up with either the traditionalistic or individualistic subcultures.

3) Go to the Houston Area Survey at http://www.houstonareasurvey.org and pretend you are a policymaker. Come up with five policy options that would deal with some of demographic trends facing Houston (and, by extension, Texas) in the future.

REVIEW QUESTIONS:

Check ☑ the correct answer:

1) Daniel Elazar
   ☐ a.   is the state demographer of Texas.
   ☐ b.   started Texas political culture in the 1800s.
   ☐ c.   studied political culture in the U.S.
   ☐ d.   developed the concept of the majority-minority.

2) Political culture
   ☐ a.   is the way that legislators are polled in Austin.
   ☐ b.   is a concept developed to study people's attitude toward government.
   ☐ c.   is a way to poll people on who they plan to vote for in the next election.
   ☐ d.   is a concept that explains the economic activity of Texans.

3) The dominant political subcultures in Texas are individualism and traditionalism.
   ☐ True
   ☐ False

4) Traditionalism
- ☐ a. encourages political participation among elites.
- ☐ b. encourages political participation among the masses.
- ☐ c. encourages political participation in rural areas.
- ☐ d. encourages political participation in urban areas.

5) Moralism
- ☐ a. is very strong in Texas.
- ☐ b. started in the northeast.
- ☐ c. started in the south.
- ☐ d. is strongest in religious communities.

6) Individualism
- ☐ a. supports rule by elites.
- ☐ b. supports minimal government.
- ☐ c. feels that every individual should actively participate in government action.
- ☐ d. feels that government programs are a solution to poverty.

7) Demographic trends in Texas indicate that Anglos will be a majority in the state until at least 2025.
- ☐ True
- ☐ False

8) Economic activity in Texas in the nineteenth century centered on
- ☐ a. cotton and cattle.
- ☐ b. oil and gas.
- ☐ c. railroads and steel.
- ☐ d. high technology.

9) Economic activity in Texas in the twentieth century centered on
- ☐ a. cotton and cattle.
- ☐ b. oil and gas.
- ☐ c. railroads and steel.
- ☐ d. high technology.

10) Agriculture currently accounts for
- ☐ a. less than 2% of the Texas workforce.
- ☐ b. more than 40% of the Texas economy.
- ☐ c. more than 10% of the Texas workforce.
- ☐ d. less than 1% of the Texas economy.

11) Oil and gas currently accounts for
☐ a.   less than 1% of the Texas workforce.
☐ b.   around 6% of the Texas economy.
☐ c.   more than 20% of the Texas economy.
☐ d.   around 30% of the Texas workforce.

12) People earning a bachelor's degrees in Texas make
☐ a.   more than the national average for their group.
☐ b.   less than the national average for their group.
☐ c.   about the national average for their group.

13) People earning only a high school diploma in Texas make less than the national average for their group.
☐ a.   true
☐ b.   false

14) Income disparity in Texas is
☐ a.   about average for the U.S.
☐ b.   more than the average for the U.S.
☐ c.   less than the average for the U.S.

15) The primary reasons African Americans and Hispanics in Texas make less than Anglos is
☐ a.   most are new to the state and tend to live in ghettos.
☐ b.   they have traditionally been denied the right to vote and lack political representation in Austin.
☐ c.   they tend to be overwhelmingly elderly and were not able to save much for retirement.
☐ d.   they are younger and less educated than the Anglo population.

16) The poverty rate in Texas
☐ a.   is higher among Hispanics than Anglos.
☐ b.   is higher among Asians than Hispanics.
☐ c.   is lower than the national average.
☐ d.   is measured differently in Texas than in the U.S.

17) The poorest parts of Texas are
☐ a.   in urban areas like Houston and Dallas.
☐ b.   in the Texas Triangle.
☐ c.   along the Gulf coast.
☐ d.   along the border with Mexico.

18) NAFTA
  ☐ a. increased poverty in Texas.
  ☐ b. is a Federal government program to alleviate poverty in the inner cities.
  ☐ c. is a free trade agreement with Canada and Mexico.
  ☐ d. is a Federal agency that measures economic growth.

19) Educational attainment
  ☐ a. is not a big concern for Texas going into the future.
  ☐ b. will have a significant impact on economic growth in Texas in the future.
  ☐ c. indicates that high school will be plenty of schooling for the future.
  ☐ d. is significantly higher in Texas than other states because of its large public university systems,

20) Minority-majority
  ☐ a. means that no one group is currently in the majority.
  ☐ b. means that Hispanics are in the majority.
  ☐ c. means that Anglos exercise control over minorities in the state.
  ☐ d. is not something that will happen in Texas anytime soon.

ESSAY QUESTIONS:

1) What is the connection between political culture and educational attainment in Texas? Be sure to also discuss how this will impact the economic future of Texas and Texans.

2) What is the connection between political culture and the level of public participation in Texas? Be sure to discuss the historical development of Texas political culture and how this has impacted whether or not people are likely to vote or participate in other ways in the state.

3) How are demographic trends likely to affect the future of Texas? Be sure to discuss the economic and political consequences of these trends over the next 30 years.

CHAPTER 22

THE TEXAS CONSTITUTION

CHAPTER OUTLINE

I. The Texas Constitution in the Federal System (pp. 686-688)
    A. What is a constitution?
        1. A **constitution** establishes the basic framework within which a government functions.
        2. A **state** constitution affects the relationship of a state to the federal government and identifies the state's relationship to its local government.
    B. The Federal System
        1. **Vertical federalism** is the relationship between the state governments and the federal government as described by the U.S. Constitution.
        2. **Horizontal federalism** is the relationship that takes place among the states and among local governments.
        3. **Judicial federalism** is when a state court interprets it's state constitution to provide more rights than are afforded by the U.S. Constitution.

II. The Origins and Development of the Texas Constitution (pp. 689-694)
    A. Constitution of the State of Coahuila y Teja
        1. Texas under the **Mexican Constitution of 1824** lived under a federal system.
        2. Under that constitution the community property system and the homestead exemption from bankruptcy were created.
        3. Texans, discontent with the state constitution of 1827, held a convention in 1832 in San Felipe de Austin. Another convention was held in 1833 and created a draft constitution written by Sam Houston.
        4. Texans declared independence from Mexico in **1836**.
    B. Constitution of the Republic of Texas, 1836
        1. The delegates met for 15 days and wrote a constitution modeled on the U.S. Constitution.
        2. It established the separation of powers into the familiar 3-branch model, a bicameral legislature, the checks and balances of each branch, a bill or rights, and the democratic selection of government officials by free Anglo and Hispanic male voters.

3. It contained several provisions from Spanish law: community property, homestead exemptions and protections, and debtor relief.

C. Texas Constitution of 1845

1. In order to gain admission to the Union a new constitution had to be drafted by January 1, 1846.
2. The new state constitution was twice as long as the Republic of Texas constitution.
3. The new constitution featured the separation of powers into three branches, a bicameral legislature, an elected governor and legislature and an appointed judiciary.

D. Constitution of 1861

1. The Secession Convention in March approved amendments to the 1845 Constitution to reflect membership in the Confederate States of America.
2. The new constitution emphasized the constitutionality of slavery and demanded states' rights.
3. Governor Sam Houston refused to sign the oath and was forced out of office.

E. The Constitution of 1866

1. A new constitution was required as part of Reconstruction at the end of the Civil War which made the Constitution of 1861 void.
2. All references to the Confederacy were removed. Slavery was abolished and certain legal rights granted to former slaves. However, it failed to provide political rights to blacks like the right to vote and hold public office.
3. The governor was granted the item veto on appropriation bills and a system for public education. It specified that a system of public schools be established for black children

F. The Constitution of 1869

1. Radical Republicans took control of the U.S. Congress and required former confederate states to redraft their constitutions and provide for universal adult male suffrage.
2. The convention was unable to come to agreement on the new constitution. The uncompleted constitution was published and ratified by Texas voters in July 1869 thereby admitting Texas back into the Union in 1870.
3. Provisions new to the constitution were: the governor was given the power to appoint the attorney general and secretary of state, a poll tax was authorized to fund schools, it declared that the U.S. constitution including the Thirteenth and Fourteenth Amendments were the supreme law of the land, created an immigration bureau, no-fee grants for homesteads to settlers, mineral rights granted to landowners, forbade slavery and declared that all people were equal before the law, the legislature was given the ability to prohibit

alcohol sales near colleges unless the college was located in the county seat and was prohibited from enacting lotteries or granting divorces.

G. Draft Constitution of 1874 and the Convention of 1875
    1. The **Constitution of 1869** was a subject of controversy resulting from the process through with it was drafted and ratified.
    2. Many believed that the constitution was too long and put too much power into the hands of the governor. A constitutional convention was finally held in September 1875.
    3. The delegates were described as "angry, frustrated and frightened." They worked to remove what many saw as excesses of the Reconstruction government.
    4. The **Constitution of 1876** is the constitution still in effect today.

III. Contents of the Texas Constitution (p. 694–706)
A. Article I – **Bill of Rights**
    1. One function of a constitution is to place limits on government's ability to coerce its people. The Bill of Rights provides these limitations.
    2. It specifies that all free men have equal rights and that the writ of habeas corpus can not be suspended or delayed.
    3. It included the right of Texans to keep and bear arms.
B. Article II – The Powers of Government - General overview of the separation of powers in the Texas government.\
C. Article III – Legislative Department - The longest of the three articles dealing with the branches of government, outlines the structure and function of the legislative branch
D. Article IV – Executive Department - Describes the structure of the executive branch of state government
E. Article V – Judicial Department
    1. Describes the structure of the judicial branch of state government
    2. The structure of county governments appears here, primarily in the discussion of the county judge and the county commissioners court
F. Article VI – Suffrage
G. Article VII – Education – The Public Free Schools
    1. Education policy is a source of controversy. Is education a state function or a local function?
    2. A State Board of Education was created composed of the governor, comptroller, and secretary of state.
    3. Created the University of Texas
    4. A 1993 amendment established that the voters must consider any income tax proposal and that the funds would be dedicated to funding public schools.
H. Article VIII – Taxation and Revenue

I. Article IX – Counties
J. Article X – Railroads
K. Article XI – Municipal Corporations
L. Article XII – Private Corporations
M. Article XIII – Spanish and Mexican Land Titles (repealed Aug. 5, 1969)
N. Article XIV – Public Lands and Land Office
O. Article XV – Impeachment
P. Article XVI – General Provisions — This is a laundry list of items dealing with the legislature, the regulation of alcoholic beverages, dueling, bribery and corruption in state and local government, public printing and contracts, fences, livestock, vacancies in office and competitive bidding on state contracts.
Q. Article XVII – Amending the Constitutions

IV. Changing the Texas Constitution (p. 701)
A. Formal amendments change the letter of the Constitution. Tradition, practice, and procedure do not effectively change the spirit of the Texas Constitution.
B. Two-thirds of all members of each chamber of the Texas legislature must approve any proposed amendment.
C. The secretary of states' office then writes explanatory statements that are certified by the attorney general.
D. The majority of Texas voters must approve the amendments.
E. Amendment votes have very low turnout. Typically below 15%.
F. The legislature amended Article XVII to allow amendments to be proposed during special sessions
G. The constitution has been amended 439 times since it was ratified in 1876.
H. One significant amendment allowed the legislature to create a state government agency to regulate railroads and it's members were appointed by the governor. Voters changed the selection process to partisan elections in 1894.
I. Many amendments are amendments of other amendments.
J. The Bill of Rights has been amended 12 times. One was the **Equal Legal Rights Amendment**, which made illegal all laws that discriminated against anyone based on sex.
K. The governor is not formally involved in the amending process.
L. It is more difficult to remove a provision than to amend it.

V. Revising the Texas Constitution (p. 706–709)
A. Amendments are an effort to make incremental, piecemeal changes to the Texas Constitution. Revisions seek to redraft the entire document.
B. In 1974 the legislature met as a constitutional convention to consider recommendations of a constitutional revision commission formed in 1971.
C. Amendments are still the preferred method of constitutional change in Texas.

VI.   Understanding the Texas Constitution (p. 709–710)
    A.   The Texas Constitution and Democracy
        1.   The extreme length and obscure provisions make it difficult to assess the democratic nature of the Texas Constitution.
        2.   The current constitution was a reaction to extremes presented by the Reconstruction era after the Civil War.
        3.   One basic principle of a constitution is that it should be easy for the people to read. It should be brief, concise, well-organized, and written in simple language. The Texas constitution is none of those.
    B.   The Texas Constitution and the Scope of Government
        1.   A constitution creates a structure of government and establishes limits on the operation of that government. The limits on Texas government are quite explicit and specific.

VII.   Summary (p. 710)

LEARNING OBJECTIVES:

After studying Chapter 22, you should be able to:

1. Describe the three major kinds of federalism in the U.S. and how they apply to Texas.
2. Trace the development of ideas in the Texas Constitution from the 1820s to the present day.
3. Identify the main structures of the Texas Constitution.
4. Describe the amendment process of the Texas Constitution.
5. Understand the impact of the Texas Constitution on the state of democracy and participation in Texas.

The following activities should help you meet these objectives:

Objective 1: Describe the three major kinds of federalism in the U.S. and how they apply to Texas.

1. Create a chart showing the functions of vertical, horizontal, and judicial federalism.

2. Use the chart created in activity 1 to identify key issues where powers overlap and potential for political conflict between the states or between the government in Washington and Austin exists.

Objective 2: Trace the development of ideas in the Texas Constitution from the 1820s to the present day.

1. Create a timeline of Texas Constitutional History.

2. Draw up a list of major characteristics of the various Texas constitutions and apply them to the timeline in Activity 1.

Objective 3: Identify the main structures of the Texas Constitution.

1. Draw a diagram of Texas government as laid out in the constitution.

2. Consider potential policy conflicts between the various parts of government specified in the Texas Constitution and make a list of issues where the structure of government has hampered efficient policymaking.

Objective 4: Describe the amendment process of the Texas Constitution.

1. Make a list of key constitutional changes as outlined in the chapter. Why were these changes necessary?

2. Research a recent slate of Constitutional Amendments. You can find a list of proposed amendments from the 2005 legislative session at: http://www.sos.state.tx.us/elections/voter/2005novconsamend.shtml. Analyze why these amendments were necessary given the structure of the Texas Constitution.

Objective 5: Understand the impact of the Texas Constitution on the state of democracy and participation in Texas.

1. Poll your friends and relatives on what they know about the Texas Constitution. Make a list documenting their knowledge. Do you think their knowledge is adequate to voting to change the Texas constitution?

2. Take the list of Amendments from http://www.sos.state.tx.us/elections/voter/2005novconsamend.shtml and ask your friends and relatives to explain them to you. Be sure that they can explain how this amendment is relevant to their lives. Consider for a moment their level of knowledge and ability to determine whether a particular provision is wise or not.

3. Look at voter participation rates for the last few special elections for Constitutional Amendments. They can be found at: http://www.sos.state.tx.us/elections/historical/70-92.shtml. What kinds of people do you think are likely to vote in these elections?

KEY TERMS:

Identify and describe:

vertical federalism

horizontal federalism

judicial federalism

Mexican Constitution of 1824

Constitution of the Republic of Texas 1836

Texas Constitution of 1846

Constitution of 1861

Constitutional Convention

Constitution of 1866

Constitution of 1869

Constitution of 1876

Bill of Rights

Amendment

Equal Legal Rights Amendment

Revision

Constitution

Compare and Contrast:

Vertical and horizontal federalism

The Constitution of 1869 and the Constitution of 1876

The Constitution of 1824 and the Constitution of 1876

The Constitution of 1836 and the Constitution of 1876

Amendment and Revision

Name that term:

1.   The first constitution specifically affecting Texas was _____.

2.   These two constitutions where specific conditions for the readmission of Texas in to the Union were _____ and _____.

3.   The only constitution of Texas as an independent country was _____.

4.   The Supremacy Clause is a key part of _____.

5.   The Texas Supreme Court declaring the public school finance system unconstitutional in 1990 is an example of _____.

6.   States are concerned about Vermont's civil union law because of _____.

7.   The current Texas Constitution has a more extensive _____ than the United States constitution.

8.   The most common way of changing the Texas constitution is through _____.

9.   The current Texas constitution is the _____.

10.   When Texas originally became a state in the United States it had to pass _____.

11.   In order to revise the fundamental laws of Texas delegates meet in a _____.

12.   1974 marked the last significant effort in Texas at constitutional _____.

13.   The fundamental laws of the state of the State of Texas are contained in the _____.

14.   Women achieved legal equality in Texas through the _____.

USING YOUR UNDERSTANDING

1. Pretend you are a delegate at a new Texas Constitutional Convention. Sketch out a structure for Texas government to achieve maximum efficiency in government policymaking so that the state government could address many of the problems described in Chapter 21. What kind of resistance do you think you would encounter in this effort?

Be sure to consider the dominant political cultures in the state and their respective attitudes toward government.

2. Research the 1974 effort at constitutional revision in Texas. Here is a good place to start: http://texaspolitics.laits.utexas.edu/html/cons/0600.html. Create a chart of proposed changes and use that to compare to a chart of features of the constitution as it currently stands. Analyze why the 1974 effort failed to revise the constitution. Consider the factors of political culture from Chapter 21 in your effort to analyze this.

REVIEW QUESTIONS:

1. A constitution
    ☐ a.   establishes the basic framework of government.
    ☐ b.   establishes the laws that govern the people of a state.
    ☐ c.   is necessary in a monarchy.
    ☐ d.   is necessary for the efficient functioning of government.

2. Texas honoring drivers licenses from Louisiana is an example of
    ☐ a.   vertical federalism.
    ☐ b.   horizontal federalism.
    ☐ c.   judicial federalism.
    ☐ d.   constitutional revision.

3. The U.S. Supreme Court mandating that Texas desegregate its schools in *Brown vs. Board of Education* is an example of
    ☐ a.   vertical federalism.
    ☐ b.   horizontal federalism.
    ☐ c.   judicial federalism.
    ☐ d.   constitutional revision.

4. The Texas Supreme Court declaring the Texas school finance system unconstitutional is an example of
    ☐ a.   vertical federalism.
    ☐ b.   horizontal federalism.
    ☐ c.   judicial federalism.
    ☐ d.   constitutional revision.

5. Texas was once combined with the state of Coahuila as a governmental entity.
    ☐ True
    ☐ False

6. The first constitution that affected Texas was the Constitution of 1836.
    ☐ True
    ☐ False

7. One feature that Texas inherited from Spanish Law was
    ☐ a.   an elected judiciary.
    ☐ b.   a state sales tax on liquor and tobacco.
    ☐ c.   an appointed judiciary.
    ☐ d.   a homestead exemption from bankruptcy.

8. Texas declared independence from Mexico because
    ☐ a.   Mexico imposed new taxes on the Anglo settlers without their consent.
    ☐ b.   Santa Ana abolished the constitution.
    ☐ c.   Mexico invaded the United States.
    ☐ d.   Santa Ana executed a number of Texan leaders.

9. The Constitution of 1836
    ☐ a.   was easy to amend.
    ☐ b.   was modeled closely on the U.S. Constitution.
    ☐ c.   was adopted while Texas was still a state of Mexico.
    ☐ d.   allowed for the election of judges.

10. The freeing of slaves was made illegal by the
    ☐ a.   Constitution of 1836.
    ☐ b.   Constitution of 1845.
    ☐ c.   Constitution of 1861.
    ☐ d.   Constitution of 1866.

11. The Constitution of 1869 provided for
    ☐ a.   the election of the secretary of state.
    ☐ b.   the appointment of judges.
    ☐ c.   the election of the attorney general.
    ☐ d.   the appointment of legislators.

12. The largest group of members of the Constitutional Convention of 1874
    ☐ a.   were former delegates to the convention of 1868.
    ☐ b.   were members of the Grange.
    ☐ c.   were Republican.
    ☐ d.   were former slaves.

13. A Bill of Rights limits
    ☐ a.   government's ability to coerce its citizens.
    ☐ b.   business's ability to coerce its workers.
    ☐ c.   the people's ability to control their government.
    ☐ d.   the power of the governor to coerce the state legislature.

14. Articles II–IV of the current Texas constitution focus on
    ☐ a.   the structure of government.
    ☐ b.   the amendment process.
    ☐ c.   local government.
    ☐ d.   education, taxation and revenue.

15. Articles VII and VIII of the current Texas constitution focus on
    ☐ a.   the structure of government.
    ☐ b.   the amendment process.
    ☐ c.   local government.
    ☐ d.   education, taxation and revenue.

16. Articles IX and XI of the current Texas constitution focus on:
    ☐ a.   the structure of government.
    ☐ b.   the amendment process.
    ☐ c.   local government.
    ☐ d.   education, taxation and revenue.

17. Article XVII of the current Texas constitution focuses on:
    ☐ a.   the structure of government.
    ☐ b.   the amendment process.
    ☐ c.   local government.
    ☐ d.   education, taxation and revenue.

18. Since the 1950s Texas constitutional amendments have been
    ☐ a.   proposed quite often.
    ☐ b.   very rare occurrences.
    ☐ c.   fail at the ballot box the overwhelming amount of the time.
    ☐ d.   usually simple and clear.

19. An example of a successful amendment to the Texas Bill of Rights was the
    ☐ a.   Equal Rights Amendment.
    ☐ b.   Equal Legal Rights Amendment.
    ☐ c.   Gay Marriage Rights Amendment.
    ☐ d.   Rural Emergency Rights Amendment.

20. The governor is an integral part of the Constitutional Amendment process
     ☐ True
     ☐ False

21. The last serious attempt at constitutional revision in Texas occurred in
     ☐ a.   2003.
     ☐ b.   1985.
     ☐ c.   1974.
     ☐ d.   1955.

22. The most recent attempt to revise the constitution through a constitutional convention was
     ☐ a.   successful.
     ☐ b.   unsuccessful.

23. The process for amending the Texas constitution
     ☐ a.   2/3 of the members of the House of Representatives approve the amendment, the governor signs it, and a majority of voters in a special election approve it.
     ☐ b.   2/3 of the members of both houses of the legislature approve the amendment, the governor signs it, and a majority of voters in a special election approve it.
     ☐ c.   2/3 of the members of both houses of the legislature approve the amendment and the governor signs it.
     ☐ d.   2/3 of the members of both houses of the legislature approve the amendment, and a majority of voters in a special election approve it.

24. The Texas constitution is "brief, concise, well-organized, and written in simple language."
     ☐ True
     ☐ False

25. The Texas constitution is so restrictive it has, at times, limited the ability of the Texas government to respond to challenges in a rapidly changing world.
     ☐ True
     ☐ False

ESSAY QUESTIONS:

1. Compare and contrast the Texas Constitutions of 1846, 1869, and 1876. How did the different contexts under which these documents were written shape the structures of state government? Be sure to consider the independence and methods of selecting the different types of government and how this would impact policymaking under the three structures.

2. Consider the implications of vertical, horizontal and judicial federalism for the ability of local constituencies to shape the policies and laws under which they are forced to live. What are the implications for democratic choice?

3. Should constitutional change in Texas be easier or more difficult to implement? Be sure to explain why you chose one over the other.

4. How does the Texas Constitution affect political participation and democracy in Texas? How could the constitution be used to encourage more political participation?

CHAPTER 23

POLITICAL PARTIES, CAMPAIGNS, ELECTIONS AND INTEREST GROUPS IN TEXAS

CHAPTER OUTLINE

I.   Political Parties in Texas (pp. 716–726)
    A.   One-Party Politics
    B.   **Yellow Dog Democrats** loyal Democrats who would vote for a yellow dog if it ran for office under the Democratic Party label
    C.   Emergence of the Republican Party
    D.   Party in the Electorate
    E.   Party in Government
    F.   Party Organization
        1.   **Permanent Organization**
            a.   **Precincts** and **Precinct Chairs**
            b.   **County Executive Committee** and the **County Chair**
            c.   **State Executive Committee** and the **State Chair** and **Vice Chair**
        2.   **Temporary Organization**
            a.   **Precinct Convention**
            b.   **County** or Senatorial **District Convention**
            c.   **State Convention** delegates certify the candidates who won the primary as the official nominee of the party, adopt a **platform** (a statement of the party's goals and policies), and elect a chair, vice chair, and a state executive committee.
            d.   National Convention
    G. The Future of the Parties in Texas
        1.   Republican Party Voting Trends
        2.   Democratic Party Voting Trends

II. Types of Elections (pp. 726–729)
    A.   **Primary Elections** voters select party nominees
        1.   Only people who registered to vote with a party can vote in the **closed primaries**.
        2.   **Open primaries** allow voters to decide the day of the election whether to vote in the Republican or Democratic primary.
        3.   Texas primaries include elements of both closed and open primaries, but more closely align with the open primary.
    B.   The top two vote recipients run against each other in a **runoff election**,

C.   **General elections** pit the parties' nominees against one another on the first Tuesday after the first Monday in November of even-numbered years.

D.   **Local Elections** include elections for most city councils, school boards, and special districts in Texas and take place in May of odd-numbered years

E.   **Special Elections** are not regularly scheduled and are called for a specific purpose.

III.   Suffrage in Texas   (pp. 726–727)
    A.   Getting the Right to Vote in Texas
       1.   **Women's suffrage** and the ratification of the **Nineteenth Amendment** to the U.S. Constitution that guarantees women the right to vote
       2.   **Minorities**
          a.   **Poll taxes** required people pay each year to register to vote
          b.   **White primaries** discriminated against minority voters because in a white primary, only whites could vote.
          c.   Equal Protection Clause of the Fourteenth Amendment to the U.S. Constitution
          d.   Restrictive Registration Requirements
    B.   Voter Turnout in Texas

IV.   The Campaign Game (pp. 727–738)
    A.   Money and Campaigning
    B.   Big Money Contributions
       1.   Individual Contributions
       2.   PAC Contributions
    C.   Media

V. Interest Groups in Texas (pp. 738–743)
    A.   How Interest Groups Try to Shape Policy
       1.   **Lobbying** involves a variety of activities, ranging from providing information to policymakers to developing a strategy to help legislators pass or defeat a measure.
       2.   **Electioneering**
          a.   PACs
          b.   Public Endorsements
       3.   **Litigation** can affect change by taking the issue to court.
       4.   **Going public** allows interest groups to get their message across to the public by sending out direct mailings, writing columns in newspapers, taking out advertisements in newspapers and magazines, posting information on their websites, and buying billboard space and commercial time on radio and television stations.

B.   Types of Interest Groups
1.   **Economic interests** are characterized by a focus on issues that potentially affect the financial well-being of individuals, organizations, and businesses.
   a.   Business Groups and Trade Associations
   b.   Agricultural Groups
   c.   Labor Groups
2.   **Professional groups** consist of doctors, dentists, lawyers, and other professionals that are often politically connected and have money and are willing to spend it to protect their profession and livelihood.
3.   **Equality** interests promote minority opportunities in education, government, politics, and the workplace.
4.   **Education** interests represent public school teachers, school administrators, urban school districts, suburban school districts, and rural school districts.
C.   Understanding Parties, Interest Groups, and Campaigns and Elections
D.   Parties, Interest Groups, Campaigns, Elections and Democracy
E.   Parties, Interest Groups, Campaigns, Elections and the Scope of Government

VI.   Summary (p. 745)

LEARNING OBJECTIVES

After studying Chapter 23, you should be able to:

1.   Discuss the history of political parties in Texas, and how the electorate has been traditionally a one-party state.

2.   Identify the different types of elections in Texas, which offer voters many opportunities to have a say in government and politics.

3.   Explain the important role that Texas interest groups play in the policymaking process to gain access and influence policymakers.

4.   Understand the constant struggle throughout Texas history over suffrage, and the ways Texas prevented people from voting, changes in the law to make voting more accessible, and the effect on voter turnout in Texas.

5.   Describe the campaign game and the two critical campaign components of money and the media.

6.   Evaluate the interaction between parties, interest groups, campaigns, and elections in Texas politics.

The following exercises will help you meet these objectives:

Objective 1: Discuss the history of political parties in Texas, and how the electorate has been traditionally a one-party state.

    1.   Make a timeline of the major changes in Texas' political parties.

    2.   How did these changes impact the electorate?

Objective 2: Identify the different types of elections in Texas, which offer voters many opportunities to have a say in government and politics.

    1.   What is a primary election?

    2.   Identify the elements of open and closed primaries that are used in Texas primary elections today.

        1.

        2.

    3.   Candidates must meet certain obligations in order to get on the general election ballot, what are they?

1. Democrats

2. Republicans

3. Independent or Third Parties

4. What is a special election and who can call a special election?

    1.

    2.

    3.

    4.

5. What are some of the reasons why a special election is called?

    1.

    2.

    3.

Objective 3: Explain the important role that Texas interest groups play in the policymaking process to gain access and influence policymakers.

1.   What activities do interest groups utilize to shape policy?

        1.

        2.

        3.

        4.

2.   The text examines four types of interest groups. Complete the following table by listing the four types of groups, identifying their issues, and giving an example for each type of group.

Interest Group Type	Issues of Importance	Example of the Group Type

Objective 4: Understand the constant struggle throughout Texas history over suffrage, and the ways Texas prevented people from voting, changes in the law to make voting more accessible, and the effect on voter turnout in Texas.

1. What impact has the U.S. Supreme Court had on suffrage? Identify the constitutional basis for their decisions?

    1.
    2.

    3.

Objective 5: Describe the campaign game and the two critical campaign components of money and the media.

1. What are some of the reasons why it is expensive to run a state-wide campaign in Texas compared to other states?

    1.

    2.

    3.

    4.

2. In Texas elections, dollar amount is not a factor in an election but rather is a sign that those candidates are going to win anyway. Why would a candidate win regardless of how much money they spent?

3.   Who can make political contributions in Texas?

    1.

    2.

4.   What types of limits are placed on campaign contributions in Texas?

Objective 6: Evaluate the interaction between parties, interest groups, campaigns, and elections in Texas politics.

    1.   What is the purpose of the four groups?

        1.   Political Parties –

        2.   Interest Groups –

        3.   Campaigns –

        4.   Elections –

    2.   How do the four groups differ in their purposes?

3.   How does their behavior change when they interact within the scope of government and in a democracy?

KEY TERMS

Identify and describe:

Yellow Dog Democrats

Temporary Organization

Permanent Organization

Precinct

Precinct Chair

County Executive Committee

County Chair

State Executive Committee

State Chair

Vice Chair

Precinct Convention

County or District Convention

State Convention

Platform

Primaries

Closed Primaries

Open Primaries

Runoff Election

General election

Nonpartisan election

Special election

Nineteenth Amendment

Poll tax

White primary

Compare and contrast:

Temporary organization and permanent organization

County Executive Committee and State Executive Committee

Precinct Convention, County or Senatorial District Convention and State Convention

Closed Primaries and Open Primaries

Name that term:

1. Conventions held every two years that allow the rank-and-file members of the party to participate in party activities

   _____

2. A committee that consists of precinct chairs and county chair, which is in charge of running the country primary and the county conventions

   _____

3. A committee consisting of two representatives from each senatorial district plus a state chair and vice chair, which plans and runs the state convention and builds the party throughout the state

   _____

4. A meeting in which people who voted in the party's primary meet the night of the primary in their precinct to participate in party activities

   _____

5. A meeting in which delegates selected from the precinct conventions vote on which delegates and resolutions to send to the state convention

   _____

6. A statement of the party's goals and policies approved by the delegates at the convention

   _____

7. An election in which voters decide who the party will nominate to run in the general election

_____

8. An election held the first Tuesday after the first Monday in November every two years between the nominees of each party

_____

9. An election in which candidates do not run under a party label

_____

10. An election in which only white voters could participate, and declared unconstitutional by the U.S. Supreme Court in 1944

_____

USING YOUR UNDERSTANDING

1. Try your hand at sketching out a chart that diagrams the temporary and permanent party organizations in Texas and the relationship between the two organizations. Be sure to indicate key election dates and how they correspond to this process. Also, include how the permanent party supports the temporary party. Briefly discuss the purpose of each level of organization. Evaluate how well this system works for Texas.

2. Although many voters believe that elections are held in November, elections in Texas are conducted throughout the year. In reading this chapter, develop a two-year timeline for elections in Texas. Take note of the differences between even numbered years and odd numbered years and the function that each election performs. Describe briefly what you have found. Use this exercise to write a timeline comparing different types of elections and their purposes.

REVIEW QUESTIONS

Check ☑ the correct answer:

1. Which of the following statements is TRUE?
   - ☐ a. Primary elections in Texas are called open primaries.
   - ☐ b. Primary elections in Texas are called closed primaries.
   - ☐ c. Primary elections in Texas are a combination of open and closed primaries.
   - ☐ d. Texas does not have primaries because it uses the caucus method of selection.

2. For most of Texas history, the battle for winning an election took place in the
   - ☐ a. primary election.
   - ☐ b. general election.
   - ☐ c. special election.
   - ☐ d. bond election.

3. Because of a Texas law passed in 1959, Lyndon Johnson, a Democrat, was able to run for reelection to the United States Senate at the same time that he ran for the vice president of the United States in 1960.
   - ☐ True
   - ☐ False

4. In 1919 Texas became the first southern state to ratify the Nineteenth Amendment to the U.S. Constitution, which was adopted in the U.S. Constitution in 1920 and guarantees
   - ☐ a. all Blacks the right to vote.
   - ☐ b. women the right to vote.
   - ☐ c. all men the right to vote.
   - ☐ d. all white men the right to vote.

5. In 1927 the Supreme Court struck down the state law requiring white primaries as a violation of the
   - ☐ a. Equal Protection Clause of the Fourteenth Amendment to the U.S. Constitution.
   - ☐ b. the Fifteenth Amendment to the U.S. Constitution that extends to African Americans the right to vote.
   - ☐ c. the Nineteenth Amendment to the U.S. Constitution.
   - ☐ d. all of the above

6. Lobbying involves
   ☐ a. electioneering and litigation
   ☐ b. going public
   ☐ c. a variety of activities, ranging from providing information to policymakers to developing a strategy to help legislators pass or defeat a measure.
   ☐ d. all of the above

7. By the middle of the 1990s, Texas was still a one-party state, as Democrats continued to expand their lead over Republicans.
   ☐ True
   ☐ False

8. The Republicans control both houses of the legislature and all statewide offices, including all 18 judges on the Texas Supreme Court and the Texas Court of Criminal Appeals.
   ☐ True
   ☐ False

9. The number of delegates that a precinct sends to the county convention and the number from each county that go to the state convention are determined by
   ☐ a. the percentage of the vote that the party's candidate for governor received within that precinct or county in the last election.
   ☐ b. the Texas Legislature.
   ☐ c. the State Parties.
   ☐ d. the Federal Election Commission.

10. A primary election is an election
    ☐ a. held the first Tuesday after the first Monday in November every two years between the nominees of each party.
    ☐ b. in which candidates do not run under a party label.
    ☐ c. in which voters decide who the party will nominate to run in the general election.
    ☐ d. that is not regularly scheduled and are called for a specific purpose.

11. Texas does not require people to register under a party affiliation, like in closed primaries, but Texas does require voters to publicly disclose on Election Day which party primary they are going to vote.
    ☐ True
    ☐ False

12. The role of the party in Texas government has traditionally been very different than in the federal government because
□ a. officeholders were of the same party, and Texas has been ruled by one party for most of its history.
□ b. party affiliation had not been an important variable in understanding the workings of Texas government.
□ c. the in fighting between the governor and legislature or within the legislature was between liberal and conservative and urban and rural.
□ d. all of the above

13. The permanent organization consists
□ a. of elected party officials and committees at the local, county, and state level that perform party building activities throughout the year.
□ b. of conventions that occur every two years at the local, county, and state levels.
□ c. both a and b
□ d. none of the above

14. Interest groups in Texas are powerful compared to the interest groups in other states because
□ a. studies show that interest groups tend to be stronger in states that traditionally have had a one-party system, a low-level of professionalism in the legislature, and a fragmented executive branch.
□ b. Texas interest groups are better organized and more actively recruiting candidates, helping candidates win elections, and expecting, once candidates are in office, that they will go along with the group's agenda.
□ c. Texas has a history of being a strong two-party system.
□ d. all of the above

15. Once a candidate is in office, an interest group's financial contributions and political support *does not* ensure the group will continue to have access to an elected official.
□ True
□ False

16. Texas lobbyists must register with the Texas Ethics Commission as lobbyists and file periodic reports of their lobbying activity.
□ True
□ False

17. Texas has no limits on how much an individual or PAC can contribute to a campaign.
☐ True
☐ False

18. Texas campaigns are expensive. In fact, some of the most expensive campaigns in the United States' history have been Texas gubernatorial elections.
☐ True
☐ False

19. Texas has incorporated many election changes to make voting more accessible, and, as a result, Texas has one of the highest voter turnouts in the nation, consistently ranking in the top 10.
☐ True
☐ False

20. In the early 1900s the Democratic Party's control over politics in Texas allowed the Democrats to institute a poll tax that required people to pay each year to register to vote.
☐ True
☐ False

ESSAY QUESTIONS

1. Texas interest groups have been able to play a key role in the policymaking process, in part because there have been few party mechanisms or efforts to enforce party rule, and party factions have struggled for supremacy. How do interest groups try to shape policy? What tactics do Texas interest groups utilize in their efforts to influence public policy? What types of interest groups operate in Texas?

2. The goal of the Democratic and Republican parties is to win elections. In Texas there are different kinds of elections that voters can participate. What are the different types of elections? When are they conducted and what is the purpose of each election?

3. Throughout American and Texas histories, there has been a constant struggle over suffrage. Write an essay that delineates the ways Texas prevented women and

minorities from voting. In your essay, include the changes in the law to make voting more accessible for women and minorities.

4. Why are money and the media two important components of the campaign game in Texas? Where does the money come from and how do candidates spend their campaign funds? Should Texas limit campaign contributions?

5. In Texas, the history of political parties has been the history of the Democratic Party and of one-party rule, and only in the last few decades has the Republican Party become competitive in Texas. Write an essay that discusses the history of political parties in Texas, which includes the Democratic Party's dominance and the emergence of the Republican Party.

CHAPTER 24

THE TEXAS LEGISLATURE

CHAPTER OUTLINE

I. Constitutional Framework of the Legislature (pp. 750–753)
    A. **Bicameral Legislature**
        1. The Texas House of Representatives has 150 members.
        2. The Texas Senate has 31 members.
    B. Legislative Sessions
        1. The Texas Constitution calls for **biennial sessions** (sessions every two years) beginning the second Tuesday in January of every odd-numbered year for 140 days.
        2. Only the governor can call a **special session**, and the governor dictates the issues that the legislature will address during a special session.
    C. Length of Legislators' Terms
        1. Texas House of Representatives serve two-year terms.
        2. Texas senators serve four-year terms.
    D. Compensation for members of the House and Senate and their presiding officers is $7,200 per year.

II. Membership and Redistricting (pp. 754–760)
    A. Qualifications for Office
    B. Membership Characteristics
    C. **Redistricting** is the process by which district lines are drawn.
        1. Every 10 years, after the census is taken, state legislatures across the nation redraw the lines of the state legislative districts and the congressional districts within their states.
        2. Redistricting sometimes leads to **gerrymandering** or the drawing of legislative district lines to benefit a certain side or political interest, such as a political party or incumbents.
    D. Redistricting State Legislative Districts in Texas
        1. Each Texas House district consists of a population of 139,012.
        2. Each Texas Senate district consists of a population of 672,639.
        3. Role of the Legislative Redistricting Board (LRB)
    E. Redistricting Texas Congressional Districts

      1.   Following the 2000 census, Texas picked up two additional seats in the United State House of Representatives to bring the total to 32.

      2.   The battle over redistricting was of course important to Texas because how districts are shaped affects which candidates will win.

III.   Legislative Leadership (pp. 760–763)

    A.   Speaker of the House

        1.   The speaker is a member of the House of Representatives who is chosen by a majority of fellow House members to be the speaker.

        2.   Members who want to be speaker try to get fellow members to sign pledges of support.

        3.   He is able to reward his supporters with benefits, ranging from a prized committee chairmanship to better office space, and punish those who oppose him by giving them poor committee assignments and ignoring their bills.

        4.   The current Speaker is Tom Craddick, a Republican from Midland.

    B.   Lieutenant Governor and the Senate

        1.   The lieutenant governor is the leader of the Senate and is elected to that position by voters in a statewide election.

        2.   The Texas lieutenant governor does not run as a team with the governor.

        3.   The lieutenant governor is the most powerful politician in the state.

        4.   Republican David Dewhurst is the current Texas Lieutenant Governor.

    C.   Powers of the Presiding Officers in the Legislative Process

        1.   Both the speaker and the lieutenant governor are given substantial powers to run their respective chambers

        2.   They appoint their respective House and Senate committee chairs and committee members, refer all bills to committees, and preside over all sessions, giving them the power to recognize those who want to speak, interpret the rules, decide when a vote takes place, and decide the outcome of a voice vote.

        3.   The speaker will vote to break a tie, or to signal to other legislators the importance of the bill to the speaker.

        4.   The lieutenant governor cannot vote in the Senate except to break a tie.

        5.   If the members do not like how their leader is exercising power they can strip the leader of many of his powers.

IV.   Committees (pp. 763–766)

    A.   Types of Committees

        1.   **Standing committees** are created by the legislature to deal with a particular policy area or responsibility.

            a.   After a bill is introduced into one of the chambers, the presiding officer assigns the bill to a committee.

      b.   The committee has almost life or death control of bills, and most bills die at this stage.

      c.   Some of the bills will be given a hearing and legislators, staffers, lobbyists, and others will gather and distribute information about the bill and try to influence the final shape the bill takes.

      d.   The committee can make changes to bills and may make so many changes that the bill's sponsor may not even recognize it at the end.

2.   Many standing committees have **subcommittees**, which are subunits of the committees, and have a specialization within the broader topic that the committee is responsible for and help share the workload of the committee.

3.   **Conference committees** are ad hoc committees organized to reconcile different versions of a bill passed by the House and the Senate.

      a.   Conference committees can only deal with the one bill to which they are assigned.

      b.   Each conference committee consists of five House members appointed by the speaker and five senators appointed by the lieutenant governor.

      c.   To reach agreement in the conference committee, three of the five House members and three of the five senators must agree on a bill.

      d.   The conference committee then sends the bill back to the House and Senate for an up or down vote of the bill the conference committee approved.

4.   **Interim committees** are standing committees appointed by the presiding officer to meet when the legislature is not in session to investigate issues, problems, and proposals for the next legislative session.

5.   **Select or special committees** are ad hoc committees formed for a specified period to examine a problem or issue and to come up with recommendations on what the state should do.

6.   In the House, in order of seniority, each legislator can select one committee he wants to be on as long as half of the committee slots on that committee are not already filled by seniority.

7.   The rest of the committee assignments and the selection of the chair and vice chair of each committee are left to the speaker's discretion.

8.   The presiding officers tend to reward their friends with choice committee assignments and committee chairs.

9.   Unlike Congress, presiding officers choose opposition party members to be committee chairs, although they usually are members who agree with the presiding officer philosophically and ideologically.

B.   Committee Chairs

1. The committee chair may decide he does not want a bill to pass so he may refuse to hold hearings on the bill.
2. The committee chair may send it to a subcommittee he knows will kill the bill.
3. And the committee chair may prevent a bill from getting out of committee when the majority of committee members want the bill passed.
4. Because of the power that committee chairs have, the selection of committee chairs is one of the important decisions presiding officers make.

V. The Legislative Process in the Texas Legislature (pp. 766–776)
  A. Types of Legislation
    1. The term "bill" describes any legislation currently in one of the chambers of the legislature.
    2. House Bills, indicated by the abbreviation HB, are the primary pieces of legislation introduced in the House. Similar bills in the Senate are called Senate Bills (SB).
    3. House Concurrent Resolutions (HCR) are a type of legislation that conveys the sentiment of the legislature. These bills are called Senate Concurrent Resolutions (SCR) in the Senate.
    4. House Joint Resolutions (HJR) and Senate Joint Resolutions (SJR) are pieces of legislation that propose changes to the Texas Constitution. Joint resolutions must be approved by two-thirds of the members of the House and two-thirds of the members of the Senate and approved by a majority of Texas voters before they become amendments to the Texas Constitution.
    5. House and Senate committees regularly rewrite bills that have been referred to them. These altered bills are called Committee Substitute House Bills (CSHB) and Committee Substitute Senate Bills (CSSB).
    6. Bills also can be classified by subject.
       a. *Local bills* are limited to a specific geographical area of the state, such as cities, counties, or school districts.
       b. *Special bills* are pieces of legislation that deal with a select or special individual or entity.
       c. All other bills are considered *general bills*.
  B. The Legislative Process in the House
    1. Anyone can write a piece of legislation, but only members of the House of Representatives may introduce the bill in the House.
    2. The Texas Legislative Council is a legislative agency that provides bill drafting services and research assistance, among other services.

3. Representatives of organized interests often write pieces of legislation and ask members of the Texas House and Senate to introduce the bills.

4. Lobbyists provide information on proposed legislation in committee hearings.
5. Interest groups mobilize public opinion through advertising campaigns.
6. After the bill has been written, the representative introduces the bill in the House.
7. House members (and Senators) may introduce bills only during the first 60 days of the 140-day regular legislative session. At the end of the 60-day period, the introduction of any bill other than a local bill or a bill dealing with an emergency declared by the governor requires the approval of at least four-fifths of the members present and voting in the House.
8. Bills that increase taxes or raise money for use by state government, for example, must be introduced in the House first.
9. When the bill is introduced, it is assigned a number and "read" the first time. The bill is not read in its entirety. Instead the clerk reads the short description of the bill, called a caption.
10. The Speaker of the House then assigns the bill to a committee.
11. The chair of each committee controls the agenda of that committee.
12. House rules allow a committee to meet in a public hearing where testimony is heard and the committee takes official action on the legislation.
13. Committees also may meet in work sessions to discuss legislation without taking official action.
14. After considering a bill, the committee may choose to take no action or it may issue a report on the bill.
    a. The committee's report outlines the committee's recommendation for further action on the bill.
    b. A detailed bill analysis complete with a **fiscal impact statement** appears in the report.
15. The bill is then sent to the Committee on Calendars or the Committee on Local.
16. When the bill is considered by the full House, it receives its second reading.
    a. The bill's caption is read and then debated by the full membership of the House.
    b. Any House member may offer an amendment to the bill.
    c. The amendment must be approved by a majority of the members present and voting.
17. If amended, the full House membership votes to pass the bill.

18. The bill is then considered on third reading and final passage; a bill may be amended during third reading, but such an amendment must be approved by a two-thirds vote of the members present and voting.
19. The Texas Constitution requires that all bills be read on three separate days.
20. The bill is considered for final passage by the House.
    a. The bill may be passed by a voice vote or a recorded vote.
    b. Recorded votes are collected by electronic device controlled by buttons located on each member's desk.
21. If a bill receives a simple majority of the vote during final passage, it is considered passed.
22. The **engrossed** House bill, which incorporates any amendments approved on the floor of the House, goes to the Senate for that chamber's consideration.

C. Legislative Process in the Senate
   1. The legislative process in the Senate is very similar to the process in the House.
   2. When the bill arrives in the Senate, it is read for the first time and then referred to committee by the lieutenant governor.
   3. The Senate committee examines the bill and can make changes to it.
      a. In the Senate, testimony may be heard and official action may be taken during any meeting of a committee or subcommittee.
      b. The committee writes a report outlining its recommendations.
   4. A favorable committee report is printed and distributed to Senators.
   5. Local and noncontroversial bills are placed on the calendar by the Senate Administration Committee.
   6. All other bills are considered by the full Senate in the order in which the bills are reported from Senate committees.
   7. Following Senate tradition, the first bill reported out of committee never goes to the Senate floor for a vote and serves as a **blocking bill**.
   8. Because bills have to be reported in the order they are received, all other bills require a suspension of the rules by a two-thirds vote in order to consider the bills out of order.
      a. Suspension of the rules requires a two-thirds majority.
      b. The level of a bill's support can be gauged before the bill comes up for third reading and final passage.
   9. The bill is read for a second time, debated, and subject to amendment by a majority vote.
   10. After amendments have been considered, the bill is voted on to pass to the third reading.

11. After the bill is read for a third time, amendments may be approved by a two-thirds vote.
12. The bill is considered for final passage by a majority vote.
13. The bill is sent back to the originating chamber, in this case the House of Representatives.

D. The Bicameral Legislative Process
1. If a bill passed both chambers in an identical format, it is printed in its final form, signed by the lieutenant governor and the speaker, and then sent to the governor.
2. If a bill returns to the originating chamber with amendments, the originating chamber may vote to agree to the amendments or it can request a conference committee to negotiate the differences between the two versions.
3. If the amendments are agreed to, the bill is put in its final form, signed by the lieutenant governor and the speaker, and sent to the governor.
4. The **conference committee**, which is temporary committees comprised of five members each from the House and the Senate, writes a report of the new language in the bill.
5. If the report is approved by both chambers, the presiding officers sign it and it is sent to the governor.

E. Gubernatorial Action
1. The governor has ten days (Sundays excepted) to decide whether to sign the bill, veto it, or allow it to become law without a signature.
   a. If the governor signs a bill, it becomes law and takes effect either immediately or at the time specified in the bill.
   b. If a governor vetoes a bill and the legislature is still in session, the bill is returned to chamber in which it originated, accompanied by a statement of the governor's objections.
   c. A two-thirds vote of the members of both chambers can override the governor's veto.
2. If a bill is sent to the governor within ten days of the end of the legislative session, and just about every bill passes the legislature in the final days of the session, the governor has twenty days after final adjournment to take action on the bill or to let it become law without a signature.
3. More than 5,600 pieces of legislation were filed in both chambers during the 2005 regular session of the 79th Legislature.
4. The legislature enacted 1,389 bills and nine joint resolutions.
5. Governor Perry vetoed 19 bills
6. Only seven bills became law without the governor's signature.
7. The current Texas Governor is Republican Rick Perry.

F. The Legislative Process Illustrated

VI. Understanding the State Legislature (pp. 776–777)
   A. The State Legislature and Democracy
      1. In a number of ways the state legislature is a democratic institution.
         a. Its members are elected from the districts they represent and remain in office by running for reelection.
         b. Texas also does not have term limits so voters can vote for a legislator and keep her in office for as long as they want.
         c. The Texas constitution tried to make the legislature democratic by keeping the legislators as much like the people they represent as possible.
            1. It does this by having the legislature meet in biennial sessions and keeping its pay to legislators low.
            2. Most people in Texas fit the constitutional requirements to serve in the legislature.
            3. The low pay has instead discouraged many people from running for the state legislature because they cannot afford to be a legislator and take several weeks off from work at a time to serve in the legislature.
      2. **Redistricting** also does not always promote democracy; it still allows those in power to draw the lines to advantage some interests and marginalize others.
   B. The State Legislature and the Scope of Government

V. Summary (p. 777)

LEARNING OBJECTIVES

After studying Chapter 24, you should be able to:

1. Discuss the constitutional framework of the Texas Legislature by comparing and contrasting the constitutional requirements for the Texas House of Representatives and Texas Senate.

2. Identify the important membership and redistricting requirements for the Texas Legislature.

3. Explain the process of how a bill becomes law and, perhaps more importantly, the many points at which a bill can fail to become law, as it travels through the Texas House and Texas Senate.

4. Understand the importance of the legislative leadership in the House and the Senate, and the differences and similarities between the powers of the Speaker of the House and the lieutenant governor.

5. Describe the different kinds of committees, their responsibilities and jurisdiction, and how they make the workload of the Texas Legislature more manageable and more efficient than if the entire legislature were doing everything.

The following exercises will help you meet these objectives:

Objective 1: Discuss the constitutional framework of the Texas Legislature by comparing and contrasting the constitutional requirements for the Texas House of Representatives and Texas Senate.

1. The text compares the differences between the Texas House of Representatives and the Texas Senate. Complete the following table by identifying the similarities and differences for each chamber.

Characteristic	Texas House	Texas Senate
Bill Approval		
Veto Power		
# of Members		
Level of Prestige		
Term of Office		
Sole Responsibilities	1. 2.	1. 2.
Compensation		

Objective 2: Identify the important membership and redistricting requirements for the Texas Legislature.

1.　The text delineates the qualifications for office for the Texas House of Representatives and the Texas Senate. Complete the following table by identifying and comparing the constitutional requirements of a Texas legislator.

Characteristic	Texas House	Texas Senate
State Residency		
District Residency		
Age Requirement		

2.　What is redistricting? How does redistricting differ from gerrymandering?

3.　How often does redistricting take place? Currently, what is the population of a House district and how does that compare to the population of a Senate district?

4. Who is responsible for redistricting? If redistricting failures occur, then, who is responsible?

Objective 3: Explain the process of how a bill becomes law and, perhaps more importantly, the many points at which a bill can fail to become law, as it travels through the Texas House and Texas Senate.

1. Assuming that a bill will pass every step of the legislative process, identify the major points a bill must pass in the House before it is sent to the Senate.

1.

2.

3.

4.

5.

6.

7.

2. Assuming that a bill passed every step of the legislative process in the House, identify the major points a bill must pass in the Senate.

1.

2.

3.

4.

5.

6.

3. Compare the two processes and identify the primary difference.

4. Once a bill passes the House and the Senate, what happens to the bill if the Senate version of the bill is amended or different from the original House version?

1.

2.

3.

4.

5.   What is an enrolled bill and what is an engrossed bill?

6.   What action can the governor take and what check does the legislature have against the governor's action?

        1.

        2.

        3.

7.   Review the legislative process and steps that you have delineated and identify where a bill could fail to become law.

Objective 4: Understand the importance of the legislative leadership in the House and the Senate, and the differences and similarities between the powers of the speaker of the House and the lieutenant governor.

        1.   The text compares the differences between the speaker of the House and the lieutenant governor. Complete the following table by identifying the similarities and differences for each legislative leadership position.

Characteristic	Speaker of the House	Lieutenant Governor
Method of Selection		
Appoint Committee Chairs		
Appoint Committee Members		
Voting Power		
Current Presiding Officer		

2. In some cases the lieutenant governor seems more powerful than the Speaker and in other cases the Speaker appears more powerful. Identify the leadership strengths of the lieutenant governor and the speaker.

Objective 5: Describe the different kinds of committees, their responsibilities and jurisdiction, and how they make the workload of the Texas Legislature more manageable and more efficient than if the entire legislature were doing everything.

1. The brunt of the work in any legislature is done in committees. List and describe in detail the types of committees the Texas Legislature uses and provide one House and Senate committee example of each committee type.

1.

2.

3.

4.

5.

KEY TERMS

Identify and describe:

Bicameral legislature
Biennial sessions

Special sessions

Redistricting

Gerrymandering

Standing committees

Subcommittees

Conference committees

Interim committees

Select or special committees

Fiscal impact statement

Engrossed
Blocking bill

Compare and contrast:

redistricting and gerrymandering

standing committees, subcommittees, and conference committees

biennial sessions and special sessions

interim committees and select or special committees

Name that term:

1. A legislature divided into two houses

    _____

2. Established for a specified period to examine problems or issues and develop recommendations on what the state should do

    _____

3. A standing committee that meets between legislative sessions to study issues, problems, and proposals in a particular policy area

    _____

4. Legislative sessions that take place once every two years

    _____

5. Legislative sessions called by the governor for whatever purpose the governor designates—can last no longer than 30 days

    _____

6. The process through which district lines are drawn

_____

7. An unimportant bill introduced in the Texas Senate that is the first bill reported out of committee; Senate rules require that all other bills have the support of two-thirds of the Senate before they may be debated on the floor

_____

8. Drawing districts in such a way as to benefit a particular interest, such as a political party

_____

9. An indication of the costs to state and local government if the bill becomes law

_____

10. The printed version of a bill as it has passed either the House of Representatives or the Senate

_____

USING YOUR UNDERSTANDING

1. Try your hand at sketching out a diagram for the legislative process. Be sure to indicate key steps in the process. Also, include any action that may cause the bill to fail and any action that may be taken to revive a bill. Keep in mind the House, the Senate and the governors' roles in the process. Briefly discuss and evaluate the effectiveness of this process.

2. Locate the Texas Constitution and that of another state, such as Louisiana, Illinois, or California. In reading the Legislative section of each constitution look for similarities or differences with the Texas Legislature. Take note of the constitutional requirements for members, the duties and responsibilities it creates, and the functions they perform. Describe briefly what you have found. Use this exercise to write a term paper comparing different types of legislatures and their effectiveness.

REVIEW QUESTIONS

Check ☑ the correct answer:

1. A bicameral legislature is a legislature that is
    - ☐ a. a one-chamber legislative branch.
    - ☐ b. divided into two houses.
    - ☐ c. empowered with both executive and legislative duties and responsibilities.
    - ☐ d. legislative session that occurs every two years.

2. Which of the following statements is TRUE regarding the Texas Legislature?
    - ☐ a. The House has 435 members elected every two years and the Senate has 100 members elected every six years.
    - ☐ b. The House has 400 members and the Senate has 40 members.
    - ☐ c. The House has 31 members elected every two years and the Senate has 150 members elected for four-year terms.
    - ☐ d. none of the above

3. The Texas Constitution calls for biennial sessions beginning the second Tuesday in January of every odd-numbered year for no longer than 140 days.
    - ☐ True
    - ☐ False

4. Only the lieutenant governor can call a special session, and the lieutenant governor dictates the issues that the legislature will address during a special session.
    - ☐ True
    - ☐ False

5. Who is the current governor of the State of Texas?
    - ☐ a. Tom Craddick
    - ☐ b. David Dewhurst
    - ☐ c. Rick Perry
    - ☐ d. Greg Abbott

6. Who is the current lieutenant governor of Texas?
    - ☐ a. Tom Craddick
    - ☐ b. David Dewhurst
    - ☐ c. Rick Perry
    - ☐ d. Greg Abbott

7. Texas legislative pay is the lowest in the United States because any increase to the annual salary for Texas legislators must be approved by the voters and voters have not approved a pay raise since 1975.
    ☐ True
    ☐ False

8. Every 10 years, after the census is taken, the state legislature redraws the lines of the state legislative districts and the congressional districts, which is called gerrymandering.
    ☐ True
    ☐ False

9. Who is the current Texas Speaker of the House?
    ☐ a.   Tom Craddick
    ☐ b.   David Dewhurst
    ☐ c.   Rick Perry
    ☐ d.   Greg Abbott

10. How is the Texas speaker of the House chosen?
    ☐ a.   The speaker is elected statewide.
    ☐ b.   The speaker is appointed by the governor.
    ☐ c.   The speaker is elected as a state representative and selected by the full House to serve as speaker.
    ☐ d.   The speaker is selected by the majority party caucus to serve as speaker.

11. The Legislative Redistricting Board consists of
    ☐ a.   the governor, the speaker of the House, the attorney general, the comptroller of public accounts, and the land commissioner.
    ☐ b.   the lieutenant governor, the speaker of the House, the agriculture commissioner, the comptroller of public accounts, and the land commissioner.
    ☐ c.   the lieutenant governor, the speaker of the House, the attorney general, the treasurer, and the land commissioner.
    ☐ d.   the lieutenant governor, the speaker of the House, the attorney general, the comptroller of public accounts, and the land commissioner.

12. Which of the following powers does the Texas Constitution grant solely to the Texas Senate?
    ☐ a. the power to confirm appointments
    ☐ b. the power to raise taxes
    ☐ c. the power to impeach state level officeholders
    ☐ d. all of the above

13. Based on the 2000 census, each House district needed to consist of a population of 139,012, and each Senate district a population of 672,639.
    ☐ True
    ☐ False

14. In the Texas Senate, committee chairs are selected
    ☐ a. on their seniority status.
    ☐ b. by appointment by the speaker.
    ☐ c. by appointment by the lieutenant.
    ☐ d. by majority vote of the Texas Senate.

15. The governor and the lieutenant governor are elected as a team, similar to the vice president and president of the United States.
    ☐ True
    ☐ False

16. An interim committee
    ☐ a. are subunits of committees.
    ☐ b. is created by the legislature to deal with a particular policy area or responsibility.
    ☐ c. are ad hoc committees organized to reconcile different versions of a bill passed by the House and the Senate.
    ☐ d. meets when the legislature is not in session to investigate issues, problems, and proposals for the next legislative session.

17. A conference committee is created in which of the following circumstances?
    ☐ a. A measure passes both houses of the legislature but is vetoed by the governor.
    ☐ b. A measure passes the House and Senate with different amendments.
    ☐ c. A measure passes the Senate but fails in the House.
    ☐ d. A measure fails both the House and Senate.

18. Committee chairs often decide the success or failure of a bill.
☐ True
☐ False

19. If the governor vetoes a piece of legislation the Texas legislature may
☐ a. override the veto by a majority vote of both the House and Senate.
☐ b. override the veto by a two-thirds vote in both the House and Senate.
☐ c. override the veto by a two-thirds vote of the entire Texas Legislature.
☐ d. not take any action, as the governor's veto cannot be overridden.

20. Anyone can write a piece of legislation, but only members of the House of Representatives may introduce the bill in the House.
☐ True
☐ False

ESSAY QUESTIONS

1. What are the qualifications to be a Texas legislator? What are the characteristics of members of the Texas legislature?

2. Discuss the process of redistricting, and the practice of gerrymandering. How has gerrymandering played or not played a role in Texas politics and the selection of legislators?

3. What are the different types of committees found in the Texas legislature? What duties and powers do they hold?

4. Describe the legislative process in both houses. How do they converge in a bicameral process?

CHAPTER 25

THE GOVERNOR AND BUREAUCRACY OF TEXAS

CHAPTER OUTLINE

I.   The Governor (pp. 782–785)
    A.   Who They Are
        1.   An American citizen
        2.   A resident of the state for at least five years
        3.   At least 30 years old
        4.   All Texas governors have been White Protestants.
        5.   All but two (Miriam Ferguson and Ann Richards) have been men.
        6.   Most have been moderate or conservative Democrats.
    B.   Compensation
        1.   Until 1954, the Constitution set the salary and increases were subject to voter approval.
        2.   In 1953 an amendment to the Constitution was passed allowing the legislature to set gubernatorial pay.
        3.   In the 2005 legislative session, the Senate passed a bill that would have raised the governor's salary from $115,345 to $150,000.
        4.   The state provides the governor with a mansion, a car, the use of state-owned planes, security detail, travel expenses, and office and personal staff.
    C.   How They Got There
        1.   Elections
            a.   The constitutional (and most common) method of selecting the governor is through elections.
            b.   The election for governor and most other elections for statewide office are held on the even-numbered years when the president of the United States is not running.
            c.   For most of Texas history, the governor was elected to a two-year term.
            d.   A constitutional amendment passed in 1972 changed the length of a term to four-years, beginning in 1974.
            e.   Since the change to a four-year term, governors have had difficulty being reelected.
            f.   There are no term limits in Texas.
        2.   Succession and Impeachment

<li>The lieutenant governor may become governor when the governor is unable to complete the term.
<ol>
<li>Resignation</li>
<li>Death</li>
<li>Impeachment and removal from office</li>
</ol>
</li>
<li>If a vacancy occurs, the lieutenant governor becomes the governor.</li>
<li>The impeachment process in Texas begins in the House of Representatives, where a majority vote is needed to impeach the governor.</li>
<li>After the impeachment, the case goes before the Senate for a trial; a two-thirds vote of the senators present is necessary to convict and remove the governor from office.</li>
<li>The state constitution does not specify what constitutes an impeachable offense.</li>
</ol>
</blockquote>

II. Gubernatorial Powers (pp. 786–791)

    A. Legislative Powers

        1. **State of the State address**

        2. The **veto** is the governor's power to sign or veto a bill the legislature passes.

            a. The governor has ten working days to sign the bill, veto the bill, or let the bill become law without his signature.

            b. If the legislature adjourns during this ten-day period, the time the governor has to consider the bill is extended to twenty days from the time the legislative session ends.

            c. The Texas governor does not have a pocket veto; a bill will become law unless the governor vetoes it.

            d. The legislature can override a veto with a two-thirds vote of both the House and the Senate.

        3. The line **item veto** allows the governor to veto portions, or lines, of a an appropriation bill without having to negate the entire bill.

            a. This affords the governor the ability to delete lines of a bill while allowing the remainder of the appropriations to go into effect.

            b. The legislature can override a line item veto the same way as it can with a regular veto.

        4. The governor has the sole authority to call a **special session**.

    B. Appointment Power

        1. During a four-year term the governor makes about 3,000 appointments.

        2. Many of these appointments are to the more than 200 administrative boards and commissions

3.   The governor may fill vacancies to elected positions if the vacancies take place between elections.
4.   The appointment power allows the governor to try to shape policy, and reward campaign contributors, friends, and supporters.
5.   Recent governors have made a greater effort to appoint people from groups that traditionally have been underrepresented.
6.   A number of restrictions on the governor's appointment power limit the governor's ability to use appointments to influence policy.
   a.   The governor is unable to fire his predecessor's appointees unless he has the approval of two-thirds vote of the Senate.
   b.   The governor's appointees must be confirmed by two-thirds of the Senate.
   c.   **Senatorial courtesy**

C.   Budgetary Powers
1.   The Texas governor has weak budgetary powers, because the Legislative Budget Board (LBB) develops the budget, more than the governor.
2.   The LBB is a permanent joint committee of the legislature that consists of five members of the House and five members of the Senate, including the speaker of the House and the lieutenant governor, who serve as co-chairs of the LBB.
3.   The governor submits a budget to the legislature, but the LBB's is usually the beginning point for the legislature.
4.   The line **item veto** assures the governor a say in the budget process.
5.   Because of changes and emergencies that take place over Texas' two-year budget cycle, some budget categories will run a surplus, while others may not have enough money.
6.   Both the governor and the LBB must agree to a reduction in spending or a transfer of money in between legislative sessions.

D.   Judicial Powers
1.   The Texas governor may only act upon the recommendations of the seven-member Board of Pardons and Paroles to grant reprieves, commutations, and pardons.
2.   The only formal power the Texas governor has to stop an execution is to issue a 30-day stay of execution.
3.   A constitutional amendment in 1936 stripped the governor of many judicial powers.

E.   Staff Support
1.   Texas governors have extensive staff support.
2.   Governors have discretion in who they hire and how they want to organize their staffs.

3. Staffers are hired because of some combination of loyalty, similar political beliefs, and/or their expertise in a particular policy area.
4. The governor hires a legislative liaison, press secretary, ethics advisor, general counsel, and chief of staff, among many others.
5. Staffers help the governor with his schedule, speeches, budget recommendations to the legislature, legal advice, economic development and tourism, to name a few.

F. Gubernatorial Power in Perspective
   1. The constitutional powers of the Texas governor are weak in comparison with other governors.
   2. But comparing gubernatorial power solely by the constitutional powers of governors does not give the full picture of gubernatorial power.

III. How the Texas Bureaucracies Are Organized (pp. 792–800)
  A. Elected Executive Officials
    1. All elected executive officials are elected to four-year terms and there are no limits on the number of terms they can serve.
    2. Framers of the Texas Constitution wanted these officials accountable to the people, not to the governor.
    3. The **lieutenant governor** does not preside over an executive department, but instead is in the unique position of being part of both the executive and legislative branches.
      a. The lieutenant governor succeeds the governor if the governor is not able to finish his term in office.
      b. The lieutenant governor serves as governor temporarily when the governor is out of the state, and he is paid the governor's salary on a pro-rated basis when the governor is out of the state.
      c. The lieutenant governor is paid the same as other legislators ($7,200).
      d. The lieutenant governor presides over the Senate, appoints all committee chairs, refers bills to committees, and interprets and enforces Senate rules..
      e. The lieutenant governor also sits on several boards and councils, including the Legislative Redistricting Board, the Legislative Budget Board, the Legislative Council, the Legislative Audit Committee, and the Legislative Education Board.
    4. The **attorney general** is the chief lawyer for the state.
      a.. The attorney general is responsible for representing the state in all legal matters.
      b. The Texas attorney general primarily deals with civil law.

    c.   Often the governor, the legislature, or a state agency will ask the attorney general to issue an opinion on the legality of a law, an agency's ruling, or some other action.

    d.   Advisory opinions issued by the attorney carries the weight of law, unless it is changed or overruled by statute, judicial decision, or a later attorney general.

    e.   Greg Abbott, the current Texas attorney general, was reelected to a second term as attorney general in November 2006.

5.   The **Comptroller of Public Accounts** is the state's chief tax administrator, collector, accountant, and revenue estimator, and plays a critical role in the legislative budget process.

    a.   Texas has a balanced budget requirement that prohibits the legislature from passing a budget that exceeds expected revenue.

    b.   Before the budget can go into effect, the comptroller must certify that the budget the legislature passed will not exceed expected revenue.

    c.   If the budget does not fall within the projections, the comptroller will not certify the budget and the legislature is forced to raise taxes, cut spending, or a combination of both to make up the difference.

    d.   The current comptroller is Susan Combs, who served two terms as agriculture commissioner before her election as comptroller in 2006.

6.   The Texas General Land Office (GLO), headed by the **land commissioner**, manages 20.4 million acres of state lands and mineral-right properties.

    a.   The GLO leases land for oil and gas production, mining, and grazing.

    b.   The revenue generated from leasing drilling rights for oil and gas production goes to the state's Permanent School Fund, an endowment established in the constitution to help finance education.

    c.   The GLO manages the Veterans Land Program, which provides low interest loans to veterans to buy land and houses.

    d.   Jerry Patterson, a former state senator, is the current land commissioner, winning reelection to another term in 2006.

7.   The **agriculture commissioner** of the Texas Department of Agriculture enforces agriculture laws and promotes and protects the agricultural interests of the state.

    a.   The department promotes Texas agricultural products and rural economic development,

<ol type="b" start="2">
<li>Regulates pesticides and herbicides, and</li>
<li>Ensures the accuracy of all weights and measures (like grocery scales or gas pumps).</li>
<li>Texans have seen the efforts of the Texas Department of Agriculture to crack down on childhood obesity by restricting the kinds of food and drinks that can be sold in schools or used at class parties.</li>
<li>Todd Staples was elected agriculture commissioner in 2006 after serving in the state House of Representatives and the state Senate.</li>
</ol>

B. Appointed Executives
1. The **secretary of state** is the only constitutional officer appointed by the governor, and is confirmed with a two-thirds vote of the Senate.
   a. The secretary of state is best known for administering the state's election laws.
   b. On election night this office gathers election returns throughout the state and provides the running totals to the public.
   c. Later the office produces the final, official tallies and certifies the election.
   d. The secretary of state protects the seal of the state of Texas and attests to the governor's signature.
   e. The secretary of state also maintains records related to Texas corporations, state laws and regulations, and publication of the *Texas Register*, which is the official record of state rules, meetings, opinions, and proclamations.
   f. The current secretary of state is Roger Williams, who was appointed by Governor Perry.
2. The governor also appoints other executive branch officials, such as the commissioner of education, commissioner of the Department of Health and Human Services, and the executive director of the Office of State-Federal Relations.

C. Elected Boards and Commissions
1. The **Railroad Commission** was created in 1891 and is the oldest regulatory agency in the state.
   a. Originally established to regulate railroads in Texas, the Railroad Commission also regulates trucking and oil and gas production.
   b. Its responsibilities include the regulation of gas utilities, oil and gas pipelines, drilling and pumping, and surface mining of coal and uranium.
   c. The commission is charged with caring for the rights of different interest owners, protecting the environment, and preventing waste of the state's natural resources.

<ol type="a" start="4">
<li>d.   The commission consists of three members elected in statewide elections to six-year, staggered terms.</li>
<li>e.   The current members are all Republicans: Michael Williams, Elizabeth A. Jones, and Victor G. Carrillo.</li>
<li>f.   The chairmanship is voted on by the members and is rotated among the commissioners.</li>
</ol>

2. The **State Board of Education** (SBOE) consists of 15 members elected to four–year, staggered terms.
   a. Each member is elected from and represents one of the 15 districts in the state.
   b. The governor selects one of the members to serve as chair.
   c. The board's responsibility is to monitor and coordinate programs and services of primary and secondary public education in Texas, and the board oversees the Texas Education Agency (TEA).
   d. The TEA is in charge of developing the statewide curriculum, administering the statewide assessment tests, collecting data on public schools, rating school districts, distributing state and federal funds to schools, and overseeing the textbook adoption process, among other things.
   e. The TEA is made up of the commissioner of education and agency staff.
   f. The commissioner is appointed by the governor, with the approval of the Senate, from three people recommended by the SBOE.
   g. The SBOE approves the textbooks for the more than 1,000 school districts in Texas.

3. *Ex officio* boards are composed of members who belong to the board because of another office they hold, and can consist either entirely or partly of *ex officio* members.

4. Most of the state bureaucracy is headed by boards and commissions whose members are appointed by the governor and confirmed with a two-thirds vote of the Senate.
   a. Most members of these boards and commissions are not paid.
   b. Most serve six-year, staggered terms.
   c. The boards hire an executive director to manage the activities of the agency.

VI. Understanding the Governor and Bureaucracy (pp. 800–805)
   A. Bureaucracy and Democracy
      1. Voters elect the different executive branch offices, which is called a **plural executive**.
      2. Most agencies are led by unelected officials.

3. As a result, the bureaucracy has to stay aware of what the electorate wants.

B. Governors Try To Control the Bureaucracy
   1. The governor has limited powers to control the bureaucracy.
   2. The plural executive precludes what would be some of the governor's most important appointments.
   3. The governor's appointment is constrained by the need to get senate approval, senatorial courtesy, staggered terms in office, and the governor's inability to fire his predecessor's appointees, as well as the difficulty in getting rid of his own.
   4. The governor makes appointments to about 3,000 positions.
   5. The budgetary power of the governor is not strong.
   6. The item veto makes the governor a player in the budget process, with the ability to eliminate different programs and in negotiations to influence the appropriations.
   7. The governor can also issue orders that can change the bureaucracy and bureaucratic behavior.
   8. These gubernatorial powers can cause agencies to placate the governor's desires in building support for the agency and its programs.

C. State Legislature Tries To Control the Bureaucracy.
   1. The Senate influences appointments because it confirms gubernatorial appointments.
   2. Agencies, not established in the Constitution, are subject to the legislature.
   3. The legislature can eliminate or reorganize an agency or can pass laws to change an agency's responsibilities and functions.
   4. The legislature controls the purse strings of agencies.
   5. Because the legislature is part-time and meets in biennial sessions, the legislature spends less time on oversight of different programs and agencies.
   6. The **sunset review** process
      a. The commission consists of 12-members chosen by the lieutenant governor and speaker of the House.
      b. The commission is mandated to review most state agencies every 12 years.
      c. About 20 and 30 agencies are reviewed for each legislative session; universities, courts, and state agencies created by the Constitution are exempt from sunset review.
      d. The Sunset Advisory Commission submits a report to the legislature with its recommendations on what to do with the agency.
      e. Recommendations may be to abolish the agency, continue the agency, or continue the agency but with changes.

    f.   The legislature does not have to follow the recommendations of the commission.

    g.   Unless the legislature votes to continue the agency under review, the agency will automatically expire and be eliminated.

    h.   The sunset process has cost the state $20 million to carry out; however, the state has saved $37 for every dollar the Sunset process has cost.

D.   The Public Tries to Control the Bureaucracy

    1.   Public attention to an agency or an issue is an important democratic control of the bureaucracy.

    2.   The public attention to the issue led an agency, the legislature, and the governor to impose changes.

    3.   Texas **open-meetings laws** require meetings of government at all levels in the state to be open to the public.

    4.   Governmental entities can hold closed-door meetings when discussing real estate transactions, personnel issues, or their involvement in litigation, although any formal action is to be open to the public.

    5.   Texas law also requires that public notices be posted for all meetings, whether open or closed.

    6.   Texas' **open records laws** force government to provide access to public records.

    7.   The Texas attorney general arbitrates conflict between the public's right to know and the government's desire to keep information off limits.

E.   The Executive Branch and the Scope of Government

    1.   Whistleblower Protection.

        a.   Bureaucrats reporting wrongdoings or mistakes in their agency

        b.   Texas public employees are protected from recrimination for reporting mistakes or wrongdoings.

        c.   If an employee is subject to reprisals, they may sue the agency.

    2.   The **revolving door** is the exchange of personnel between state agencies and those industries they regulate.

        a.   Employees of a state agency gain experience and contacts through work and quit the agency to get a better-paying job with the industry that his former agency regulated.

        b.   Individuals who work in an industry quit and work for the agency that regulates the industry they were in.

V.   Summary (p. 805)

LEARNING OBJECTIVES

After studying Chapter 25, you should be able to:

1. Discuss the constitutional requirements to be governor, the profiles of a typical Texas governor, the compensation of the governor, and the selection and removal of the governor.

2. Identify the various powers of the governor and describe how much power the governor has.

3. Explain the organizational structure of the Texas bureaucracy and the plural executive by identifying the important components of the elected executives, appointed executives, elected boards and commissions, *ex officio* boards, and appointed boards and commissions.

4. Understand the differences between gubernatorial control, legislative control and public control of the bureaucracy.

5. Evaluate the decentralized and fragmented nature of the Texas bureaucracy as a reflection of the desire of the framers of the Texas Constitution to protect against the concentration of political power.

The following exercises will help you meet these objectives:

Objective 1:   Discuss the constitutional requirements to be governor, the profiles of a typical Texas governor, the compensation of the governor, and the selection and removal of the governor.

1. Make a list of the requirements to be governor.

    1.

    2.

    3.

2. What is the profile of a typical Texas governor and how does that compare to the last four governors of Texas?

3.   Make a list of the types of compensation the governor receives.

       1.

       2.

       3.

       4.

       5.

       6.

       7.

       8.

4.   What is the most common method of selecting the governor, what is the term of office for the governor, and when does the selection occur?

5.   Explain the circumstances that require the lieutenant governor to serve as a governor.

Objective 2: Identify the various powers of the governor and describe how much power the governor has.

1.   The text examines four legislative powers of the governor established by the Texas Constitution. Complete the following table, listing these powers, defining them, and giving an example for each.

Legislative Power	Definition	Example

2.   Are the appointment powers of the governor a powerful tool in controlling the bureaucracy? List the pros and cons for the governor and his power to make appointments and shape policy, and evaluate the

Pros
   1.

   2.

   3.

   4.

   5.

Cons

    6.

    7.

    8.

3.   What is the roll of the Legislative Budget Board (LBB) as it relates to the Texas governor's weak budgetary powers? What one power does the governor wield with regard to his budgetary powers?

4.   What two judicial powers does the governor of Texas have? List the one formal power and the one limited power. Explain the reason for the governor's limited judicial powers.

    1.

    2.

    3.

Objective 3: Explain the organizational structure of the Texas bureaucracy and the plural executive by identifying the important components of the elected executives, appointed executives, elected boards and commissions, *ex officio* boards, and appointed boards and commissions.

1. The text examines the five elected executive offices of the Texas bureaucracy. Complete the following table, listing these offices, identifying their primary duties and responsibilities, and naming the current officeholder for each office.

Elected Executive Office	Duties and Responsibilities	Current Officeholder

2. Who is the only constitutional officer appointed by the governor? Identify the name of the office and the four primary responsibilities of this office.

   1.

   2.

   3.

   4.

   5.

3.   The text examines two elected boards and commissions in the Texas bureaucracy. Complete the following table, each office, identifying the number of members and their term of office, and primary responsibilities.

Board/Commission	Number of Members And Term of Office	Primary Responsibilities

4.   What is an *ex officio* board member?

5   What is the process for a Texas citizen to become a member of an appointed commission? Typically, what is the salary and term of office for such appointments?

Objective 4.   Understand the differences between gubernatorial control, legislative control and public control of the bureaucracy.

1.   The text examines the powers of the governor and how governors try to control the bureaucracy. List the various ways a governor's powers are limited when attempting to control the bureaucracy.

1.

2.

3.

2. List the various powers a governor utilizes to control the bureaucracy.

1.

2.

3.

3. The text examines how the legislature attempts to control the bureaucracy. List the various powers of the legislature with regard to their ability to control the bureaucracy.

1.

2.

3.

4.

5.

4.   The text examines how the public tries to control the bureaucracy. List the
        various tactics the public uses to control the bureaucracy.

        1.

        2.

        3.

Objective 5.   Evaluate the decentralized and fragmented nature of the Texas bureaucracy as a
reflection of the desire of the framers of the Texas Constitution to protect against the
concentration of political power.

        1.   Based on your findings in objectives 2-4, evaluate the power of the governor. Is
                the Texas governor strong or weak? Support your argument with your findings.

KEY TERMS

Identify and describe:

Plural executive

State of the state address

Veto

Item veto

Special session

Senatorial courtesy

Lieutenant governor

Attorney general

Comptroller

Land Commissioner

Agriculture Commissioner

Secretary of state

Sunset process

Open meetings requirements

Open records requirements

Revolving door

Compare and contrast:

Veto and Item veto

State of the state address and a special session

Plural executive and Senatorial courtesy

Governor and lieutenant governor

Attorney general, comptroller and secretary of state

The Land Commissioner and the Agriculture Commissioner

Open meetings requirements and open records requirements

Revolving door and sunset process

Name that term:

1. A structure of government in which independently-elected officeholders make up the executive branch.

   _____

2. The constitutional power of the governor to reject a bill passed by the legislature

   _____

3. Second in line of succession if a vacancy occurs before the governor's term is up and presides over the Texas Senate

   _____

4. The power of the governor to reject portions of an appropriations bill without rejecting the bill entirely

   _____

5. A custom in the state Senate whereby the senator from the district the governor's nominee is from can block the governor's nominee from being confirmed

   _____

6.   Manages state lands and mineral-right properties

              _____

7.   Promotes and protects the agricultural interests of the state and enforces agriculture, weights and measures laws

              _____

8.   Serves as the state's chief election administrator

              _____

9.   A process in which most state agencies are evaluated every 12 years, and should the legislature fail to reauthorize the agency after the review, the agency expires

              _____

10.   The exchange of personnel between state agencies and those industries they regulate

              _____

USING YOUR UNDERSTANDING

1.   Try your hand at sketching out a diagram for the executive branch. Be sure to indicate key officials, their duties, and responsibilities. Also, include how the officials are selected. Keep in mind the voters, the House, the Senate and the governors' roles in government. Briefly discuss and evaluate the effectiveness of this plural executive system.

2.   Locate the Texas Constitution and that of another state, such as Louisiana, Illinois, or California. In reading the Executive section of each constitution look for similarities or differences with the Texas Executive. Take note of the constitutional requirements for members of the Executive Branch, the duties and responsibilities it creates, and the functions they perform. Describe briefly what you have found. Use this exercise to write a term paper comparing different types of executive branches and their effectiveness.

REVIEW QUESTIONS

Check ☑ the correct answer:

1. Which of the following officeholders is required by the Texas Constitution to certify the budget and estimate state revenues for the upcoming two-year budget cycle?
   ☐ a. Attorney General
   ☐ b. Governor
   ☐ c. Comptroller
   ☐ d. Texas Legislature

2. The election for governor and most other elections for statewide office are
   ☐ a. held on the even-numbered years when the president of the United States is running.
   ☐ b. held on the even-numbered years when the president of the United States is not running.
   ☐ c. held on odd-numbered years during the spring.
   ☐ d. held on odd-numbered years in November.

3. The plural executive is
   ☐ a. a structure of government in which independently elected officeholders make up the executive branch.
   ☐ b. a legislature that is divided into two chambers.
   ☐ c. similar to the president and vice president of the United States because the governor and lieutenant governor run as a team.
   ☐ d. none of the above

4. Who is the current attorney general of the State of Texas?
   ☐ a. Greg Abbott
   ☐ b. Susan Combs
   ☐ c. Jerry Patterson
   ☐ d. Elizabeth A. Jones

5. Who is the current comptroller of public Accounts for the State of Texas?
   ☐ a. Greg Abbott
   ☐ b. Susan Combs
   ☐ c. Jerry Patterson
   ☐ d. Elizabeth A. Jones

6. Which of the following individuals serves as a member of the Texas Railroad Commission?
- a. Greg Abbott
- b. Susan Combs
- c. Jerry Patterson
- d. Elizabeth A. Jones

7. A 28-year-old American citizen who was born and raised in Texas and lives in Boerne, Texas would be qualified to run for Texas governor.
- True
- False

8. The Texas governor is limited to serving two four-year terms.
- True
- False

9. If a vacancy occurs in the governorship
- a. the state legislature selects the new governor by a majority vote.
- b. the state legislature selects the new governor by a two-thirds vote.
- c. the lieutenant governor becomes the governor.
- d. the members of the executive branch selects a new governor and the voters must approve their selection.

10. The veto allows governors to veto portions, or lines, of a bill without having to negate the entire bill.
- True
- False

11. Which of the following are TRUE regarding a special session?
- a. Only the governor can call a special session
- b. Only the governor can set the agenda for the special session.
- c. A special session can last for no longer than 30 days.
- d. all of the above.

12. The Texas governor has weak budgetary powers compared to the president of the United States and the governors in most other states
    ☐ a. because the comptroller sets the biennium budget for Texas.
    ☐ b. because the treasurer sets the biennium budget for Texas.
    ☐ c. because the governor is completely removed from the process, and the legislature has power to set the budget.
    ☐ d. because the Legislative Budget Board (LBB) has more power than the governor in developing the budget.

13. Who is the current commissioner of the Texas GLO?
    ☐ a. Greg Abbott
    ☐ b. Susan Combs
    ☐ c. Jerry Patterson
    ☐ d. Elizabeth A. Jones

14. The lieutenant governor enjoys both executive and legislative branch powers.
    ☐ True
    ☐ False

15. The Texas governor has the power to commute sentences.
    ☐ True
    ☐ False

16. Texas open meetings laws require
    ☐ a. meetings of government at all levels in the state to be open to the public.
    ☐ b. governmental entities to hold closed-door meetings when discussing real estate transactions, personnel issues, or their involvement in litigation.
    ☐ c. a public notice to be posted for all meetings, whether open or closed.
    ☐ d. all of the above

17. The revolving door is
    ☐ a. the exchange of personnel between state agencies and those industries they regulate.
    ☐ b. when people who work in an industry quit and work for the agency that regulates the industry they were in.
    ☐ c. a and b
    ☐ d. none of the above

18.   *Ex Officio* Boards are composed of members who belong to the board because of another office they hold.
        ☐ True
        ☐ False

19.   Which office manages the 20.4 million acres of state lands and mineral-right properties?
        ☐ a.   Agriculture Commissioner
        ☐ b.   Railroad Commission
        ☐ c.   General Land Office Commissioner
        ☐ d.   Texas Real Estate Board

20.   When the attorney general issues an advisory opinion, it carries the weight of law.
        ☐ True
        ☐ False

ESSAY QUESTIONS

1.   Explain how the legislature can use their powers as a means for controlling the state bureaucracy.

2.   Explain the Texas plural executive as a system that strengthens or weakens the office of governor. Be sure to explain the reasoning that supports your argument.

3.   Who is the most important elected state executive office holder? Be sure to explain the reasoning that supports your argument.

4.   If an individual desires to become governor of Texas, what requirements would they need to meet and what is the most common method of selection?

5.   Texas voters have more involvement in trying to control the bureaucracy than voters do with the federal government and in many other states. Explain the powers of the public as a means for controlling the state bureaucracy.

CHAPTER 26

TEXAS COURT SYSTEM

CHAPTER OUTLINE

I.   The Structure of the Texas Judiciary (pp. 810–815)
  A.   Jurisdiction
    1.   Jurisdiction is the power of a court to consider and decide a particular type of case.
    2.   Courts with original jurisdiction hear the facts of a case and apply the law to decide the outcome of the case.
  B.   Inferior Courts
    1.   Two separate court systems make up the inferior courts: the justice of the peace courts and the municipal courts.
    2.   **Justice of the peace** courts have original jurisdiction in misdemeanor criminal cases that involve simple crimes and punishment which consist of a fine and/or jail time of less than one year.
      a.   The Texas Constitution requires each county to maintain between one and eight justice of the peace (JP) precincts, depending on the county's population and on the precinct's population.
      b.   JP courts have exclusive civil jurisdiction when the amount in controversy does not exceed $200, and concurrent jurisdiction with county courts when the amount exceeds $200 but less than $5,000.
      c.   JP courts operate as small claims courts that involve less than $5,000.
      d.   JP courts serve as magistrates, issuing warrants for the apprehension and arrest of persons charged with felony or misdemeanor offenses.
      e.   The JP serves as the coroner in counties that do not have a medical examiner and may perform marriage ceremonies.
      f.   JPs are elected in partisan elections and serve four-year terms.
    3.   **Municipal courts** have original and exclusive jurisdiction over criminal violations of municipal **ordinances**.
      a.   Most of the cases heard by municipal courts involve traffic violations.
      b.   They have concurrent jurisdiction with justice of the peace courts in certain misdemeanor criminal cases.
      c.   The judge has the authority to issue arrest warrants.
      d.   Most municipal courts do not keep a record of their cases.
      e.   Most municipal court judges are appointed by the governing body of the municipality; others are elected by the voters in a city.

C. County-level Courts
    1. The Constitution established a county-level trial court in each of the 254 counties in the state, with judges who are elected to four-year terms.
    2. The **constitutional county courts** hear appeals from the inferior courts, and have jurisdiction over higher-level misdemeanors, probate matters, and civil claims controversies between $200.01 and $5,000.
        a. The county judge serves a legislative function as the presiding officer of the county commissioners' court.
        b. In more populous counties, the county judge may spend most of his or her time on the administration of county government.

D. County courts-at-law
    1. Statutory county courts have either civil or criminal jurisdiction.
    2. Civil jurisdiction is over cases involving less than $100,000.
    3. Criminal jurisdiction includes serious misdemeanors with a punishment of a jail sentence or a fine over $500.
    4. Qualifications for becoming a statutory county judge depend on the statute that created the court and usually include at least four years experience as a practicing attorney.
    5. Statutory county court judges are elected to four-year terms.
    6. **Probate courts** determine the disposition of wills and operate in 10 counties to relieve the county judge of some judicial functions.

E. District Courts
    1. The **district courts** are the chief trial courts of the state.
    2. Each court has one judge, who must be at least 25 years of age, a resident of the district for at least two years, a citizen of the United States, and a licensed practicing attorney or judge for four years.
    3. District judges are elected to four-year terms.
    4. District courts have general jurisdiction over felony criminal cases and misdemeanors involving official misconduct, divorce cases, and election contests.
    5. They also have jurisdiction over civil cases that exceed $200.
    6. Juvenile cases are also usually tried in district courts.
    7. More populous counties have many district courts.
    8. District courts in metropolitan areas tend to specialize in criminal, civil, juvenile, or family law matters.

F. Appellate Courts
    1. The **courts of appeals,** which make up the intermediate appellate courts, hear appeals in both civil and criminal cases from the district- and county-level courts in their region, with the exception of death penalty cases.
        a. The state is divided into 14 districts, each with a court of appeals with a chief justice and at least two other justices.
        b. Each justice serves a four-year term.
        c. There are currently 80 justices serving on the 14 intermediate courts of appeals.

2.   The **Court of Criminal Appeals** hears appeals from death-penalty convictions and denials of bail, and is the court of last resort for criminal appeals.
     a.   It has discretion to review decisions in criminal cases appealed from the courts of appeal, but the Court has the right to refuse to hear an appeal without explanation.
     b.   The presiding judge and eight associate judges serve staggered six-year terms.
3.   The Texas **Supreme Court** is the court of last resort in civil and juvenile cases.
     a.   The Court's caseload is directly affected by the structure and jurisdiction of Texas' appellate court system.
     b.   The Court's chief justice and eight justices are elected in state-wide elections to staggered six-year terms.

II.   Judicial Selection and Removal (pp. 815–820)
A.   Elected Judges
      1.   All judges in the state of Texas, with the exception of municipal court judges in a few cities, are selected in partisan elections.
      2.   Opponents of judicial elections argue that elections make judges less independent and more willing to rule in favor of whoever provides the largest campaign contribution.
      3.   **Elective-appointive** occurs when judges will retire or resign their seats before their term expires, allowing for a replacement to be appointed.
      4.   Incumbent candidates for judicial positions rarely lose.
      5.   In response to the rising costs of campaigns, the Texas Legislature passed the **Judicial Campaign Fairness Act** in 1995, which limits individual contributions to candidates.
B.   Appointed Judges
      1.   Municipal judges are frequently appointed by the local governments that they serve.
      2.   The governor can make appointments to fill vacancies in the district and appellate courts. These appointees must be approved by the consent of the Senate.
      3.   Supporters of the appointment method argue that the governor is better positioned to gauge the qualifications of potential judges.
      4.   Opponents argue the governor will appoint only his or her friends or wealthy campaign contributors.
C.   Merit Selection
      1.   **Merit selection**, also known as the Missouri Plan, is a hybrid of the other two selection methods that combines gubernatorial appointment with elections.
      2.   This method is used in a number of states, but not in Texas.

D. Reforming Judicial Selection
E. Retirement and Removal of Judges
   1. District court judges and judges and justices of the appellate courts must retire when they reach the age of 75.
   2. Judges may be removed from office, suspended, censured, or disciplined by the State Commission on Judicial Conduct.

III. Judges and Justices in the Texas Judiciary (pp. 820–823)
   A. Qualifications
      1. Justices and judges in the appeals courts of Texas must have been licensed to practice law for at least ten years, be citizens of the United States and of Texas, and be at least 35-years old.
      2. District judges must have been licensed to practice law in Texas for at least four years, be residents of the judicial district in which they serve for at least two years, and be citizens of the state.
      3. Statutory county court judges and probate judges are governed by the statutes that created the courts and must be 25-years old, licensed to practice law, must be residents of the county they will serve, and have some experience as practicing attorneys.
      4. Most constitutional county court judges are not attorneys.
      5. No constitutional or statutory qualifications exist to serve as a justice of the peace.
      6. All judges of municipal courts of record must be licensed attorneys, but judges in other municipal courts do not need to be licensed to practice law.
   B. Diversity in the Texas Judiciary
      1. The Texas judiciary is largely composed of men (70 percent) and Caucasians (82 percent).
      2. Women and members of minority groups are underrepresented, but the number of women has been growing faster than the number of minority members.
      3. As the Republican Party gained strength in the 1980s and 1990s, more Republican judges were elected.
      4. Voters rely on political party as a guide in casting their vote.

IV. The Law and Legal Process (pp. 823–830)
   A. Criminal Justice System
      1. Law enforcement consists primarily of municipal police, county sheriffs, and the Texas Department of Public Safety.
      2. Criminal prosecution functions are performed by district attorneys offices.
      3. The criminal trial and appeals process involves the court system, public defenders, juries, and other court activities.
      4. Criminal justice involves punishment that includes incarceration, parole, and capital punishment.
      5. Crime

a. There are two types of crimes: felonies, which are serious crimes; and misdemeanors, which are minor crimes.

b. The rules of criminal procedure and the penal code in Texas are written by the legislature and are rarely updated.

6. The Trial

   a. Before a serious criminal case goes to trial, the accused must be indicted for the crime by a grand jury.

   b. A prosecuting attorney prepares a formal accusation and presents it to a grand jury.

   c. If there is enough evidence, the grand jury will issue an indictment, and if not, the accused is released.

   d. If a person is indicted, he or she may request to be released from custody for the duration of the trial.

   e. Before a case goes to trial, the accused is asked to enter a plea of guilty, not guilty, or *nolo contendere*

   f. The first step in a trial is the selection of a jury.

   g. The jury is then presented with the indictment.

   h. Opening statements are made by both sides and then the state (the prosecution) presents its case.

   i. The defense makes its case and both sides are allowed to present testimony that challenges the testimony presented by the other side.

   j. The judge instructs the jury and the jury moves to the jury room to deliberate.

   k. If the jury finds that the state proved beyond a reasonable doubt that the defendant committed the offense charged, the trial then proceeds to the punishment phase.

   l. If the defendant is found not guilty, he or she is free to go.

3. Punishment

   a. The convicted person could be assessed a monetary fine, incarceration in a correctional facility, or both.

   b. Misdemeanors carry a fine only or both a fine and incarceration, depending on the crime.

   c. Fines typically are the only punishment assessed for minor crimes.

   d. Formerly known as probation, **community supervision** allows a convicted person to live in his or her home as long as he or she complies with court-ordered terms of probation.

   e. **Deferred adjudication** requires the defendant to enter a plea of guilty; however, there is no finding of guilt by a court, but the defendant must comply with conditions similar to those of a person under community supervision.

4. Parole

   a. **Parole** is early release from prison before a full sentence has been served.

        b.   The decision whether to grant parole is made by the Texas Board of Pardons and Paroles, and they determine the conditions of release, imposing any special conditions for parole.

        c.   The board's seven members are appointed by the governor, with the advice and consent of the Texas Senate, to serve six-year terms.

B.   Civil Law in Texas

    1.   A civil lawsuit is brought by a plaintiff, the person allegedly harmed by the actions of the defendant.

    2.   The plaintiff outlines the complaint in the lawsuit and the type of remedy sought, and the defendant responds by writing a pleading.

    3.   The defendant has the opportunity to make counter-claims and even ask for damages.

    4.   In discovery, the plaintiff and defendant ask for and receive information about the incident or incidents at controversy in the suit.

    5.   A civil trial may have a trial by jury or judge.

    6.   The end result of a civil trial is a finding of whether or not the defendant was negligent in dealing with the plaintiff and how much reimbursement the defendant may owe to the plaintiff for that negligence.

C.   Appeals

    1.   An appeal generally occurs after a conviction when the defendant asks a higher court to determine whether errors were committed during the trial.

    2.   The appellate courts do not decide guilt or innocence, but instead decide questions of procedure about the prior trial.

    3.   If the court finds errors were committed during the trial, the original conviction is thrown out and a new trial ordered.

    4.   The prosecutor may determine that he or she does not have enough evidence remaining and will decide to throw out the charge.

    5.   Civil appeals usually are filed by the losing side, and may take many years before a final decision is reached.

D.   Jury Duty

    1.   Jury service begins with a summons.

    2.   Failure to answer a jury summons may result in a fine and potential criminal penalty.

    3.   Names are randomly selected from a list of registered voters and people who have registered their cars.

    4.   A juror must be a citizen of the United States and of the state of Texas, be at least 18 years of age, reside in the county of jury service, be able to read and write, and be of sound mind.

    5.   Persons who have been convicted of a felony or any type of theft cannot serve on a jury.

    6.   The process of selecting the jurors is called *voir dire*, whereby both sides of the case try to eliminate jurors they believe may be prejudiced toward the parties or have some connection with the parties in the case.

7.   The jurors listen to both sides present their cases.
8.   After closing arguments, the judge instructs the jurors on what they are to deliberate.
   a.   In civil cases, jurors usually are asked to answer a series of questions about the degree of negligence permitted by the defendant.
   b.   In criminal cases, jurors are asked to make a general statement of guilt.
   c.   Jurors in capital murder cases also may be asked to determine the punishment of the convicted person.
10.   Employers are not required to pay people while they miss work to serve on a jury, and they may not fire a person for missing work to serve on a jury.
11.   Jurors are paid $6 for the first day of service and $40 after the first day of service.

V.   Understanding the Texas Court System (pp. 830–833)
   A.   Democracy and Reforming the Texas Court System
   B.   The Texas Judiciary and Policymaking
      1.   Candidates for Texas judicial positions often campaign on their unwillingness to use their positions to enact policy positions.
      2.   The Texas Supreme Court has increasingly played an active role in shaping broader public policies and addressing significant constitutional issues.

VI.   Summary (p. 833)

LEARNING OBJECTIVES

After studying Chapter 26, you should be able to:

1.   Discuss the important differences between the inferior courts, the county courts, district courts, Intermediate Appellate Courts, and the State Highest Appellate Courts.

2.   Identify the different methods of judicial selection and explain the reasons why a judge would leave the bench.

3.   Explain the qualifications potential candidates must meet if they wish to become a Texas judge and discuss the diversity in the Texas judiciary.

4.   Understand the Texas legal system by explaining the differences between a civil case and a criminal case, as well as, a juror's responsibilities and duties.

5.   Describe the appeals process filed by the losing side to review the procedures of the prior trial.

The following exercises will help you meet these objectives:

Objective 1:   Discuss the important differences between the inferior courts, the county courts, district courts, Intermediate Appellate Courts, and the State Highest Appellate Courts.

1. Complete the list below by identifying the two types of inferior courts and explaining their primary function, criminal jurisdiction, civil jurisdiction, method of judicial selection, and term of office for the judge.

1.

Primary function:

Criminal jurisdiction:

Civil jurisdiction:

Method of judicial selection:

Term of office for the judge:

2.

Primary function:

Criminal jurisdiction:

Civil jurisdiction:

Method of judicial selection:

Term of office for the judge:

2.   Complete the list below by explaining the primary function, criminal jurisdiction, civil jurisdiction, method of judicial selection, and term of office for a judge sitting on the county level courts.

     1.

     Primary function:

     Criminal jurisdiction:

     Civil jurisdiction:

     Method of judicial selection:

     Term of office for the judge:

3.   Complete the list below by identifying the three types of county courts at law and explaining their primary function, jurisdiction, method of judicial selection, and term of office for the judge.

1.

Primary function:

Jurisdiction:

Method of judicial selection:

Term of office for the judge:

2.

Primary function:

Jurisdiction:

Method of judicial selection:

Term of office for the judge:

3.

Primary function:

Jurisdiction:

Method of judicial selection:

Term of office for the judge:

4.   Complete the list below by identifying the three types of appellate courts and explaining their primary function, jurisdiction, method of judicial selection, and term of office for the judge.

1.

Primary function:

Criminal jurisdiction:

Civil jurisdiction:

Method of judicial selection:

Term of office for the judge:

5.   Complete the list below by explaining the primary function, jurisdiction, method of judicial selection, and term of office for a judge sitting on the state district courts.

1.

Primary function:

Jurisdiction:

Method of judicial selection:

Term of office for the judge:

2.

Primary function:

Jurisdiction:

Method of judicial selection:

Term of office for the judge:

3.

Primary function:

Jurisdiction:

Method of judicial selection:

Term of office for the judge:

Objective 2:   Identify the different methods of judicial selection and explain the reasons why a judge would leave the bench.

1.   The text examines three methods of judicial selection. Complete the following table, listing each method, defining the method, and listing the pros and cons for each.

Method	Definition	Pros	Cons

2.   The text examines several reasons why a judge might leave his bench. Describe the circumstances that would require this to happen.

        1.

        2.

        3.

3.   What authority does the State Commission on Judicial Conduct have over Texas judges and what action may it take against them?

Objective 3:   Explain the qualifications potential candidates must meet if they wish to become a Texas judge and discuss the diversity in the Texas judiciary.

        1.   List the judicial qualifications for the following Texas judges.

                1.   appeals courts

                        a.

                        b.

                        c.

                2.   district courts

                        a.

                        b.

                        c.

3.   statutory county courts

        a.

        b.

        c.

        d.

4.   justice of the peace

        a.

5.   municipal courts of record

        a.

6.   municipal courts

        a.

2.   How diverse is the Texas judiciary? Compare the number of men and women on
        the bench, as well as, the number of racial minorities. Explain your findings.

Objective 4:   Understand the Texas legal system by explaining the differences between a criminal case and a civil case, as well as, a juror's qualifications, responsibilities, and duties.

1.   What are the primary components of the criminal justice system?

1.

2.

3.

4.

5.

2.   How are crimes classified?

1.

2.

3.   Explain the events that take place before a criminal case goes to trial.

4.   List the steps of a criminal trial.

1.

2.

3.

4.

5.

6.

7.

8.

9.

5.   List the steps of a civil trial.

1.

2.

3.

4.

5.

6.

7.

6.   The text examines the different types of punishment for the losers in civil and criminal cases. What type of punishment may a defendant in a criminal case receive and how does that compare to the defendant who loses a civil case?

7.   Who is qualified to be a Texas juror and what would disqualify someone from serving as a juror?

       1.

       2.

       3.

       4.

       5.

       6.

       7.

       8.

8.   Suppose you fail to show up for jury duty, what would happen?

9.   What is the responsibility of a juror?

Objective 5:   Describe the appeals process filed by the losing side to review the procedures of the prior trial.

    1.   Why would a defendant in a criminal or civil case appeal a case if the appellate courts do not decide guilt or innocence?

    2.   Are civil cases or criminal cases more likely to be appealed?

    3.   What are the steps of a criminal appeal that does not involve the death penalty?

KEY TERMS

Identify and describe:

jurisdiction

Justice of the peace courts

court of record

de novo

municipal courts

ordinance

Constitutional county court

county courts at law

probate courts

district courts

courts of appeals

Court of Criminal Appeals

Supreme Court

elective-appointive

Judicial Campaign Fairness Act

Merit selection

Retention election

Community supervision

Deferred adjudication

parole

voir dire

Compare and contrast:

jurisdiction and court of record

Justice of the peace courts and municipal courts

county courts at law and probate courts

district courts and courts of appeals

Court of Criminal Appeals and Supreme Court

Judicial Campaign Fairness Act and community supervision

elective-appointive, merit selection, and retention election

deferred adjudication and parole

Name that term:

1. An informal process in which a judge leaves office before his or her term expires allowing the succeeding judge to run for reelection as an incumbent.

   _____

2. A plea bargain agreement between a defendant and a Texas criminal court in which formal judgment of guilt is withheld pending the outcome of the probation period.

   _____

3. An intermediate appellate courts in the state of Texas that hear appeals from the district courts.

   _____

4. A trial court of general jurisdiction in the state of Texas.

   _____

5.   A local court whose jurisdiction includes adjudicating violations of city ordinances.

        _____

6.   A court that maintains a permanent record of its proceedings.

        _____

7.   A local court that administers criminal or civil justice in minor cases, administer oaths, fix bail, perform marriages, and so on.

        _____

8.   The types of cases that courts may hear.

        _____

9.   The process of questioning prospective jurors with the intent to determine if they could be fair and impartial.

        _____

10.   A new trial.

        _____

USING YOUR UNDERSTANDING

1.   Try your hand at sketching out a diagram for the court structure of Texas. Be sure to indicate the five levels of courts. Also, include the court's civil or criminal jurisdiction, whether the court is a trial court or an appellate court and illustrate the appeals process for civil and criminal lawsuits. Briefly discuss and evaluate the effectiveness of this process.

2.   Locate the Texas Constitution and that of another state, such as Louisiana, Illinois, or California. In reading the judicial section of each constitution look for similarities or differences with the Texas judiciary. Take note of the constitutional requirements for judges, method of selection, the duties and responsibilities it creates, and the functions the courts perform. Describe briefly what you have found. Use this exercise to write a term paper comparing different types of judicial branches and their effectiveness.

REVIEW QUESTIONS

Check ☑ the correct answer:

1. The loser of a civil lawsuit tried in a state district court could appeal the decision to which of the following courts?
   - ☐ a.   U.S. Supreme Court
   - ☐ b.   Texas Supreme Court
   - ☐ c.   Texas Civil District Court
   - ☐ d.   Texas Court of Appeals

2. The highest civil appellate court in the state of Texas is the
   - ☐ a.   Texas Court of Appeals.
   - ☐ b.   U.S. Supreme Court.
   - ☐ c.   Texas Circuit Court.
   - ☐ d.   Teas Supreme Court.

3. A state district judge resigns three years into his four-year term. What is the method used to select a new judge?
   - ☐ a.   The governor calls a special election to fill the vacancy.
   - ☐ b.   The bench remains vacant until the next election.
   - ☐ c.   The County Commissioners Court fills the vacancy
   - ☐ d.   The governor appoints a replacement who must run for election at the end of the unexpired term.

4. The municipal courts would hear a case involving the violation of a city ordinance.
   - ☐ True
   - ☐ False

5. John Smith is charged with a serous felony offense, such as murder, and would be tried in which of the following Texas court?
   - ☐ a.   JP court
   - ☐ b.   county court
   - ☐ c.   Texas Court of Criminal Appeals
   - ☐ d.   district court

6. A routine traffic offense would involve
   - ☐ a.   the district courts.
   - ☐ b.   the court of appeals.
   - ☐ c.   the traffic court of appeals.
   - ☐ d.   the JP courts.

7.   Which of the following courts has jurisdiction over felony criminal cases?
☐ a.   JP court
☐ b.   county court
☐ c.   Texas Court of Criminal Appeals
☐ d.   district court

8.   Death penalty appeals always go directly to the Texas Court of Criminal Appeals.
☐ True
☐ False

9.   Which of the following actions would never happen during the appeals process?
☐ a.   a jury deliberating a defendant's guilt
☐ b.   a panel of judges ruling on a point of law
☐ c.   both a and b
☐ d.   none of the above

10.   Which of the following actions would never happen during the trial process?
☐ a.   a lawyer cross-examining a witness
☐ b.   a verdict of guilty
☐ c.   a panel of judges ruling on a point of law
☐ d.   a jury deliberating a defendant's guilt

11.   Which of the following events would never happen in a criminal case?
☐ a.   The defendant is sentenced to 5 years in prison.
☐ b.   They jury awards $100,000 in damages to the plaintiff.
☐ c.   The defendant appeals the outcome of the case to a higher court.
☐ d.   The defendant agrees to a plea bargain before the trial.

12.   Which of the following events would never happen in a civil case?
☐ a.   The defendant is sentenced to 5 years in prison.
☐ b.   They jury awards $100,000 in damages to the plaintiff.
☐ c.   The defendant appeals the outcome of the case to a higher court.
☐ d.   The defendant agrees to a settlement before the trial.

13.   Courts with original jurisdiction hear the facts of a case and apply the law to decide the outcome of the case.
☐ True
☐ False

14.   The elective-appointive situation occurs because the governor can decide whether or not to appoint a judicial candidate to a bench or call a special election for the vacancy.
☐ True
☐ False

15. Most Texas judges are selected by partisan elections.
    ☐ True
    ☐ False

16. Which of the following individuals is qualified to become a justice of the peace?
    ☐ a. A 25-year-old practicing attorney, who is a 15-year Texas resident.
    ☐ b. A 30-year-old non-licensed attorney, who is a 10-year Texas resident.
    ☐ c. A 40-year-old non practicing attorney, who is a 40-year Texas resident.
    ☐ d. all of the above

17. Under community supervision,
    ☐ a. a convicted person may be allowed to live in his or her home as long as he or she complies with court-ordered terms of probation.
    ☐ b. the defendant enters a plea of guilty but there is no finding of guilt by a court.
    ☐ c. a prisoner can earn time off his or her sentence through the award of "good conduct time."
    ☐ d. none of the above

18. The State Commission on Judicial Conduct has the power to remove from office.
    ☐ True
    ☐ False

19. The process of selecting jurors is called
    ☐ a. *nolo contendere.*
    ☐ b. *de novo.*
    ☐ c. *habeas corpus.*
    ☐ d. *voir dire.*

20. When a judge reaches the age of 65 they must retire.
    ☐ True
    ☐ False

ESSAY QUESTIONS

1. What is the difference between a civil trial and a criminal trial? What events occur during both a civil and criminal trial, and what events are unique to civil cases and exclusive to criminal cases?

2. What is the difference between a trial and an appeal? Explain the general process of each.

3.   What method of selection should be used to choose Texas judges? Consider the current method and compare it with other methods. What are the pros and cons of each? You be the policymaker. What would you do? Be sure to explain your reasoning.

4.   What happens after you receive a jury summons? Explain the process of jury selection. What is a juror's responsibility once they are selected to serve?

5.   Explain the process by which a court case loser would appeal a decision. What is the process for a criminal defendant? How does that differ from a civil defendant's appeal?

CHAPTER 27

LOCAL GOVERNMENT IN TEXAS

CHAPTER OUTLINE

I.   The Diversity of Local Governments in Texas (pp. 837–839)
       A. Texas ranks third among the 50 states in number of local units, with 4,784 as of June 2002.
       B. The large number of governments means that the average Texan may be governed by a number of different local governments, including city and county governments and numerous special district governments.

II.   **Counties** (pp. 839–844)
       A. Counties serve as the local administrative arm of the state government. A county is a political subdivision of state government with a set of government officials who administer state functions while also providing local services.
       B. Counties are the oldest form of local government in Texas.
       C. County Functions
              1. Responsibilities include:
                  a. Road construction and maintenance,
                  b. Law enforcement
                  c. Tax collection.
                  d. Maintenance of records and licenses.
                  e. As populations increase services expand to include health and social welfare, solid-waste management, and housing and community development.
                  f. Many of these services are provided free of charge or for a small fee.
       D. Structure of County Government
              1. **County Commissioners Court** is the chief governing body.
                  a. The Texas Constitution specifies that the commissioner's court consist of a county judge and four county commissioners.
                  b. The court divides the county into four individual commissioners precincts, which must be roughly equal in size based on population.
              2. Terms of office
                  a. The county judge is elected to a four-year term.
                  b. The county commissioners are elected to staggered four-year terms with two commissioners elected every two years.

3. The Texas Local Government Code contains the provisions that direct the commissioners court in carrying out it's duties in operating county government
4. The chief executive officer of the county is the county judge.
    a. Serves as the county's Emergency Management Director
    b. The county judge also has responsibilities relating to the creation and operation of special districts.
5. **County attorney** is elected to a four-year term and is the chief prosecuting officer for the county courts and also serves as a legal advisor to the county commissioners court. The county attorney is elected only in counties without a criminal district attorney.
6. Counties that are also a criminal district also have an elected district attorney in addition to the county attorney.
7. The **county sheriff**
    a. Chief law enforcement officer for the county
    b. Responsible for operating county jails, investigating crimes, making judgments, and maintaining communications with other law enforcement organizations.
8. The **county clerk**
    a. Clerk for the county courts, including probate courts, and the commissioner's court
    b. Chief record keeper for the county.
9. The **tax assessor-collector** is a constitutionally required office for counties over 10,000 people.
    a. Collects taxes for the county
    b. Responsible for motor vehicle registration
    c. Responsible for voter registration
10. The **county treasurer** is elected for a term of four years at the same time as the governor. The treasurer signs paychecks and supervises the county's bank account. Some counties have abolished the office of treasurer.

III. Municipalities (pp. 844–853)
   A. There are two categories of cities in Texas. General **law cities** and **home rule cities**.
      1. General law cities are small cities with less than 5,00 inhabitants. There are 3 types of general law cities: Type A, Type B, and Type C.
         a. Type A has populations over 600.
            i) May use either **aldermanic** or **commission** forms of government.
            ii) Governing body is known as the "City Council" and varies in size depending on whether or not the city has been divided into wards. A ward is a geographic subdivision of a city into districts of equal population.

          iii)   If the city has been divided into wards then the council consists of a mayor and two council members elected from each ward.

    b.   Type B is how most new cities start out with populations from 201-599. They operate as either aldermanic or commission government.

          i)   Aldermanic governments have a governing body called the "Board of Aldermen" and include six members: the mayor and fiver aldermen. All officials are elected on an at-large basis.

          ii)   Commission governments have a governing body called the "board of commissioners" and always consist of a mayor and two commissioners.

    c.   Type C has between 201–4,999 residents and uses a commission form of government.

  2.   Home rule cities are directed on what they cannot do rather than told what to do by the legislature. Towns of more than 5,000 residents can draw up a city charter and declare home rule

    a. A city's charter is the basic law of a city government in much the same way that the U.S. Constitution is the nation's basic law. A city charter describes the city's governmental powers.

    b. Powers and Limits of Home Rule Cities.

       i.   The government structure of a home rule city is left to the discretion of the city's voters.

       ii. Voters chose from 3 forms of government: Mayor-council, council-manager, or commission.

       iii. One of the most significant inherent powers held by home rule cities is the power to annex adjoining areas. They can do this without the permission of the persons who reside in the area.

    c. In 1999 Annexation was amended

       i.   Cities now have to hold hearings in the affected areas

       ii. Cities must provide a plan to provide services to the affected areas

    d. There are limits on home rule powers, imposed by sate and federal laws. Every city must obey the Texas Constitution and statutory requirements.

B. Forms of Municipal Government

  1.   The **commission form** of government originated in the early 1900s but no city in Texas uses it at present. It is also known as the Galveston Plan. Voters elect a small governing commission, typically five or seven members, on an at-large basis. They are the

legislative body of the city responsible for taxation, appropriations, ordinance, and other government functions. Individually, each commissioner is in charge of a specific aspect of city affairs, like public works, finance or public safety

    2.   The **council-manager** form of city government is the newest of the three forms. Residents of the city elect the city council, which then hires a professional city manager to administer the day-to-day activities of city government. The council operates as a legislative body and establishes policy.

    3.   The **mayor-council** government has a mayor and a number of council members or aldermen. The mayor is elected from the city at large and the aldermen may be elected at large but they are usually elected from single-member districts called wards.

C. Municipal Elections come in three classifications. **At-Large**, **Single-Member District**, and **Mixed** (hybrid)

    1.   In at large elections, all council members are voted on by all city voters

    2.   Single-member districts limit each voter's choice to a single contest. A voter must choose from the list of candidates who have filed to run to represent the district, which the voter resides. This favors neighborhood groups, ethnic and racial groups and other community groups.

    3.   A mixed election allows for a number of members of the city council to be elected in an at-large citywide election and others by single-member districts.

IV. **Special Districts** (pp. 853–855)

A. Sometimes referred to as "invisible government" because they do not attract much public attention.

    1.   Organized entities, possessing a structural form, and official name, perpetual succession and the right to sue and be sued, to make contracts and to obtain and dispose of property.

    2.   Have officers who are popularly elected or are chosen by other public officials.

    3.   Special districts usually provide only one or two functions.

B. Types of Special District Government

    1.   School districts

    2.   Irrigation

    3.   Hospital

    4.   Fire

    5.   Water conservation

    6.   Utilities

    7.   Others

C. Structure and rationale of Special District Governments

1. Easy to establish and operate
2. Offer greater flexibility to solve specific problems
3. Are a way to get around constitutional and statutory restrictions place on counties and municipalities
4. Due to their technical nature they are difficult to hold accountable to the public.

D. School Districts
1. Have a unique history and a common mission to provide public education to all Texans
2. Texas Education Agency enforces regulations and guidelines established by the state
3. School boards are generally elected at large by numbered place.

V. Local Government Cooperation (pp. 855–856)
A. **Councils of Government**, regional planning commissions, are political subdivision of the state in Texas law.
1. COGs are voluntary, area-wide association of local governments to foster local cooperation
2. Serve as forums for intergovernmental problem solving and by planning governmental programs and facilities on a regional basis
3. Councils of government work on problems that involve numerous local governments or cross-jurisdictional lines.

B. **Interlocal** cooperation contract
1. Improve the efficiency and effectiveness of local governments by authorizing the fullest possible range of inter-governmental contracting authority at
2. Allow for greater efficiency by pooling resources from various local government entities

VI. Financing Local Government in Texas (pp. 856–859)
A. Property tax is the largest source of revenue
B. Other sources include sales taxes, fees for services, tolls, fines, special taxes are others.
C. Counties can issue bonds to raise funds.
1. Public improvement bonds, which would be paid through property taxes and must have voter approval.
2. Enterprise bonds are called revenue bonds and do not require voter approval.
D. Special districts are allowed to levy property taxes and some special districts may collect a sales tax.

LEARNING OBJECTIVES (5-7):

After studying Chapter 27, you should be able to:

1. Discuss and understand county government in the state of Texas.

2. Discuss and understand municipal government in the state of Texas.

3. Discuss and understand special district government in the state of Texas.

4. Discuss the implications of the number and complexity of local government for democracy in the state of Texas.

The following exercises will help you meet these objectives:

Objective 1: Discuss and understand county government in the state of Texas.

1. Make a chart of county government functions using this text as well as the website of your local county.

2. Investigate how many people work in your local county government and that are required to carry out these tasks.

3. Look at the budget of your county (should be available on your local county's website) and compare it to the budget of your local school district (on the district website). Which entity spends more money? Which entity has a greater number of tasks to fulfill?

Objective 2: Discuss and understand municipal government in the state of Texas.

1. Fill in the following table with the three closest municipalities to you. A complete list is available at http://usplaces.info/TX_municipalities.

NAME	Population	Type of Government	List of Departments
1:			
2:			

3:			

2. Look at the chart you made in Activity 1. What key responsibilities are missing from your local municipalities and who do you think handles them? Pretend you are looking for one of the missing responsibilities and research the Internet to find out where that service is offered.

3. Look for the nearest home rule city to you. See if you can find any information on annexation plans on its website. What kinds of conditions does it list for annexation?

Objective 3: Discuss and understand special district government in the state of Texas.

1. Research to see what kind of special district governments apply to your residence. Make a list of these governments.

2. Make a list of taxes and services that these governments offer to you.

3. Make a list of how officials are chosen for the special district governments that affect you.

Objective 4: Discuss the implications of the number and complexity of local government for democracy in the state of Texas.

1. Attend a meeting of a local government near you (county commissioner's court, city council, special district government). What kinds of issues are discussed? How many people attend the meeting?
2. Look up the most recent ballot for your area. How many local officials are on the ballot? How many are running unopposed? Research how many of these officials were re-elected in the last election.

KEY TERMS:

Identify and Describe:

county

county commissioners court

county judge

county commissioners

special districts

county attorney

district attorney

county sheriff

county clerk

tax assessor-collector

county treasurer

general law cities

home rule cities

charter

aldermanic government

mayor-council government

council-manager government

commission government

annexation

at-large elections

single-member district elections

mixed (hybrid) elections

councils of government

interlocal cooperation contract

unfunded mandate

Compare and Contrast:

County attorney and district attorney

General law city and home rule city

Mayor-council and council-manager government

Single-member district elections and at-large elections

Councils of Government and interlocal cooperation contracts

Special Districts and Counties

Counties and municipalities

Name that term:

1. This local government is headed by a judge: _____

2. This government body consists of five commissioners and a judge: _____

3. In small counties this official has both judicial and executive functions: _____

4. There are always four of these officials per county and they are elected from geographical districts: _____

5. School districts and taxing districts are examples of _____.

6. Counties without a criminal district attorney must elect a _____.

7. Each criminal district in Texas must elect a _____.

8. In counties of less than 10,000 people this official can double as the tax assessor-collector: _____

9. This official tabulates unofficial election returns: _____

10. This official determines the value of property within a given county: _____

11. Some counties have abolished this position but it has required an amendment of the Texas constitution to do so: _____

12. Before 1912 all cities in Texas were _____.

13. Cities that can establish all rules not specifically prohibited to it by the state is called a _____.

14. A document establishing the guidelines for the operation of a home rule city is called a _____.

15. A type of general law city with a mayor and six aldermen is called a _____.

16. This type of city government separates executive and legislative functions: _____

17. This type of city government hires a bureaucrat to oversee administrative functions of the city: _____

18. This form of government was invented in Texas but is not practiced by any of our larger municipalities today: _____

19. The Kingwood case resulted in fewer _____ by Home Rule cities.

20. One way to reduce minority representation in government is through _____ .

21. Critics of this form of government argue that it favors parochial interests over the interests of the city at large _____ .

22. In this type of system, city councilmen and women are elected through two types of electoral systems, single-member and at-large _____ .

23. These are voluntary cooperative organizations between local governments sanctioned by the state government: _____

24. These are agreements among local governments to pool resources in order to maximize their utilization: _____

25. When the state requires county government to provide services without providing for them in the state budget it is called: _____

USING YOUR UNDERSTANDING

1) Research how many local governments you are subject to at your residence. Make a diagram showing what part of your life they govern and whether or not you pay taxes directly to them. Include in the diagram the names of the officials responsible for these functions and whether or not they are elected.

2) Pick one of the local governments from your diagram for activity 1 and list five recent decisions they have reached. For each of these decisions analyze their impact on your life – either through taxes or fees you might have to pay or services you might use.

REVIEW QUESTIONS:

1) This type of local government is considered to be a local administrative arm of state government:
   - ☐ a. County
   - ☐ b. Municipality
   - ☐ c. Special District
   - ☐ d. City

2) The largest county in Texas has over 3.4 million inhabitants and the smallest county in the state has less than 67 inhabitants.
   - ☐ True
   - ☐ False

3) If you need to research records and licenses, the best place to do in Texas is the
   - [ ] a. state clerk's office.
   - [ ] b. county clerk's office.
   - [ ] c. city clerk's office.

4) The county commissioner's court consists of
   - [ ] a. the county clerk, tax assessor-collector, sheriff, and county judge.
   - [ ] b. four elected commissioners.
   - [ ] c. four elected commissioners and the county judge.
   - [ ] d. four county judges and three elected commissioners.

5) Every county has the freedom to set up its own governmental structure.
   - [ ] True
   - [ ] False

6) The chief executive officer of the county is the
   - [ ] a. county clerk.
   - [ ] b. county sheriff.
   - [ ] c. mayor.
   - [ ] d. county judge.

7) Every county has a county attorney.
   - [ ] True
   - [ ] False

8) This official can be the county tax assessor-collector in counties with less than 10,000 inhabitants.
   - [ ] a. county clerk
   - [ ] b. county attorney
   - [ ] c. county judge
   - [ ] d. county sheriff

9) Deeds are kept by the
   - [ ] a. county clerk
   - [ ] b. county attorney
   - [ ] c. county tax assessor-collector
   - [ ] d. county sheriff

10) Voter registration is the responsibility of the
   - [ ] a. county clerk
   - [ ] b. county attorney
   - [ ] c. county tax assessor-collector
   - [ ] d. county sheriff

11) State law only specifies what this local government can't do.
  - ☐ a. home rule city
  - ☐ b. general law city
  - ☐ c. county
  - ☐ d. school district

12) A type of municipality whose structure is carefully structured by state law is called:
  - ☐ a. home rule city
  - ☐ b. general law city
  - ☐ c. county
  - ☐ d. school district

13) Which of the following is a key issue for home rule cities?
  - ☐ a. school finance
  - ☐ b. maintenance of voting machines
  - ☐ c. the formation of hospital districts
  - ☐ d. annexation

14) The most common form of municipal government in Texas is
  - ☐ a. council-manager government.
  - ☐ b. strong mayor government.
  - ☐ c. mayor-council government.
  - ☐ d. commission government.

15) Which form of municipal election is most likely to result in minority representation on city council?
  - ☐ a. commission elections
  - ☐ b. at-large elections
  - ☐ c. single-member district elections
  - ☐ d. mixed (hybrid) elections

16) Which of the following is considered a special district government?
  - ☐ a. home rule city
  - ☐ b. single-member district city council
  - ☐ c. school district
  - ☐ d. commission government.

17) Voluntary regional organizations of local government are called
  - ☐ a. charters.
  - ☐ b. county commissioners courts.
  - ☐ c. aldermanic government.
  - ☐ d. Councils of Government.

18) The main sources of revenue for local governments are
- ☐ a.   property taxes.
- ☐ b.   sales taxes.
- ☐ c.   income taxes.
- ☐ d.   fees.

19) An example of enterprise fund would be
- ☐ a.   an enterprise bond.
- ☐ b.   the Harris County Hospital District.
- ☐ c.   the Aviation Department of the City of Houston.
- ☐ d.   the Texas Lottery.

20) The largest source of revenue for the public schools is
- ☐ a.   the Texas Lottery.
- ☐ b.   the State of Texas.
- ☐ c.   property taxes.
- ☐ d.   sales taxes.

ESSAY QUESTIONS:

1) Should Texas decrease the number of local governments in the state? Why or why not?

2) Analyze how the number of local governments impacts political participation in the state of Texas. Does it make it more or less likely that Texans will participate in their government decision-making processes? Why or why not?

3) How does the number of local governments impact the funding of state services? Be sure to consider the funding limitations of counties, the problem of unfunded mandates, as well as the problems of school finance in your answer.

4) Analyze how the local government structures of Texas reflect the political cultures dominant in our state (from Chapter 21). How are traditionalism and individualism apparent in how we structure this particular aspect of our government?

ANSWERS TO REVIEW QUESTIONS

CHAPTER 1

INTRODUCTION

1. d (p. 4)
2. a (p. 5)
3. b (p. 8)
4. a (p. 9)
5. a (p. 9)
6. T (p. 10)
7. a (p. 10)
8. a (p. 10)
9. F (p. 10)
10. d (p. 10)
11. T (p. 11)
12. a (p. 11)
13. d (p. 11)
14. c (p. 11)
15. F (p. 12)
16. b (p. 12)
17. d (p. 13)
18. d (p. 13)
19. c (p. 13)
20. c (p. 14)
21. d (p. 14)
22. c (p. 14)
23. c (p. 15)
24. a (p. 15)
25. T (p. 15)
26. b (p. 16)
27. a (p. 16)
28. c (p. 16)
29. F (p. 17)
30. d (p. 18)
31. b (p. 18)
32. F (p. 18)
33. c (p. 19)
34. T (p. 19)
35. c (p. 19)
36. b (p. 19)
37. d (p. 19)
38. F (p. 20)
39. a (p. 21)
40. F (p. 22)
41. c (p. 24)
42. d (p. 24
43. b (p. 24)

CHAPTER 2

THE CONSTITUTION

1. d (p. 32)
2. b (p. 32)
3. c (p. 33)
4. b (p. 34)
5. d (p. 35)
6. c (p. 36)
7. F (p. 37)
8. T (p. 37)
9. a (p. 38)
10. d (p. 38)
11. a (p. 38)
12. d (p. 39)
13. b (p. 39)
14. c (p. 41)
15. F (p. 42)
16. c (p. 42)
17. b (p. 43)
18. a (p. 44)
19. d (p. 44)
20. T (p. 44)
21. d (p. 46)
22. c (p. 46)
23. T (p. 48)
24. a (p. 48)
25. T (p. 49)
26. d (p. 49)
27. b (p. 49)
28. a (p. 50)
29. c (p. 51)
30. F (p. 51)
31. b (p. 51)
32. d (p. 52)
33. F (p. 52)
34. c (p. 54)
35. a (p. 55)
36. a (p. 55)
37. T (p. 55)
38. a (p. 56)
39. T (p. 57)
40. d (p. 57)
41. a (p. 59)
42. b (p. 60)
43. T (p. 60)
44. c (p. 60)
45. T (p. 62)
46. c (p. 62)
47. c (p. 64)
48. d (p. 65)

CHAPTER 3

FEDERALISM

1.	c (p. 70)	26.	c (p. 80)
2.	F (p. 70)	27.	F (p. 80)
3.	d (p. 70)	28.	c (p. 81)
4.	T (p. 70)	29.	b (p. 81)
5.	F (p. 72)	30.	b (p. 81)
6.	d (p. 72)	31.	a (p. 82)
7.	F (p. 73)	32.	b (p. 85)
8.	T (p. 73)	33.	F (p. 85)
9.	c (p. 73)	34.	a (p. 86)
10.	F (p. 74)	35.	b (p. 86)
11.	b (p. 74)	36.	c (p. 87)
12.	d (p. 74)	37.	a (p. 87)
13.	a (p. 75)	38.	b (p. 87)
14.	d (p. 75)	39.	T (p. 88)
15.	c (p. 75)	40.	T (p. 88)
16.	d (p. 76)	41.	F (p. 88)
17.	c (p. 76)	42.	c (p. 88)
18.	b (p. 76)	43.	d (p. 90)
19.	T (p. 77)	44.	F (p. 92)
20.	b (p. 77)	45.	b (p. 92)
21.	a (p. 77)	46.	c (p. 93)
22.	b (p. 77)	47.	c (p. 94)
23.	a (p. 78)	48.	F (p. 94)
24.	d (p. 78)	49.	a (p. 95)
25.	b (p. 80)		

CHAPTER 4

CIVIL LIBERTIES AND PUBLIC POLICY

1.	b (p. 100)	26.	T (p. 117)
2.	a (p. 100)	27.	d (p. 117)
3.	F (p. 100)	28.	T (p. 117)
4.	c (p. 101)	29.	b (p. 118)
5.	b (p. 102)	30.	T (p. 119)
6.	T (p. 102)	31.	b (p. 119)
7.	c (p. 102)	32.	F (p. 120)
8.	c (p. 102)	33.	F (p. 120)
9.	c (p. 104)	34.	T (p. 122)
10.	b (p. 104)	35.	d (p. 122)
11.	F (p. 105)	36.	a (p. 124)
12.	b (p. 106)	37.	a (p. 124)
13.	T (p. 107)	38.	c (p. 126)
14.	a (p. 109)	39.	d (p. 126)
15.	c (p. 109)	40.	b (p. 127)
16.	d (p. 110)	41.	T (p. 128)
17.	b (p. 110)	42.	b (p. 128)
18.	T (p. 112)	43.	a (p. 128)
19.	c (p. 114)	44.	a (p. 130)
20.	T (p. 114)	45.	F (p. 131)
21.	a (p. 114)	46.	d (p. 133)
22.	d (p. 115)	47.	c (p. 134)
23.	b (p. 116)	48.	b (p. 136)
24.	T (p. 117)	49.	T (p. 136)
25.	b (p. 117)		

CHAPTER 5

CIVIL RIGHTS AND PUBLIC POLICY

1. a (p. 142)
2. c (p. 142)
3. a (p. 142)
4. c (p. 142)
5. T (p. 143)
6. c (p. 143)
7. c (p. 143)
8. T (p. 144)
9. a (p. 145)
10. c (p. 145)
11. T (p. 146)
12. d (p. 146)
13. b (p. 147)
14. F (p. 148)
15. d (p. 148)
16. b (p. 148)
17. T(p. 149)
18. c (p. 149)
19. d (p. 149)
20. b (p. 150)
21. T (p. 151)
22. b (p. 151)
23. a (p. 151)
24. F (p. 152)
25. d (p. 152)
26. d (p. 152)
27. b (p. 152)
28. d (p. 154)
29. T (p. 155)
30. c (p. 156)
31. F (p. 157)
32. c (p. 157)
33. F (p. 158)
34. a (p. 158)
35. T (p. 158)
36. a (p. 159)
37. d (p. 160)
38. T (p. 161)
39. c (p. 161)
40. c (p. 161)
41. b (p. 162)
42. T (p. 162)
43. F (p. 163)
44. F (p. 165)
45. d (p. 166)
46. d (p. 167)
47. T (p. 168)
48. c (p. 169)
49. F (p. 169)
50. c (p. 169)
51. c (p. 171)
52. d (p. 173)

CHAPTER 6

PUBLIC OPINION AND POLITICAL ACTION

1. T (p. 178)
2. c (p. 178)
3. c (p. 178)
4. b (p. 178)
5. F (p. 178)
6. d (p. 179)
7. d (p. 179)
8. b (p. 180)
9. T (p. 180)
10. b (p. 181)
11. c (p. 181)
12. c (p. 183)
13. b (p. 183)
14. a (p. 183)
15. a (p. 183)
16. F (p. 183)
17. T (p. 184)
18. b (p. 185)
19. F (p. 185)
20. d (p. 185)
21. a (p. 185)
22. b (p. 185)
23. b (p. 188)
24. c (p. 189)
25. a (p. 189)
26. b (p. 189)
27. d (p. 189)
28. a (p. 190)
29. F (p. 190)
30. T (p. 191)
31. c (p. 191)
32. c (p. 192)
33. c (p. 192)
34. b (p. 192)
35. d (p. 193)
36. a (p. 193)
37. F (p. 196)
38. a (p. 196)
39. d (p. 196)
40. F (p. 197)
41. a (p. 197)
42. d (p. 199)
43. c (p. 199)
44. F (p. 199)
45. a (p. 201)
46. c (p. 202)
47. F (p. 202)
48. b (p. 203)
49. T (p. 203)
50. b (p. 206)
51. a (p. 206)
52. T (p. 207)

CHAPTER 7

THE MASS MEDIA AND THE POLITICAL AGENDA

1. T (p. 212)
2. c (p. 212)
3. F (p. 212)
4. F (p. 212)
5. b (p. 213)
6. d (p. 213)
7. T (p. 213)
8. a (p. 213)
9. b (p. 214)
10. F (p. 214)
11. d (p. 215)
12. d (p. 215)
13. c (p. 217)
14. d (p. 217)
15. T (p. 218)
16. T (p. 218)
17. a (p. 218)
18. F (p. 218)
19. d (p. 218)
20. c (p. 218)
21. b (p. 221)
22. a (p. 222)
23. b (p. 224)

24. F (p. 226)
25. c (p. 226)
26. T (p. 226)
27. c (p. 226)
28. d (p. 228)
29. b (p. 228)
30. c (p. 231)
31. d (p. 231)
32. a (p. 232)
33. b (p. 232)
34. T (p. 233)
35. c (p. 233)
36. T (p. 234)
37. F (p. 234)
38. F (p. 234)
39. c (p. 234)
40. d (p. 235)
41. T (p. 235)
42. b (p. 236)
43. F (p. 236)
44. F (p. 236)
45. d (p. 236)
46. T (p. 236)

CHAPTER 8

POLITICAL PARTIES

1. F (p. 241)
2. b (p. 241)
3. a (p. 241)
4. b (p. 242)
5. d (p. 243)
6. d (p. 243)
7. c (p. 243)
8. F (p. 244)
9. c (p. 244)
10. T (p. 244)
11. c (p. 245)
12. c (p. 247)
13. F (p. 247)
14. d (p. 248)
15. T (p. 249)
16. F (p. 249)
17. b (p. 249)
18. b (p. 251)
19. c (p. 251)
20. d (p. 252)
21. T (p. 252)
22. c (p. 252)
23. c (p. 254)
24. T (p. 254)

25. a (p. 254)
26. F (p. 254)
27. c (p. 254)
28. b (p. 254)
29. d (p. 255)
30. a (p. 256)
31. c (p. 256)
32. d (p. 257)
33. b (p. 257)
34. b (p. 25)
35. T (p. 259)
36. a (p. 259)
37. d (p. 260)
38. c (p. 260)
39. b (p. 261)
40. T (p. 261)
41. a (p. 262)
42. b (p. 262)
43. c (p. 262)
44. b (p. 263)
45. a (p. 263)
46. T (p. 264)
47. b (p. 264)

CHAPTER 9

NOMINATIONS AND CAMPAIGNS

1.	d (p. 270)	21.	c (p. 277)
2.	c (p. 270)	22.	F (p. 277)
3.	c (p. 270)	23.	T (p. 277)
4.	b (p. 270)	24.	d (p. 279)
5.	F (p. 270)	25.	b (p. 281)
6.	b (p. 270)	26.	F (p. 281)
7.	d (p. 271)	27.	F (p. 281)
8.	T (p. 271)	28.	d (p. 284)
9.	d (p. 271)	29.	a (p. 286)
10.	d (p. 271)	30.	a (p. 287)
11.	c (p. 272)	31.	b (p. 287)
12.	b (p. 273)	32.	F (p. 288)
13.	F (p. 273)	33.	b (p. 288)
14.	F (p. 273)	34.	c (p. 289)
15.	b (p. 273)	35.	a (p. 290)
16.	d (p. 274)	36.	a (p. 291)
17.	T (p. 275)	37.	c (p. 291)
18.	b (p. 275)	38.	d (p. 291)
19.	F (p. 275)	39.	F (p. 292)
20.	F (p. 276)	40.	T (p. 293)
		41.	c (p. 293)

CHAPTER 10

ELECTIONS AND VOTING BEHAVIOR

1.	d (p. 298)	21.	F (p. 310)
2.	d (p. 298)	22.	a (p. 310)
3.	a (p. 298)	23.	c (p. 311)
4.	T (p. 298)	24.	c (p. 313)
5.	c (p. 300)	25.	d (p. 313)
6.	b (p. 300)	26.	c (p. 313)
7.	d (p. 300)	27.	T (p. 314)
8.	d (p. 301)	28.	d (p. 315)
9.	c (p. 301)	29.	a (p. 315)
10.	T (p. 302)	30.	F (p. 316)
11.	T (p. 303)	31.	d (p. 316)
12.	c (p. 303)	32.	b (p. 316)
13.	a (p. 304)	33.	T (p. 316)
14.	T (p. 305)	34.	T (p. 317)
15.	b (p. 305)	35.	a (p. 317)
16.	a (p. 305)	36.	b (p. 317)
17.	c (p. 306)	37.	b (p. 318)
18.	T (p. 306)	38.	c (p. 318)
19.	b (p. 308)	39.	T (p. 319)
20.	T (p. 308)		

CHAPTER 11

INTEREST GROUPS

1. F (p. 324)	26. T (p. 334)
2. F (p. 324)	27. d (p. 335)
3. b (p. 326)	28. a (p. 335)
4. b (p. 326)	29. b (p. 335)
5. c (p. 326)	30. T (p. 336)
6. a (p. 326)	31. d (p. 336)
7. T (p. 327)	32. c (p. 337)
8. d (p. 328)	33. F (p. 337)
9. b (p. 328)	34. b (p. 338)
10. T (p. 328)	35. d (p. 338)
11. b (p. 328)	36. b (p. 338)
12. c (p. 328)	37. F (p. 339)
13. d (p. 329)	38. d (p. 341)
14. c (p. 330)	39. a (p. 342)
15. F (p. 330)	40. T (p. 342)
16. a (p. 330)	41. b (p. 343)
17. d (p. 330)	42. T (p. 344)
18. c (p. 330)	43. a (p. 344)
19. d (p. 330)	44. a (p. 344)
20. c (p. 330)	45. T (p. 345)
21. b (p. 331)	46. b (p. 346)
22. a (p. 332)	47. b (p. 346)
23. T (p. 332)	48. c (p. 347)
24. T (p. 333)	49. a (p. 348)
25. b (p. 333)	50. F (p. 349)

CHAPTER 12

CONGRESS

1. T (p. 354)	27. T (p. 368)
2. a (p. 354)	28. c (p. 369)
3. c (p. 354)	29. d (p. 369)
4. c (p. 355)	30. d (p. 369)
5. c (p. 356)	31. a (p. 370)
6. T (p. 358)	32. b (p. 370)
7. b (p. 358)	33. F (p. 371)
8. c (p. 358)	34. d (p. 372)
9. T (p. 359)	35. c (p. 373)
10. d (p. 359)	36. d (p. 373)
11. c (p. 360)	37. c (p. 373)
12. F (p. 362)	38. b (p. 374)
13. d (p. 362)	39. d (p. 375)
14. c (p. 362)	40. b (p. 376)
15. T (p. 362)	41. c (p. 378)
16. b (p. 362)	42. a (p. 379)
17. F (p. 363)	43. T (p. 379)
18. T (p. 364)	44. c (p. 381)
19. b (p. 365)	45. c (p. 381)
20. d (p. 365)	46. b (p. 382)
21. a (p. 365)	47. c (p. 383)
22. d (p. 365)	48. T (p. 383)
23. c (p. 366)	49. b (p. 383)
24. a (p. 366)	50. T (p. 384)
25. c (p. 367)	51. T (p. 385)
26. d (p. 368)	

CHAPTER 13

THE PRESIDENCY

1.	b (p. 391)	31.	T (p. 410)
2.	d (p. 392)	32.	b (p. 411)
3.	b (p. 392)	33.	T (p. 412)
4.	c (p. 392)	34.	c (p. 413)
5.	a (p. 393)	35.	T (p. 413)
6.	d (p. 395)	36.	d (p. 414)
7.	b (p. 395)	37.	b (p. 414)
8.	F (p. 395)	38.	T (p. 414)
9.	T (p. 397)	39.	c (p. 416)
10.	a (p. 397)	40.	F (p. 417)
11.	F (p. 397)	41.	b (p. 418)
12.	T (p. 398)	42.	b (p. 419)
13.	d (p. 399)	43.	d (p. 419)
14.	b (p. 399)	44.	T (p. 419)
15.	a (p. 400)	45.	F (p. 420)
16.	F (p. 400)	46.	b (p. 421)
17.	b (p. 401)	47.	T (p. 421)
18.	c (p. 402)	48.	a (p. 422)
19.	F (p. 402)	49.	b (p. 423)
20.	d (p. 404)	50.	F (p. 423)
21.	b (p. 404)	51.	d (p. 424)
22.	b (p. 404)	52.	F (p. 425)
23.	a (p. 406)	53.	T (p. 425)
24.	c (p. 406)	54.	c (p. 425)
25.	T (p. 406)	55.	d (p. 428)
26.	F (p. 408)	56.	T (p. 428)
27.	b (p. 408)	57.	c (p. 428)
28.	a (p. 408)	58.	F (p. 429)
29.	a (p. 410)	59.	F (p. 431)
30.	d (p. 410)	60.	b (p. 431)

CHAPTER 14

THE CONGRESS, THE PRESIDENT, AND THE BUDGET: THE POLITICS OF TAXING AND SPENDING

1.	b (p. 436)	28.	a (p. 452)
2.	b (p. 437)	29.	a (p. 452)
3.	b (p. 438)	30.	F (p. 452)
4.	b (p. 438)	31.	d (p. 453)
5.	F (p. 438)	32.	a (p. 453)
6.	d (p. 438)	33.	c (p. 454)
7.	b (p. 439)	34.	c (p. 454)
8.	F (p. 440)	35.	c (p. 454)
9.	d (p. 440)	36.	T (p. 454)
10.	T (p. 440)	37.	d (p. 455)
11.	c (p. 441)	38.	b (p. 455)
12.	F (p. 441)	39.	c (p. 456)
13.	d (p. 441)	40.	d (p. 456)
14.	b (p. 442)	41.	c (p. 457)
15.	d (p. 445)	42.	F (p. 457)
16.	T (p. 445)	43.	a (p. 457)
17.	b (p. 446)	44.	d (p. 457)
18.	T (p. 447)	45.	F (p. 458)
19.	F (p. 447)	46.	b (p. 459)
20.	d (p. 447)	47.	T (p. 460)
21.	F (p. 449)	48.	b (p. 460)
22.	c (p. 449)	49.	b (p. 461)
23.	F (p. 450)	50.	b (p. 462)
24.	b (p. 451)	51.	T (p. 462)
25.	c (p. 451)	52.	T (p. 462)
26.	d (p. 451)	53.	d (p. 462)
27.	T (p. 451)		

CHAPTER 15

THE FEDERAL BUREAUCRACY

1.	F (p. 467)	27.	T (p. 483)
2.	a (p. 468)	28.	a (p. 484)
3.	a (p. 468)	29.	d (p. 484)
4.	c (p. 468)	30.	a (p. 485)
5.	T (p. 470)	31.	T (p. 485)
6.	a (p. 470)	32.	c (p. 485)
7.	F (p. 470)	33.	d (p. 486)
8.	b (p. 472)	34.	b (p. 487)
9.	c (p. 472)	35.	d (p. 488)
10.	c (p. 473)	36.	a (p. 488)
11.	d (p. 473)	37.	b (p. 489)
12.	b (p. 473)	38.	a (p. 491)
13.	c (p. 474)	39.	F (p. 491)
14.	d (p. 474)	40.	c (p. 491)
15.	a (p. 475)	41.	d (p. 491)
16.	b (p. 475)	42.	d (p. 491)
17.	b (p. 477)	43.	T (p. 492)
18.	T (p. 478)	44.	F (p. 493)
19.	c (p. 478)	45.	a (p. 493)
20.	d (p. 479)	46.	T (p. 495)
21.	d (p. 479)	47.	d (p. 495)
22.	b (p. 479)	48.	c (p. 496)
23.	F (p. 480)	49.	c (p. 496)
24.	d (p. 481)	50.	b (p. 496)
25.	a (p. 481)	51.	c (p. 499)
26.	F (p. 481)		

CHAPTER 16

THE FEDERAL COURTS

1.	F (p. 504)	31.	F (p. 516)
2.	d (p. 504)	32.	T (p. 518)
3.	b (p. 504)	33.	d (p. 518)
4.	T (p. 504)	34.	d (p. 519)
5.	a (p. 505)	35.	c (p. 520)
6.	b (p. 505)	36.	a (p. 521)
7.	a (p. 505)	37.	d (p. 522)
8.	c (p. 505)	38.	c (p. 522)
9.	F (p. 505)	39.	a (p. 522)
10.	c (p. 506)	40.	b (p. 523)
11.	a (p. 507)	41.	d (p. 523)
12.	c (p. 507)	42.	T (p. 523)
13.	b (p. 507)	43.	F (p. 524)
14.	T (p. 507)	44.	b (p. 525)
15.	a (p. 508)	45.	c (p. 526)
16.	c (p. 508)	46.	d (p. 526)
17.	b (p. 508)	47.	T (p. 527)
18.	b (p. 509)	48.	a (p. 529)
19.	c (p. 510)	49.	a (p. 530)
20.	T (p. 510)	50.	a (p. 531)
21.	c (p. 511)	51.	a (p. 532)
22.	a (p. 511)	52.	d (p. 532)
23.	b (p. 511)	53.	F (p. 532)
24.	F (p. 512)	54.	c (p. 532)
25.	d (p. 512)	55.	d (p. 535)
26.	T (p. 513)	56.	b (p. 535)
27.	b (p. 513)	57.	F (p. 535)
28.	F (p. 513)	58.	d (p. 535)
29.	d (p. 516)	59.	d (p. 536)
30.	b (p. 516)		

CHAPTER 17

ECONOMIC POLICYMAKING

1.	c (p. 542)	24.	F (p. 551)
2.	b (p. 542)	25.	a (p. 553)
3.	T (p. 542)	26.	b (p. 555)
4.	d (p. 543)	27.	d (p. 556)
5.	b (p. 543)	28.	b (p. 556)
6.	T (p. 546)	29.	a (p. 557)
7.	a (p. 546)	30.	c (p. 557)
8.	a (p. 546)	31.	c (p. 557)
9.	a (p. 546)	32.	a (p. 557)
10.	F (p. 547)	33.	c (p. 557)
11.	a (p. 549)	34.	d (p. 557)
12.	a (p. 549)	35.	a (p. 558)
13.	b (p. 549)	36.	c (p. 558)
14.	c (p. 549)	37.	c (p. 558)
15.	c (p. 550)	38.	d (p. 558)
16.	a (p. 550)	39.	d (p. 558)
17.	d (p. 550)	40.	T (p. 558)
18.	F (p. 550)	41.	F (p. 559)
19.	c (p. 550)	42.	b (p. 560)
20.	a (p. 550)	43.	F (p. 560)
21.	c (p. 551)	44.	F (p. 560)
22.	b (p. 551)	45.	b (p. 560)
23.	c (p. 551)		

CHAPTER 18

SOCIAL WELFARE POLICYMAKING

1.	b (p. 566)	20.	F (p. 574)
2.	c (p. 568)	21.	c (p. 575)
3.	F (p. 568)	22.	b (p. 575)
4.	a (p. 568)	23.	b (p. 575)
5.	d (p. 568)	24.	d (p. 575)
6.	d (p. 568)	25.	c (p. 575)
7.	b (p. 569)	26.	d (p. 576)
8.	b (p. 570)	27.	F (p. 576)
9.	d (p. 571)	28.	d (p. 577)
10.	a (p. 571)	29.	T (p. 578)
11.	d (p. 573)	30.	d (p. 579)
12.	c (p. 573)	31.	T (p. 580)
13.	a (p. 573)	32.	b (p. 581)
14.	F (p. 573)	33.	T (p. 582)
15.	c (p. 573)	34.	a (p. 583)
16.	a (p. 573)	35.	d (p. 583)
17.	d (p. 573)	36.	T (p. 584)
18.	T (p. 573)	37.	F (p. 584)
19.	d (p. 573)	38.	d (p. 585)

CHAPTER 19

POLICYMAKING FOR HEALTH CARE AND THE ENVIRONMENT

1. F (p. 590)
2. a (p. 590)
3. c (p. 591)
4. d (p. 591)
5. c (p. 592)
6. T (p. 592)
7. b (p. 592)
8. T (p. 593)
9. d (p. 593)
10. c (p. 593)
11. b (p. 594)
12. c (p. 595)
13. d (p. 595)
14. a (p. 596)
15. T (p. 596)
16. d (p. 597)
17. d (p. 598)
18. c (p. 598)
19. F (p. 599)
20. d (p. 600)
21. T (p. 600)

22. T (p. 601)
23. T (p. 601)
24. b (p. 601)
25. d (p. 601)
26. c (p. 602)
27. T (p. 603)
28. a (p. 603)
29. b (p. 603)
30. d (p. 603)
31. a (p. 603)
32. a (p. 605)
33. T (p. 606)
34. d (p. 607)
35. T (p. 607)
36. d (p. 608)
37. d (p. 609)
38. b (p. 609)
39. c (p. 610)
40. c (p. 611)
41. F (p. 611)

CHAPTER 20

FOREIGN AND DEFENSE POLICYMAKING

1. F (p. 616)
2. d (p. 616)
3. F (p. 616)
4. c (p. 616)
5. c (p. 617)
6. a (p. 618)
7. b (p. 618)
8. b (p. 618)
9. d (p. 619)
10. a (p. 620)
11. T (p. 620)
12. a (p. 621)
13. d (p. 622)
14. b (p. 623)
15. d (p. 624)
16. b (p. 625)
17. c (p. 625)
18. a (p. 626)
19. c (p. 626)
20. F (p. 627)
21. d (p. 628)
22. c (p. 628)
23. F (p.628)
24. c (p. 628)
25. T (p. 629)
26. b (p. 629)
27. T (p. 629)

28. b (p. 629)
29. d (p. 630)
30. F (p. 630)
31. c (p. 631)
32. d (p. 633)
33. a (p. 634)
34. b (p. 635)
35. c (p. 635)
36. T (p. 635)
37. d (p. 636)
38. d (p. 637)
39. d (p. 637)
40. c (p. 638)
41. T (p. 638)
42. F (p. 639)
43. b (p. 640)
44. a (p. 641)
45. c (p. 642)
46. b (p. 643)
47. d (p. 645)
48. b (p. 647)
49. c (p. 647)
50. F (p. 647)
51. d (p. 648)
52. F (p. 649)
53. d (p. 650)
54. F. (p. 650)

CHAPTER 21

THE NEW FACE OF STATE AND LOCAL GOVERNMENT

1. T (p. 656)
2. b (p. 656)
3. d (p. 657)
4. F (p. 657)
5. d (p. 657)
6. a (p. 659)
7. F (p. 659)
8. c (p. 660)
9. d (p. 660)
10. T (p. 661)
11. F (p. 662)
12. d (p. 662)
13. T (p. 665)
14. a (p. 666)
15. c (p. 666)
16. T (p. 666)
17. d (p. 667)
18. b (p. 669)
19. d (p. 670)
20. d (p. 670)
21. F (p. 671)
22. c (p. 672)
23. c (p. 673)
24. b (p. 674)
25. c (p. 675)
26. c (p. 676)

27. b (p. 677)
28. a (p. 678)
29. b (p. 678)
30. c (p. 678)
31. a (p. 679)
32. c (p. 679)
33. a (p. 680)
34. T (p. 680)
35. d (p. 680)
36. c (p. 681)
37. c (p. 682)
38. T (p. 682)
39. T (p. 683)
40. d (p. 683)
41. F (p. 683)
42. b (p. 685)
43. b (p. 686)
44. b (p. 686)
45. c (p. 687)
46. d (p. 688)
47. T (p. 688)
48. d (p. 690)
49. c (p. 691)
50. F (p. 691)
51. c (p. 691)

TEXAS CHAPTER 21

INTRODUCING GOVERNMENT IN TEXAS

1. c (p. 656)
2. T (p. 656)
3. c (p. 659)
4. a. (p. 658)
5. b (p. 657)
6. b (p. 656)
7. F (p. 662)
8. a (p. 668)
9. b. (p. 668)
10. a (p. 671)
11. b (p. 678)
12. a (p. 678)
13. T (p. 676)
14. b (p. 672)
15. d (p. 678)
16. a (p. 675)
17. d (p. 675)
18. c (p. 671)
19. b (p. 677)
20 a (p. 662)

TEXAS CHAPTER 22

THE TEXAS CONSTITUTION

1. a (p. 686)
2. b (p. 688)
3. a (p. 687)
4. c (p. 688)
5. T (p. 689)
6. F (p. 689)
7. d (p. 689)
8. b (p. 690)
9. b (p. 690)
10. c (p. 692)
11. b (p. 693)
12. c (p. 694)
13. a (p. 697)
14. a (p. 698)
15. d (p. 699)
16. c (p. 700)
17. b (p. 700)
18. a (pp. 703-704)
19. b (p. 704)
20. F (p. 706)
21. c (p. 708)
22. b (p. 709)
23. d (p. 701)
24. F (pp. 709-710)
25. T (p. 710)

TEXAS CHAPTER 23

POLITICAL PARTIES, CAMPAIGNS, ELECTIONS AND INTEREST GROUPS IN TEXAS

1. c (p. 726)
2. a (p. 717)
3. T (p. 719)
4. b (p. 729)
5. a (p. 730)
6. d (p. 739-742)
7. F (p. 721)
8. T (p. 723)
9. a (p. 725)
10. c (p. 726)
11. T (p. 726)
12. a (p. 723)
13. a (p. 723)
14. a. (p. 738)
15. F (p. 739)
16. T (p. 739)
17. T (p. 732)
18. F (p. 731)
19. F (p. 730)
20. T (p. 729)

TEXAS CHAPTER 24

THE TEXAS LEGISLATURE

1. b (p. 750)
2. d (p. 750)
3. T (p. 751)
4. F (p. 751
5. c (p. 749)
6. b (p. 762)
7. T (p. 752)
8. F (p. 755)
9. a (p. 761)
10. c (p. 760)
11. d (p. 756)
12. a (p. 750)
13. T (p. 757)
14. c (p. 763)
15. F (p. 761)
16. d (p. 765)
17. b (p. 765)
18. T (p. 766)
19. b (p. 771)
20. T (p. 786)

TEXAS CHAPTER 25

THE GOVERNOR AND BUREAUCRACY OF TEXAS

1. c (p. 793)
2. b (p. 783)
3. a (p. 781)
4. a (p. 793)
5. b (p. 795)
6. d (p. 798)
7. F (p. 782)
8. F (p. 783)
9. c (p. 785)
10. F (p. 787)
11. d (p. 787)
12. d (p. 788)
13. c (p. 796
14. T (p. 792)
15. F (p. 788)
16. d (p. 803-804)
17. c (p. 804)
18. T (p. 799)
19. c (p.796)
20. T (p. 792)

TEXAS CHAPTER 26

THE TEXAS COURT SYSTEM

1. d (pp. 813-814)
2. d (p. 815)
3. d (p. 816)
4. T (p. 812)
5. d (p. 813)
6. d (pp. 810-811)
7. d (p. 813)
8. T. (p. 814)
9. a (p. 828)
10. d (p. 825)
11. b (pp. 825-827)
12. a (p. 828)
13. T (p. 810)
14. F (p. 816)
15. T (p. 816)
16. d (pp. 820-821)
17. a (p. 827)
18. T (p. 819)
19. d (p. 829)
20. F (p. 819)

CHAPTER 27

LOCAL GOVERNMENT IN TEXAS

1) a (p. 838)
2) T (p. 840)
3) b (p. 840)
4) c (p. 841)
5) F (p. 841)
6) d (p. 842)
7) F (p. 842)
8) d (p. 843)
9) a (p. 843)
10) b (p. 843)
11) a (p. 844)
12) b (pp. 845-46)
13) d (p. 848)
14) a (p. 849)
15) d (p. 852)
16) c (p. 853)
17) d (p. 855)
18) a (p. 856)
19) c (p. 857)
20) c (p. 858)